Mental Health Law and Practice for Social Workers

David Anderson-Ford LL.B, Dip.CL
Senior Lecturer in Law, West London Institute of Higher Education

Michael D Halsey LL.B (Hons) (London)
Senior Assistant Solicitor, North Tyneside
Metropolitan Borough Council

London
Butterworths
1984

England	Butterworth & Co (Publishers) Ltd, 88 Kingsway, LONDON WC2B 6AB
Australia	Butterworths Pty Ltd, SYDNEY, MELBOURNE, BRISBANE, ADELAIDE, PERTH, CANBERRA and HOBART
Canada	Butterworth & Co (Canada) Ltd, TORONTO and VANCOUVER
New Zealand	Butterworths of New Zealand Ltd, WELLINGTON and AUCKLAND
Singapore	Butterworth & Co (Asia) Pte Ltd, SINGAPORE
South Africa	Butterworth Publishers (Pty) Ltd, DURBAN and PRETORIA
USA	Butterworth Legal Publishers, ST PAUL, Minnesota, SEATTLE, Washington, BOSTON, Massachusetts, AUSTIN, Texas and D & S Publishers, CLEARWATER, Florida

ISBN 0 406 25980 1

Typesetting by Lin-Art, Ashford, Kent.
Printed and bound in Great Britain by Billing and Sons Ltd, Worcester.

Preface

This book is concerned with the Mental Health Act 1983 which can be described as a series of amendments to a blue-print – the Mental Health Act 1959. The earlier Act was rightly considered radical in its day – emphasising as it did the fact that patients suffering from mental disorder should wherever possible be treated on an informal basis – and adopted a medical model almost entirely unfettered by the notion of personal legal rights attributable to the patient. This element, missing from the 1959 Act, has formed the basis of much controversy and pressure for change since that time.

The amendments contain important implications for the medical and legal professions, but it is perhaps the social worker who will be the most acutely affected by the new statutory requirements in relation to assessment procedures, the increased emphasis on treatment of the patient in the community (bearing in mind that the definition of medical treatment contained in the Act includes 'care', 'habilitation' and 'rehabilitation') and in relation to the social work training requirements to be undertaken in order to acquire the status of approved social worker.

In writing this book we have pursued two main objectives: (1) to provide a clear guide to a complex piece of legislation and (2) to raise and discuss issues inherent in the legislation which have direct practical significance for social workers in mental health work.

The approach we have adopted to meet our first objective is to select for detailed consideration only those sections of the 1983 Act which are of particular significance for social workers employed by local authorities in England and Wales. In our search for clarity and simplification a number of sections which are not, in our opinion, of direct practical importance to social workers are not referred to at all. We would refer those readers who require a comprehensive guide to the 149 sections and six schedules of the 1983 Act to existing works which satisfy this requirement, and to the relevant Regulations and statutory forms (see para 1.3).

Part Eleven of the book attempts to satisfy our second objective. The case studies are an essential component and whilst we hope that they will be of particular assistance to those involved in mental health training programmes, we further hope that all mental health practitioners will find them useful in handling the everyday legal problems which they encounter in the field.

There are 'grey areas' and illogicalities in the Act and an attempt has been made to explore these fully with the purpose of presenting suggestions for further reform. Emphasis is also given to the Parliamentary debates from which the changes came.

The authors have considerable experience in the legal aspects of the education and training of social workers and indeed, the book has been written during a period of intense activity on our part in in-service training in connection with the Act. We would like to thank those audiences of long-suffering social workers and training officers up and down England and Wales who have had to endure our struggles to divine on their behalf the, often convoluted, meaning of the text of the Act! Much of the comment and discussion which has arisen during these courses has been distilled into the text.

Mike Hewitt, Training Officer, Birmingham City Council Social Services Department, deserves special mention in this regard for his invaluable assistance in formulating the case studies, as do the late Pat Offord and the late Peter Kendall for their unfailing support and encouragement. They will both be greatly missed. We would also like to place on record our appreciation of the help we have received from Ian Forster, also of Birmingham Social Services Department, and Danny Veitch of North Tyneside Social Services Department.

Many hands were employed in the typing of the early drafts, for which special thanks must go to Rosemary Halsey, Moira Ford and Renee Churchill, Ray Knudsen and Joyce Roberts (the latter two being responsible for introducing one of us to the wonders of word processing!), and thanks, as always, must also go to Glenys, Tilley, Daniel and Matthew. Butterworths deserve the last word for their tolerance and understanding in the incorporation of late changes.

We have sought to state the law as it stands on 31 July 1984, and unless otherwise stated references in the text are to the Mental Health Act 1983. For any errors, of course, we alone are responsible.

July 1984   D A-F
  M D H

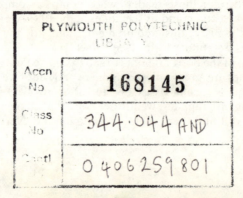

Contents

1 Historical perspectives and the classification of mental disorder

1.1 General introduction

1.1.1 The Mental Health Act 1959 was a landmark in the development of care for the mentally disordered. It established many important principles. Among these are those that where care treatment in hospital are needed, they are given upon a voluntary basis wherever that is possible and that in those few cases where compulsion does prove necessary it must be subject to strict controls . . . this Bill seeks to amend the 1959 Act but it does not challenge those principles.

> The Bill does not seek in any way to overturn the principles of the 1959 Act. It seeks to build on them and to take account of the developments which have occurred since 1959.

The above extracts from the Parliamentary debates on the Mental Health (Amendment) Bill 1982 set out the Government's intentions in promoting the Bill. The Bill was passed and was eventually incorporated within the consolidating Act, the Mental Health Act 1983. So to understand the objectives of the 1983 Act we must first look at the 1959 Act and at what it set out to achieve.

1.1.2 The Preamble to the 1959 Act stated that it was 'An Act to repeal the Lunacy and Mental Treatment Acts 1890 to 1930, and the Mental Deficiency Acts, 1913 to 1938, and to make fresh provision with respect to the treatment and care of mentally disordered persons and with respect to their property and affairs...'.

It was no longer considered socially or medically appropriate to refer to mental disorder in such terms as 'idiocy' or 'lunacy'. But the 1959 Act did not merely substitute new terminology for old. The main provisions of the 1959 Act reflected a distrust of the legalism of the past – the concept of Victorian paternalistic control and an over-emphasis on administrative detail, inspection and legal procedures leading to admission to an asylum. This over-emphasis on legal procedures was particularly evident in the Lunacy Act 1890, described by Professor Kathleen Jones as the 'triumph of legalism'. The 1890 Act prevented patients from receiving treatment on a voluntary basis because the only way in which an asylum could receive patients was (except in urgent cases) under the authority of a reception order authorised by a JP. This prevented early diagnosis or treatment because for a reception order to be granted the patient had to be exhibiting symptoms of unsoundness of mind which were obvious and detectable by a lay JP. However once a reception order had been signed the custodial emphasis of the 1890 Act meant that the patient's situation was ignored by the law. He had no right to apply for his discharge or refuse treatment – the law concerned itself entirely with pre-admission procedures and controls.

It may be thought that the 1983 Act, with its emphasis on patients' legal rights and the legal regulation of medical treatment, marks a return to nineteenth century legislation. But this ignores those provisions of the 1983 Act which require the Secretary of State to set standards of good medical and social work practice by issuing Codes of Practice after consultation with the multi-disciplinary Mental Health Act Commission and also the obligations upon local authorities to appoint sufficient specialist social workers who have proved their competence in mental health work. It also ignores the important retention of the patient's right to receive treatment on a voluntary as opposed to a compulsory basis, a provision which was not contained in the 1890 Act. Voluntary status did not appear until 1930 in the Mental Treatment Act.

By 1959 psychiatry had established a position of respect within the medical profession. It appeared that some success in treating mental illness was being achieved, particularly through the use of drugs popularly described as tranquillisers. There was a considerable amount of social and medical optimism about psychiatry in general and in the light of this the Mental Health Act 1959 reflected an almost exclusively medical, clinical model. Legal constraints in respect of treatment and attention to the rights of the patient remained minimal until 30 September 1983, so a lawyer examining the statutory procedures leading to compulsory detention of patients in hospital for treatment looked in vain for a legal procedure similar to that which existed for the detention of persons convicted of criminal activity. He looked for, but did not find, a process of investigation, presentation of evidence under rigidly applied formal procedures to an independent tribunal, and appeal rights. The process leading to compulsory detention of patients for treatment under the 1959 Act bore little resemblance to criminal procedures.

1.1.3   Indeed the role of the courts in mental health legislation had been minimal for some time and remained so after the 1959 Act. To some extent this limited role arose from the statutory provisions which prevented patients from starting legal proceedings in respect of action taken under the mental health legislation without permission from the High Court. But more important was the difficulty experienced by the courts in handling the terminology and imprecise concepts of mental disorder. This is particularly well illustrated by two cases in 1959 and 1973. In the former a judge in a divorce case was asked to decide upon the meaning of the phrase 'incurably of unsound mind' in divorce legislation. He stated that if ' . . . a man can hope to resume a normal married life and to manage himself and his affairs, no ordinary person would describe him as incurably of unsound mind or insane because he has to take a drug once a week or once a day'. The judge elaborated upon difficulties he had experienced in the case in the following passage from his judgment:

> My task would be comparatively easy if the doctors were prepared to assess the prospects of a 'cure' or to assess the patient's state in terms of 'curability' or 'incurability' but these are not the terms in which they are prepared to give their evidence. The medical terms 'clinical', 'social' and 'semi-social' recovery are terms which the doctors understand and which involve a practical criterion against which they can assess the mental state of a patient. I am faced with the difficulty of reconciling the terms which they use with the terms used by Parliament – namely 'incurably of unsound mind'. Moreover I must bear in mind that the modern tendency is to discharge patients from hospital more freely than in the past. A patient is often discharged where arrangements can be made for his care outside hospital and where further treatment is unlikely to improve his mental state, whom, nevertheless, few people would describe as normal

or cured.

The 1973 case was directly concerned with the 1959 Act and here the Court of Appeal was required to define the words 'mental illness' which had been deliberately left undefined in the 1959 Act. In this case the court was asked to decide whether a man who had tortured and killed several family pets was mentally ill. This is how one of the judges approached the problem:

> . . . there is no definition of 'mental illness'. The words are ordinary words of the English language. They have no particular medical significance. They have no particular legal significance. How should the court construe them? The answer is . . . that ordinary words of the English language should be construed in the way that ordinary sensible people would construe them. That being, in my judgment, the right test, then I ask myself, what would the ordinary sensible person have said about the patient's condition in this case if he had been informed of his behaviour to the dogs, the cat and his wife? In my judgment such a person would have said: 'Well, the fellow is obviously mentally ill'.

That, combined with medical opinion was, and is, the legal view as to what constitutes mental illness. It is particularly well described by Brenda Hoggett in *Mental Health* (Sweet and Maxwell: 1st edn 1976; 2nd edn 1984) as 'the man must be mad ' test.

1.1.4   The 1959 Act did not concern itself at all with the legal rights of the patient although Mental Health Review Tribunals were established to allow detained patients and certain of their relatives to apply for discharge from compulsory detention. But even this right was surrounded with problems. The MHRT's powers were limited to ordering discharge or continuing a patient's detention, and as if to emphasise the irrelevance of legal procedures, detention under the non-criminal procedures of the 1959 Act was one of the few custodial sentences to which a person could be subjected without entitlement to legal aid. Yet if any group of prisoners could lay claim to the greatest need for professional advice and assistance in putting forward their case for release it must surely have been persons detained for treatment under the 1959 Act. Legal aid for representation in MHRTs was not introduced until the end of 1982, and only after strong pressure had been placed on the Government during the passage of the 1982 Amendment Bill through Parliament were the necessary regulations made to provide legal aid for applicants to MHRTs.

A major limitation of MHRTs was that their powers were so

narrowly drawn. The patient either did or did not come within the definition of mental disorder in section 4 of the 1959 Act. If the patient did not so qualify the Tribunal was obliged to order his discharge no matter how many years he had spent in hospital as a detained patient. There was no intermediate provision, such as a power to delay discharge by placing a patient under guardianship. Further difficulties existed in relation to the patient's lack of access to reports provided for the benefit of the Tribunal and, perhaps most controversially, the whole question of consent to treatment.

1.1.5 Criticism also centred around the fact that the tribunal composition and procedure tended to reflect the almost total medical model which the 1959 Act sought to create. The chairmen of tribunals were lawyers, but given the lack of attention devoted to the legal rights of the patient in the 1959 Act the 'evidence' provided tended to be almost exclusively clinical, and therefore perceptions made of the condition of the patient remained clinical.

Nonetheless the Mental Health Act of 1959 was a considerable improvement upon the previous law, particularly in its emphasis on informal admissions; section 5 of the Act made it quite plain that compulsory detention should be a matter of last resort:

> **Section 5** (1) Nothing in this Act shall be construed as preventing a patient who requires treatment for mental disorder from being admitted to any hospital or mental nursing home in pursuance of arrangements made in that behalf and without any application, order or direction rendering him liable to be detained under this Act, or from remaining in any hospital or mental nursing home in pursuance of such arrangements after he has ceased to be liable to be detained.

And it is true that since 1959 in excess of 90% of all patients are apparently being treated on an informal basis. However the distinction between formal and informal status has traditionally been blurred; there is also the difficulty of assessing how many patients who were originally admitted informally are ultimately unable to leave by virtue of the fact that they have become totally dependent upon the hospital and thus 'institutionalised'.

Other major and beneficial features of the 1959 Act included the limiting of compulsory detention to those patients who really would not be treated voluntarily and whose disorder required hospital treatment, ie those suffering from a mental disorder 'of a nature or degree which warrants the detention of the patient in a hospital for medical treatment' (section 26). Also in the 1959 Act a parallel of comprehensive orders in relation to the criminal offender were created, particularly hospital and guardianship orders, thus creating similar powers of detention for offender and non-offender patients.

1.1.6 Central to the working of the 1959 Act were the admission procedures, particularly the choice between different procedures – eg an emergency admission provision (section 29); a slightly longer term procedure for observation (section 25); and then the long term detention power for treatment (section 26).

So advances were made in 1959 – an attempt was made to remove the stigmatisation associated with the terminology of mental disorder, such as lunacy and mental deficiency. 'Subnormality' was at that time considered to be a liberalising influence, and successful in terms of the large increase in the number of informal admissions under section 5. However, the trust placed in the hands of the psychiatric profession (the medical model) was not tempered by a reciprocal focus on the patient as an individual living within a society and on the legal rights which, in normal circumstances, would attach to such an individual (the legal model). The patient remained on an unequal footing in relation to those rights, even to the point of being legally prevented from voting, or in some cases being prevented from sending or receiving postal communications. There are parallels here between psychiatry and sociology. Sociology had its glittering period in the 1960s. Claims to objectivity failed the test of close analysis. In the 1960s pressure for change entered its first stage, and became more developed and sophisticated in the 1970s. Those who advocated reform saw the Mental Health Act 1959 as an exercise in liberating the psychiatrist and in some cases, conferring freedom to do nothing as far as the treatment of the patient was concerned. It represented a 'wholly medical and therapeutic approach to the question of hospital admission and treatment' (Hoggett *Public Law Journal* (1983) 173).

1.1.7 There were parallel criticisms in America and it was there that change was initially effected. In the 1960s and 1970s an attempt was made to 'insert' a legal model within the purely clinical model. This meant moving the focus away from those who administered the treatment, away from those who detain compulsorily, to the patient as the starting point – the individual. And over the past 20 years, litigation in the American courts has assumed that focus and the courts have responded by taking the view that compulsory detention of the individual on the grounds of mental disorder is, in law, a matter of absolute last resort. The liberty of the individual is not to be lightly denied. The perception of mental disorder as an illness led to a heavy emphasis on treatment in the community rather than in hospital and this was assisted by a strong civil libertarian lobby which confirmed that this should be the case. At first glance such reform, couched in terms of civil liberty, is a wholly acceptable advance. There is, however, room for criticism which may counter its initial appeal. There has developed in the American Tribunals and courts an obsessive attention to the interpretation of rules, an exhaustive defining and redefining of terminology, which has resulted in the ability (to use the parlance of the criminal law) to 'get the patient off on a technicality'. This perhaps marks a return to legalism which was the cause of so many problems in the UK in the late nineteenth and early twentieth centuries.

The result of numerous 'test cases' was that patients were released into the community, because of the work of lawyers inserting or trying to insert a legal model into the medical model. This is not to deny the value of such an approach, providing the community is well-provided in terms of resources – day-care, out-patient facilities, community psychiatric nursing support, etc. Indeed legislation in America, and the 1959 Act, positively stressed that treatment should be provided in the community unless, as a last resort, it has to be within the context of an institution. However it has been the American experience that resources have not been adequately provided to assist with the care and treatment of patients within the community rather than by compulsory detention in hospital. Legislation in both countries attempted to strike a balance between the interests of the health or safety of the patient and what is necessary for the protection of other persons, between the patient and his care and protection and the care and protection of the community as a whole (see section 26(2)(b) of the 1959 Act). This balance is easier to strike if there is considerable degree of resource within the community. The necessary resources have not been provided in America with the result that there are a considerable number of persons in the community who are a danger to themselves and a danger to others.

It is submitted that the new legislation in the UK has more of the appearance of the civil libertarian model than has hitherto been the case: there is an attempt in this new legislation to address exactly the same problem in exactly the same way. One indication of this, perhaps comparatively insignificant if taken in isolation, is the new power to request legal aid for representation in MHRTs. The availability of legal aid for tribunal work should make it more attractive to the legal profession and a new area of legal expertise should eventually be created. A promising sign is the initiative taken by the Law Society in establishing a panel of solicitors with experience and interest in tribunal work. This may well lead to a significant change in the manner in which tribunals conduct their proceedings – perhaps towards a more formal approach. Legal representation in itself may do no more than satisfy a long held desire for patients to be provided with an effective 'mouth-piece', but there are likely to be other consequences such as an increase in the number of patients' cases which reach the courts. This could lead to a second 'triumph of legalism' imposed by the courts as opposed to legislation. If more patients succeed in securing their discharge from hospital more demands will be placed upon community based services.

1983
Act

1.1.8 Previous legislation has placed little or no emphasis on the need for after-care facilities and the 1983 Act takes a small, hesitant and wholly inadequate step in this direction in section 117 where statutory duties in relation to after-care provisions have been built in. Provided sufficient finance is made available (unlikely in present circumstances) to allow for resourcing in terms of people and facilities, a useful balance between the liberty of the individual and protection of the community will be achieved.

A further reason for pressure for amending legislation in the UK was a series of highly-publicised inquiries into the care and treatment of patients compulsorily detained in institutions – Ely Hospital in Cardiff, Fairley Hospital, Whittingham Hospital, Normansfield, Rampton. Staff of these institutions were prosecuted for alleged offences against patients and some prosecutions resulted in convictions. A picture was painted of a dark and sinister form of institutionalisation whose detained population was being casually and cynically exploited, and it was this picture together with the influential work of MIND and other pressure groups that persuaded parties on both sides of the Houses of Parliament that the 1959 Act should be looked at again with a view to reform.

At the end of the 1970s two White Papers were produced, the most significant being 'Reform of Mental Health Legislation' 1981 (Cmnd 8405) which immediately preceded an Amendment Bill. Of this the White Paper stated: 'The Bill is about the status and legal position of those mentally disordered people who need special protection and control' and further, 'the Bill improves and safeguards the position of staff looking after them and removes uncertainties in the law'. It should be remembered that what followed was not entirely new legislation and much of the phraseology that has emerged in the 1983 Act is in exactly the same terms as those of the 1959 Act. Parliament did not sit down with a clean piece of paper and start again in relation to mental health. The original blue-print remains intact, but at least some of the amendments, particularly those relating to the rights of the patient, represent a new emphasis not present in the 1959 Act.

1.2 The main provisions of the new law

1.2.1 The basic framework divided into civil and criminal provisions remains. The three types of civil applications for compulsory detention in hospital – emergency short term power (72 hours), medium term power (28 days), both for assessment, and long term power (six months initially) for treatment remain virtually identical to those in the 1959 Act. The applications are still procedural in nature: there is no judicial involvement in the procedure, no return to certification by a JP as under the pre-1959 legislation although there is the possibility of subsequent examination of the procedure followed in individual cases by the Mental Health Act Commission.

There are changes in the grounds for applications for treatment. Most important is the introduction of a treatability test for psychopathic or mentally impaired patients. Other changes are procedural in nature – the redefinition of 'three days' or '72 hours'. So criticisms of the misuse of the emergency admission procedure for observation under section 29 of the 1959 Act will still apply. The less than knowledgeable GP pressing for admission to hospital, hasty diagnoses and 'trigger-happy' Mental Welfare Officers are not entirely banished under the 1983 Act. Reference to the high proportion of emergency applications made under section 29 of the 1959 Act can be found in the 1976 Review which states at paragraph 2.6: 'In practice section 29 has been the most widely used compulsory form of admission procedure and in some regions has constituted over 80% of all compulsory admissions'. Whilst heavy use of the section 29 procedure does not of itself point to abuse, the research by Barton and Hander into the use of section 29 in one

9

hospital over a three-year period showed that only 72 out of 182 admissions were properly made, that is 40%.

1.2.2 In relation to the criminal offender, the amendments are perhaps more significant. The law relating to hospital and guardianship orders has been revised and new orders, such as remands to hospital for reports and treatment, will be introduced. Further, restriction orders (which restrict discharge under section 65 of the 1959 Act and which have hitherto been the subject of much criticism) become subject to appeal to Tribunals. For the first time, the conditionally discharged patient may apply to a Tribunal for the removal or variation of the conditions of discharge.

1.2.3 As previously suggested, where the Act does depart significantly from the 1959 Act is in relation to the rights of patients and the most widely publicised feature of this departure lies in the new consent to treatment provisions. As will be seen the provisions are narrowly drawn and whether the battle waged by MIND and others in relation to the issue of consent to treatment has actually been won remains in doubt.

A further change is represented by the new duty placed on hospital management to ensure that patients are provided, as soon as possible after admission, with written details of their rights (now available in the form of DHSS leaflets), and someone (possibly an approved social worker) has a duty to sit down with the patient and explain exactly what those rights are.

1.2.4 The work of tribunals will be considerably increased by the fact that the time periods during which patients can apply for discharge are exactly halved. Put another way this means that patients' rights to apply to tribunals are doubled in the 1983 Act. The increase estimated by the Government is from 1000 to 5000 applications per year. To maintain efficiency the number of persons qualified to undertake tribunal duties has been increased. The tribunals' powers have also been increased under the new Act – the delayed discharge provision in particular should be borne in mind. Previously a tribunal could only consider whether or not to order discharge. The delay mechanism enables the tribunal to recommend, for example, guardianship and to further consider the case in the event of the recommendation not being acted upon. To enable tribunals to carry out their new and revised powers the 1960

Tribunal Rules have been repealed and replaced by the Mental Health Review Tribunal Rules 1983. The most significant changes are:

(a) the rules no longer prescribe statutory forms;
(b) the tribunal must hold a hearing within seven days of an application by a patient detained for assessment, and
(c) the Responsible Authority's statement must contain an 'up to date social circumstances report'.

Finally patients under 16 have the same rights to apply to a Tribunal as patients over 16.

1.2.5 A major problem will be to ensure that the rights of the patient are actually upheld. The solution in the 1983 Act (some may say it is merely digging into the past and disinterring an old idea) is an inspectorate, the Mental Health Act Commission, which met for the first time on 1 September 1983 and started operating on the 30 September 1983. MHAC is a body of 72 persons, drawn from the ranks of the medical, nursing, legal and social work professions with heavy representation from the medical profession (well over half being psychiatrists or suitably qualified nursing staff). Thus the medical, legal and social work models are represented. MHAC will perform a number of central tasks, all of which will be examined in detail later. Essentially it is an inspectorate, an investigative body, and it is our opinion that this is the lynchpin of the new legislation. If the medical model is to contain within it legal safeguards against abuse, there must necessarily be an element of independent supervision, otherwise most of these changes (particularly in relation to consent to treatment) are going to be reduced to paper exercises and thus rendered meaningless. However, having recognised this, whether 72 people, 'inspecting 300 or so local hospitals and mental nursing homes in England and Wales by visiting once or twice a year and making around one visit per month to the 4 Special Hospitals' (White Paper 1981) can efficiently 'make themselves available to detained patients who wish to see them, ensure that staff are helping patients to understand their legal position and their rights . . . look at patients' records of admission and renewal of detention and at records relating to treatment' (White Paper) remains to be seen. We have seen other inspectorates in the past that have been less than efficient (the Health and Safety Inspectorate, for example, hampered as it is by lack of resources).

1.2.6 The role of the 'nearest relative' is preserved and indeed strengthened. Some concern has been expressed about this in the light of the fact that, in most cases, the nearest relative will look to the Approved Social Worker to make an application. The number of people involved who would wish to take an independent stance from the social worker and/or the GP are likely to be few. There was pressure at the Bill stage of the 1982 Amendment Act to remove the nearest relative's powers but it failed and we see instead increased powers for particular categories of relative.

1.2.7 The professional independence of social workers has been strengthened and clarified. The broad areas of change outlined above became embodied in the Mental Health (Amendment) Act 1982 which reached the statute book on 28 October in that year. None of the provisions came into force on that date except one that directly affected social workers and local social services authorities employing them. This provision, now part of the 1983 Act, reads as follows:

> **Section 114** (1) A local social services authority shall appoint a sufficient number of approved social workers for the purpose of discharging the functions conferred on them by this Act.
>
> (2) No person shall be appointed by a local social services authority as an approved social worker unless he is approved by the authority as having appropriate competence in dealing with persons who are suffering from mental disorder.
>
> (3) In approving a person for appointment as an approved social worker a local social services authority shall have regard to such matters as the Secretary of State may direct.

1.2.8 Local social services authorities have been given a two-year transitional period (October 1982 to October 1984) to appoint sufficient approved social workers to carry out the duties formerly performed by mental welfare officers. The DHSS and latterly, CCETSW, have had to deal with the problem of how 'appropriate competence' should be assessed. The DHSS produced a modular training programme (see para 12.4) involving local authority training departments and educational institutions. This programme was opposed mainly by the Local Authority Associations on the grounds that the transitional period was too short and the proposed programme would be too costly. The outcome of this debate has been a phased series of one day national examinations prepared and assessed by CCETSW. A more complete picture is provided in DHSS circular LAC (83) 7 which states in paragraph 4-6:

4. The Secretary of State directs that any person to be approved from 28 October 1984 to carry out statutory duties under the Mental Health Act 1983 shall have received appropriate training and shall have succeeded in a system of assessment organised in relation to the Act by the Central Council for Education and Training in Social Work. This direction does not imply that any person who has received such training and has succeeded in such an assessment should automatically become an approved social worker. Approval to carry out the duties rests with the employing social services authority.

5. The Secretary of State directs that the period for which approval by a local authority can be given under paragraph 4 above shall not exceed 5 years. Social workers may be re-approved at the end of the 5 year period after appropriate re-appraisal by the local authority. Social workers moving from one employing authority to another must be re-approved by the new authority which must be satisfied that such persons have met whatever requirement CCETSW specifies.

6. The Secretary of State directs, that, except for mental welfare officers in post on 28 October 1982 (the date the Mental Health (Amendment) Act was passed), all candidates for assessment by CCETSW and for approval by social services authorities shall hold the Certificate of Qualification in Social Work or a qualification recognised as comparable by CCETSW.

The Circular also provides a broad summary of the duties of approved social workers in paragraph 12 which is referred to at paragraph 2.8.11 following.

1.2.9 The implications involved in the change to approved social worker status have been hotly debated. It has been viewed by many as an indictment of the current training and qualification of social workers at both national and local level. It has also been seen as an initial attempt to break down the generic basis from which individual social workers have operated since the changes recommended in the Seebohm Report (1969), and therefore as an attempt to enforce an increased specialisation. The same may now happen in relation to child care. The change has been attacked as being divisive in employment terms – for example, will approved social workers rank higher in status than other social workers?

Whatever the operational and professional implications of the new law may be, it quite clearly places local social services authorities under a duty to appoint sufficient approved social workers by October 1984 to carry out work currently performed by mental welfare officers. The test of competence proposed by the Secretary of State and CCETSW has not been well received by social workers who will be expected to put themselves forward for assessment. At the time of writing the indications are that it is unlikely that sufficient numbers of social workers will take the examinations in time to be in post as approved social workers by October 1984. It also seems likely that the examination will be replaced by an assessment system.See Part 12 for further details.

1.2.10 What will be the consequences for a local social services authority if it cannot appoint sufficient approved social workers in time for the implementation of section 114 because of their opposition to the assessment scheme? Undoubtedly such an authority would be in breach of its statutory duty if insufficient workers are in post by October 1984, and the default powers in section 124 could be used by the Secretary of State. If however, as seems more likely, some social workers do take the necessary examinations and are approved by their employing authorities under section 114 it is doubtful that the social services authority will be in breach of its duty.

Whether or not the number of approved social workers appointed by a local social services authority is 'sufficient' is a question to be answered by reference to the particular local circumstances prevailing within an individual authority's area. There are no statutory or DHSS guidelines upon the number of approved social workers which should be appointed; therefore this must be a matter left to the discretion of the local social services authority. One of the main aims of the 1983 Act is to encourage local authorities to establish teams of specialist mental health workers. As a result it would be reasonable to expect that the overall number of approved social workers will ultimately be less than the current number of mental welfare officers, who are often engaged in other areas of social work.

1.2.11 Where a local social services authority fails to carry out a statutory duty the proper procedure is for a complaint to be made to the Secretary of State who must consider whether or not to exercise his default power. An individual who seeks to require an authority to carry out its statutory social services duties must first complain to the Secretary of State. The courts have shown in the past that they will not intervene where there is a default power unless the Secretary of State fails or refuses to exercise his default power. The creation of a trained group of social workers possessing specialist skills in mental health work will undoubtedly lead to greater accountability for practitioners and (possibly) their employers. The 1983 Act requires the Secretary of State to give guidance to doctors, hospitals and approved social workers in the form of a Code of Practice and the MHAC has been directed to submit proposals for the Code. Whilst the Code will not have the force of law we feel that it will have great significance for approved social workers faced with litigation by a patient. Failure to follow the Code without good reason could amount to a prima facie case of professional negligence. Such a prima facie case may prove sufficient grounds for the High Court to grant a patient leave to bring legal proceedings in negligence against an approved social worker.

1.3   Summary

1.3.1   The 1983 Act can be described as a series of amendments to the 1959 Act – most significantly, in relation to the rights of the patient, the powers of tribunals, the Mental Health Act Commission and powers and duties of approved social workers. Only time will tell how the 1983 Act will serve the benefit of the patient and the benefit of the community. In May 1983 the amendments to the 1959 Act were consolidated in the Mental Health Act 1983 and the majority of the provisions came into force on 30 September 1983. This was not the case for a few provisions, eg the statutory duty on local social services authorities to appoint approved social workers referred to above. Other exceptions relate to new criminal offender provisions increasing the range of orders that the courts may make. These will probably come into force on 1 October 1984 following the creation of new secure units.

Since the debate upon the reform of mental health legislation began in the 1970s a substantial amount of consultative material, White Papers, Acts and explanatory material has been published to implement and amplify the new legislation. Reference is made to these documents throughout this work and a selection is set out below with abbreviated references in brackets where appropriate:

1.3.2   Acts

The Mental Health Act 1959 (the 1959 Act)
The Mental Health (Amendment) Act 1982 (the 1982 Amendment Act)
The Mental Health Act 1983 (the 1983 Act)

1.3.3 Statutory Instruments

The Mental Health (Amendment) Act 1982 (Commencement No 1) Order 1983 – 1983 No 890

The Mental Health (Nurses) Order 1983 - 1983 No 891

The Mental Health Act Commission (Establishment and Constitution) Order 1983 - 1983 No 892

The Mental Health Act (Hospital, Guardianship and Consent to Treatment) Regulations 1983 - 1983 No 893 ('the 1983 Regulations')

The Mental Health Act Commission Regulations 1983 - 1983 No 894

The Nursing Homes and Mental Nursing Homes (Amendment) Regulations 1983 - 1983 No 901

The Mental Health Review Tribunal Rules 1983 - 1983 No 942 ('the 1983 Rules')

1.3.4 Circulars

Mental Health (Amendment) Act 1982. Mental Health Act 1983. – Approved Social Workers. LAC (83) 7

Representation of the People Act 1983 – Electoral Registration in Mental Illness and Mental Handicap Hospitals ('Health Circular August 1983')

Mental Health Act 1983 – Notes for General Medical Practitioners. HN(FP) (83)31

1.3.5 Memoranda

Mental Health Act 1983 – Explanatory Memorandum (DHSS June 1983, 'DHSS Guide')

1.3.6 Parliamentary Papers

A Review of The Mental Health Act 1959 – DHSS 1976 ('the 1976 Review')

Review of the Mental Health Act 1959 – Cmnd 7320 ('the 1978 Review')

Reform of Mental Health Legislation – Cmnd 8405 ('the 1981 White Paper')

The Mental Health (Amendment) Bill – ('1982 Amendment Bill')

House of Commons Official Report – Special Standing Committee ('Commons Committee')

1.4 Mental disorder – legal classifications

1.4.1 Section 1 (2) In this Act –

'mental disorder' means mental illness, arrested or incomplete development of mind, psychopathic disorder and any other disorder or disability of mind and 'mentally disordered' shall be construed accordingly.

1.4.2 This paragraph sets out the various categories of mental disorder with which the Act is concerned and the categories are apparently unchanged. We will see when we consider the definitions more closely that some important changes have been made and others have not. As in the 1959 Act, again, the law remains silent as to the meaning of mental illness. Those critical of the power of psychiatrists will find little comfort in the fact that this remains almost entirely a matter of clinical judgment. Yet we have seen earlier (at para 1.1.3) in the 1973 case the consequences of the failure of the 1959 Act to define this term. The 1976 Review contained a possible definition but the 1978 Review rejected the idea of defining mental illness on the ground that there was little evidence that the lack of definition had caused many problems. The result is that the definition of mental illness in the 1973 case still applies.

A more fundamental issue is whether or not the term mental disorder should be defined at all. In considering the arguments for and against changes in the definition the 1976 Review identified three options:

  (a) abolishing the sub-categories altogether producing the following definition:
     'In this Act "mental disorder" means mental illness, arrested or incomplete development of mind and any other disorder or disability of mind however caused or manifested and "mentally disordered" shall be construed accordingly.'
  (b) a closed definition which would define mental disorder in precise detail and which would allow no flexibility
  (c) modifying the present sub-categories.

1.4.3 Surprisingly both the Royal College of Psychiatrists and MIND were in agreement to some extent (for different reasons) over the need to remove the sub-categories. The Royal College of Psychiatrists wished to avoid use of the term psychopathy whilst MIND felt that compulsory detention should be based on the need to protect the patient, individuals or the public from the patient's dangerousness or vulnerability rather than the type of mental disorder from which the patient is suffering. The 1978 Review preferred the third option of retaining the 1959 Act categories whilst revising the definitions and terminology and eventually this option was adopted and incorporated within the 1983 Act. The phrase 'and any other disorder or disability of mind' provides considerable freedom in clinical diagnosis. The clinical model would appear to have been preserved intact. This status quo retained in the 1982 Amendment Bill was the subject of considerable Parliamentary debate. There was concern that 'any other disorder or disability of mind' might cover almost any abnormality, perception of ethnic difference, religious belief or individual eccentricity. Was it acceptable that individuals could be rendered liable to compulsory detention on such ill-defined grounds?

The advantage of retaining this widely drawn category was that it allows certain conditions such as disordered brain damage, to be covered by the compulsory admission procedures. Few people have been admitted to hospital under this part of the definition – fewer than 100 at any time – and removal of it might force those responsible for diagnosis to make hasty judgments about a patient's condition if it was thought necessary for him to be detained. The latter argument prevailed and the suggested amendments in Parliament were withdrawn.

1.4.4 **Section 1** (2) 'severe mental impairment' means a state of arrested or incomplete development of mind which includes severe impairment of intelligence and social functioning and is associated with abnormally aggressive or seriously irresponsible conduct on the part of the person concerned and 'severely mentally impaired' shall be construed accordingly;

'mental impairment' means a state of arrested or incomplete development of mind (not amounting to severe mental impairment) which includes significant impairment of intelligence and social functioning and is associated with abnormally aggressive or seriously irresponsible conduct on the part of the person concerned and 'mentally impaired' shall be construed accordingly;

The terms 'severe mental impairment' and 'mental impairment' are substituted for 'severe subnormality' and 'subnormality', the terminology used in the 1959 Act. As mentioned earlier, those terms replaced other terms such as 'lunacy' and 'mental deficiency' in an attempt to de-stigmatise the individual. The term 'impairment' represents a further move in this direction. At first sight it appears to be a merely cosmetic change but impairment must be considered at a deeper level. It is an attempt to remove most cases of mental handicap from the legislation. This is stated Government policy. The White Paper 'Reform of Mental Health Legislation' Cmnd 8405, stated at paragraphs 8 and 9:

> 8. The Government shares the concern which is widely felt that mental handicap should not be confused with mental illness and that the needs of different groups of people should be recognised. They have also considered with great care whether it is still appropriate to provide compulsory powers in respect of any mentally handicapped people and if so how this should be done.
>
> 9. The weight of professional opinion is that there is a very small minority of mentally handicapped people without any other mental disorder, who do need to be detained in hospital – usually for their own safety. The Government recognises the importance of stressing that this is only a small minority. While, therefore, the Bill continues to provide for the compulsory detention which is required, subject to all safeguards provided, it does make a change in the words used. 'Severe subnormality' and 'subnormality' are to be replaced by the more up to date terms 'severe mental handicap' and 'mental handicap'.

Whether the new terminology will actually bring that policy to fruition remains to be seen. The 1982 Amendment Bill began its Parliamentary life using the terms 'mental handicap' and 'severe mental handicap'. During its passage through the Lords the term 'impairment' was introduced to replace 'handicap' in an attempt to respond to pressure from Lord Renton, chairman of MENCAP. This pressure sought to remove mentally handicapped people from the ambit of the compulsory detention provisions of the Act because mental handicap is not a treatable condition but rather it is, to quote Lord Elton, speaking for the Government in the Lords' Second Reading debate, 'an unalterable condition, usually acquired before birth, whereas mental illness is a treatable condition acquired at any age. The conditions are not the same and to have them lumped together in one Act of Parliament obscures the difference.' So no useful purpose could be served by detaining mentally handicapped patients in hospital. The Government, whilst accepting that there was a problem, refused to go all the way with Lord Renton. The outcome was a compromise which seemingly satisfied the mentally handicapped lobby. This compromise was to substitute the terms 'impairment' and 'severe impairment' for 'subnormality' and 'severe subnormality' and to alter the definitions of these terms.

1.4.5 Can the mentally handicapped always be treated in the community? It was the expressed opinion of the Royal College of Psychiatrists in 1979 that there was a small minority of mentally handicapped people, who did not suffer from any other form of mental disorder, and who needed to be detained in hospital because they were either violent or vulnerable if left alone in the community. This opinion was not shared by many psychiatrists and it was heavily criticised even before it was published. Nonetheless the argument against total removal of the mentally handicapped from the scope of the Act prevailed and in order to satisfy critics, the term 'impairment' was inserted in the Bill. The origins of this term lie in its use by the World Health Organisation to describe any case of abnormality of psychological, physiological or anatomical structure or function. It occurs in the International Classification of Impairments, Disabilities and Handicaps published by WHO in Geneva in 1980. The problem that remains if the term impairment is used is to restrict the scope of the Act to those violent or vulnerable people who require detention. This is achieved by providing that it is not sufficient for a patient's development of mind to be impaired or severely impaired. The condition must be associated with aggressive or irresponsible conduct. Doubts have been expressed as to the effectiveness of this safeguard. In particular there is concern over whether the phrase will be interpreted in a subjective or an objective manner. The distinction is clearly important – it is the difference between asking 'Has the patient behaved abnormally aggressively or seriously irresponsibly in the past?' and 'Is the diagnosed condition normally associated with abnormally aggressive or seriously irresponsible behaviour?' An attempt to strengthen the objective nature of the test by inserting a requirement that the conduct must be recent was defeated and we therefore retain some doubt that the apparent safeguards will prove effective enough to restrict the scope of the Act to those mentally impaired patients who need to be covered by the compulsory provisions. It is perhaps an area for the Mental Health Act Commission to monitor.

1.4.6   **Section 1** (2) 'psychopathic disorder' means a persistent disorder or disability of mind (whether or not including significant impairment of intelligence) which results in abnormally aggressive or seriously irresponsible conduct on the part of the person concerned.

The White Paper stated that:

12. The Government has considered whether psychopathic disorder should be excluded from the Act, bearing in mind the discussion in the

Butler Report on Mentally Abnormal Offenders (Cmnd 6244). The weight of current medical opinion is that most psychopaths are not likely to benefit from treatment in hospital and are for the penal system to deal with when they do commit offences, but that there are some persons suffering from psychopathic disorder who can be helped by detention in hospital. For this reason this category is not excluded in the Act.

1.4.7   The main issue here is whether psychopathic disorder should be included as a category of mental disorder at all. To quote the 1978 Review: 'There is doubt about whether psychopathic disorder should be included within the scope of the Act at all since it is questionable whether the Health Service can at present offer effective treatment to the generality of people suffering from this disorder'. In an attempt to remove the stigma associated with the term psychopathic disorder the Butler Committee suggested that it should be replaced by 'personality disorder' but there was little support for this change in terminology or for the Butler Committee's suggested definition (which would apply in criminal proceedings only):

(a) That a previous mental or organic illness or an identifiable psychological or physical defect, relevant to the disorder is known or suspected; and

(b) there is an expectation of therapeutic benefit from hospital admission.

The consequences of removing psychopathic disorder completely from the Act would have been significant, since nearly 10% of detained patients are classified as suffering from psychopathic disorder, and a small number of psychopathic offenders are made subject to hospital orders, It was thought unwise to remove these patients from the scope of the Act and therefore the sub-category remains although the definition is changed.

Under the 1959 Act, one of the limitations on compulsory admission powers was that they could only be applied to mentally subnormal and psychopathic patients if they were under 21 (although once admitted they could continue after the age of 25 if they were considered dangerous). The origin of the age limit lay in medical opinion that mentally handicapped or psychopathic adults were unlikely to benefit from hospital treatment. It is now generally accepted that such age limits are arbitrary and they have been removed under the new Act, in order to allow for the greater possibility of treatment (see below section 3) and the informed view is that attempts should be made to treat psychopaths of all ages.

1.4.8 The disorder must:

(a) be persistent,
(b) may or may not include *'significant'* impairment of intelligence (rather than 'subnormality of intelligence' as under the 1959 Act) and
(c) the disorder or disability must *result* in (rather than be 'associated with') abnormal aggression or seriously irresponsible conduct.

1.4.9 **Section 1** (3) Nothing in subsection (2) above shall be construed as implying that a person may be dealt with under this Act as suffering from mental disorder, or from any form of mental disorder described in this section by reason only of promiscuity or other immoral conduct, sexual deviancy or dependence on alcohol or drugs.

The 1959 Act excluded only 'promiscuity or other immoral conduct' from the definition of mental disorder which was a liberal measure designed to prevent compulsory detention of so-called 'moral defectives'. Three further categories are added to the 1959 Act exclusions:- sexual deviancy (undefined therefore a matter for clinical judgement), dependence on alcohol and dependence on drugs. This is a significant change in that it extends the circumstances which alone do not constitute mental disorder unless related to one of the specific categories of mental disorder in section 1(2).

1.4.10 Reclassification of Patients

Section 16 (1) If in the case of a patient who is for the time being detained in a hospital in pursuance of an application for admission for treatment, or subject to guardianship in pursuance of a guardianship application, it appears to the appropriate medical officer that the patient is suffering from a form of mental disorder other than the form or forms specified in the application, he may furnish to the managers of the hospital, or to the guardian, as the case may be, a report to that effect; and where a report is so furnished, the application shall have effect as if that other form of mental disorder were specified in it.

(2) Where a report under subsection (1) above in respect of a patient detained in a hospital is to the effect that he is suffering from psychopathic disorder or mental impairment but not from mental illness or severe mental impairment the appropriate medical officer shall include in the report a statement of his opinion whether further medical treatment in hospital is likely to alleviate or prevent a deterioration of the patient's condition; and if he states that in his opinion such treatment is not likely to have that effect the authority of the managers to detain the patient shall cease.

(3) Before furnishing a report under subsection (1) above the appropriate medical officer shall consult one or more other persons who have been professionally concerned with the patient's medical treatment.

(4) Where a report is furnished under this section in respect of a patient, the managers or guardian shall cause the patient and the nearest relative to be informed.

(5) In this section 'appropriate medical officer' means—

(a) in the case of a patient who is subject to the guardianship of a person other than a local social services authority, the nominated medical attendant of the patient; and

(b) in any other case, the responsible medical officer.

This section gives the doctor in charge of a patient's treatment the power to reflect changes in the diagnosis of the patient's mental condition by reclassifying him. It applies only to patients in hospital under an application to detain for treatment or patients subject to guardianship. It is important to note that:

(a) the 'treatability' test must be satisfied if a patient is reclassified to psychopathic disorder or mental impairment. If this test is not satisfied the authority to detain the patient ends;

(b) the doctor must consult with those who have been 'professionally concerned with the patient's medical treatment' before reclassifying the patient;

(c) the patient and his nearest relative have, on reclassification, the right to be informed and to apply to a tribunal for the patient's discharge within 28 days of being informed (the Mental Health Act 1983, section 66; see para 6.2 following).

For some case studies relating to this Part see para **11.2.1** *in Part 11 following.*

Into hospital

2.1 Introduction

This is the most crucial part of the legislation, as far as the social worker, approved or otherwise, is concerned and contains within it the following aspects:

(1) Compulsory admission procedures .... (sections 2-6)
(2) General provisions as to applications and
    medical recommendations .... (sections 11-15)
(3) Duration of detention and discharge .... (sections 20-25)
(4) Functions of relatives of patients .... (sections 26-30)
(5) Role of the approved social worker .... (section 13)
(6) Role of the police .... (sections 135-136)

Some of the sections interrelate closely with one another and these will be identified as the text proceeds.

2.2 Admission for assessment (Forms 1 to 4, 1983 Regulations)

Section 2 (1) A patient may be admitted to a hospital and detained there for the period allowed by subsection (4) below in pursuance of an application (in this Act referred to as 'an application for admission for assessment') made in accordance with subsection (2) and (3) below.

(2) An application for admission for assessment may be made in respect of a patient on the grounds that—

    (a) he is suffering from mental disorder of a nature or degree which warrants the detention of the patient in a hospital for assessment (or for assessment followed by medical treatment) for at least a limited period; and

(b) he ought to be so detained in the interests of his own health or safety or with a view to the protection of other persons.

2.2.1 The new term 'assessment' which replaces 'observation' contained in the 1959 Act, implies a more active evaluation and intervention than was hitherto the case. The change answers the call from the medical profession for express authority for psychiatrists to treat patients detained for observation. This problem has now been resolved in subsection (2)(a) which allows treatment other than that used in assessment procedures to be given to patients detained for assessment. Some unease has been expressed with regard to this change. Compared to section 3 (admission for treatment, see para 2.3) the grounds for admission for assessment in section 2 are wider and therefore open to potential abuse. This could take the form of attempting to use section 2 as a device for making repeated short-term admissions for assessment – virtually the equivalent of long-term admission under detention for treatment. It is to be presumed that the Mental Health Act Commission will seek to monitor admissions procedures and identify cases of repeated use of this section in relation to particular patients. The consent to treatment provisions (see para 4.2) will apply to patients detained for assessment and such patients can now apply to a Mental Health Review Tribunal for discharge.

> **Section 2** (3) An application for admission for assessment shall be founded on the written recommendations in the prescribed form of two registered medical practitioners, including in each case a statement that in the opinion of the practitioner the conditions set out in subsection (2) above are complied with.

The subsection does not state who may make an application for admission for assessment or who the two recommending doctors should be. Since this problem will arise in relation to other forms of admission it will be appropriate to discuss the matter here.

2.2.2 Who may make an application?

> **Section 11** (1) Subject to the provisions of this section, an application for admission for assessment, an application for admission for treatment and a guardianship application may be made either by the nearest relative of the patient or by an approved social worker, and every such application shall specify the qualification of the applicant to make the application.
>
> (2) Every application for admission shall be addressed to the managers of the hospital to which admission is sought and every guardianship application shall be forwarded to the local social services authority named in the application as guardian, or, as the case may be, to

the local social services authority for the area in which the person so named resides.

The applicant must be either an approved social worker (not any social worker) or the nearest relative of the patient (not any relative). The identity of the nearest relative will be a matter considered later at para 2.7.2. Note that a nearest relative can only object to an approved social worker making an application for admission for treatment and not an application for admission for assessment.

2.2.3   Who may make the medical recommendations?

Section 12 (1) The recommendations required for the purposes of an application for the admission of a patient under this Part of this Act (in this Act referred to as 'medical recommendations') shall be signed on or before the date of the application, and shall be given by practitioners who have personally examined the patient either together or separately, but where they have examined the patient separately not more than five days must have elapsed between the days on which the separate examinations took place.

(2) Of the medical recommendations given for the purposes of any such application, one shall be given by a practitioner approved for the purposes of this section by the Secretary of State as having special experience in the diagnosis or treatment of mental disorder; and unless that practitioner has previous acquaintance with the patient, the other such recommendation shall, if practicable, be given by a registered medical practitioner who has such previous acquaintance.

If the examinations take place separately, not more than five days must separate them. This period was seven days in the 1959 Act.

The two recommending doctors must be:

(a) an approved doctor (ie a psychiatrist).

Although reference is made to approval by the Secretary of State, this power has been delegated to District Health Authorities, and it is usual for the District Health Authorities to supply their local social services authorities with lists of approved doctors;

(b) a registered medical practitioner (usually the patient's GP).

If such a doctor is unavailable within the 5 day period (or if the patient has no GP) then any doctor may give the second recommendation.

2.2.4   When must the application be made?

Section 11 (5) None of the applications mentioned in subsection (1) above shall be made by any person in respect of a patient unless that person has personally seen the patient within the period of 14 days ending with the date of the application.

An approved social worker or a nearest relative must apply within 14 days of the last time they saw the patient. The application must be based upon the medical recommendations therefore the application should *not* be made until the medical recommendation(s) have been signed by the doctor(s). This view is also supported by section 12(1) which refers to the medical recommendations as being signed on or before the date of the application.

2.2.5 The relationship between the timing of applications and their supporting recommendations is most important. The problems which arose in *Townley v Rushworth,* a case in 1964 under the 1959 Act provisions, may still arise under the 1983 Act.

In this case a wife signed an application for the emergency admission of her husband to hospital. The family GP was then asked to provide the medical recommendation required under the 1959 Act. The wife left the family home to protect herself from her husband's violent behaviour. The doctor went to the family home with the husband's brother-in-law and two policemen. The doctor took with him the wife's signed application and an uncompleted medical recommendation and, as required by the Act, was not prepared to sign the medical recommendation until he had examined the husband. The husband allowed all concerned to enter the house but when the doctor informed him that he would have to go to hospital and began to prepare an injection the husband asked them to leave. The husband went to his bedroom and was prevented from leaving it by the first policeman. The second policeman came upstairs with the doctor to assist in restraining the husband whilst he was being sedated. The husband thought he was about to be attacked and assaulted the second policeman, breaking his nose. The doctor then examined the husband, sedated him, called an ambulance and *then* signed the medical recommendation. The husband was charged with assault and convicted by magistrates who held that although the medical recommendation had not been completed the husband had no reasonable ground for believing that he was about to be attacked. On appeal, it was held that since the medical recommendation had not been signed, none of the persons present in the family home had authority to be present under the 1959 Act and were therefore trespassers. The conviction for assault was quashed. The importance of the case lies in the court's decision that the signed application was not sufficient authority to prevent the persons present in the family home becoming trespassers once they were asked to leave by the husband and this was because the medical recommendation had not been signed. We offer guidance upon the correct procedure to follow in cases such as this at paragraphs 2.6 and 2.9 below.

2.2.6 Effect of an application

Section 6 (1) An application for the admission of a patient to a hospital under this Part of the Act, duly completed in accordance with the provisions of this Part of this Act, shall be sufficient authority for the applicant, or any person authorised by the applicant, to take the patient and convey him to the hospital at any time within the following period, that is to say—

(a) in the case of an application other than an emergency application, the period of 14 days beginning with the date on which the patient was last examined by a registered medical practitioner before giving a medical recommendation for the purposes of the application;

It should also be noted that the application and medical recommendation forms are sufficient authority to take the patient to hospital within a 14-day period beginning with the date on which the patient was last medically examined.

2.2.7 **Section 2** (4) Subject to the provisions of section 29(4) below, a patient admitted to hospital in pursuance of an application for assessment may be detained for a period not exceeding 28 days beginning with the day on which he is admitted, but shall not be detained after the expiration of that period unless before it has expired he has become liable to be detained by virtue of a subsequent application, order or direction under the following provisions of this Act.

A 28-day period of detention in hospital is created and this period existed in the 1959 Act. This period can be extended if an application to displace a nearest relative is made under section 29(4) (see para 2.7.8 below).

There is no other way in which an admission for assessment can be extended under the Act. However it is possible to make an application for detention for treatment in respect of a patient already in hospital (see para 2.5.9 below). Such an application must be made before the 28-day period has expired since after this time there will be no authority to detain the patient.

2.2.8 The rights of the patient and nearest relative following admission to hospital

The patient must be informed of his rights as soon as practicable following admission (see section 132, para 4.1.2) and it is particularly important that this is done quickly for patients admitted for assessment because their right to apply to a tribunal for discharge must be exercised within 14 days of admission. As legal aid and advice is now available for tribunal proceedings (subject to the usual means tests) this new right of patients to apply for discharge is likely to create a considerable increase in the tribunals' work-load. The White Paper commented:

> For practical reasons application must be made within the first 14 days of detention and the hearing will take place shortly afterwards. For these short-term cases the Tribunal will of necessity have to evolve new arrangements and will usually have to rely largely on the medical and social workers' reports made at the time of admission, with perhaps an oral report from the patient's responsible medical officer.

Rule 31(a) of the Tribunal Rules states that the date of the hearing '[shall be] not later than 7 days from the date on which the application was received...'.
Further, the 1983 Rules indicate that reports, including an up-to-date social circumstances report, are required to be in the possession of the Tribunal by the date of the hearing.

2.2.9 In relation to the nearest relative, the provisions of section 132 also apply unless the patient otherwise requests, so the hospital managers must take such steps as are practicable to give to the nearest relative a copy of the information given to the patient. In addition to this, the approved social worker will need to bear in mind the provisions of section 11(3):

> **Section 11** (3) Before or within a reasonable time after an application for the admission of a patient for assessment is made by an approved social worker, that social worker shall take such steps as are practicable to inform the person (if any) appearing to be the nearest relative of the patient that the application is to be or has been made and of the power of the nearest relative under section 23(2)(a) below.

This amendment to the provisions of the 1959 Act possibly only reflects what should have been good practice in any event. The difference now is that this becomes a statutory duty where the application has been or is to be made by the approved social worker. Not only must the nearest relative be informed by the approved social worker of the fact of the application, but he must also be informed of his power to order the patient's discharge and by implication how he may exercise this power:

2.2.10 **Section 23** (2) An order for discharge may be made in respect of a patient—

(a) where the patient is liable to be detained in a hospital in pursuance of an application for assessment or for treatment by the responsible medical officer, by the managers or by the nearest relative of the patient;

Regulation 15 (1) Any order made by the nearest relative of the patient under section 23 for the discharge of a patient who is liable to be detained under Part II of the Act shall be served upon the managers of the hospital where the patient is liable to be detained and may be in the form set out in Form 34.

2.2.11 If the responsible medical officer or the managers of the hospital do not do so, the nearest relative may exercise the power to discharge the patient. Regulation 15 states how this power may be exercised and a form is prescribed but is not mandatory.

Section 24 (1) For the purpose of advising as to the exercise by the nearest relative of a patient who is liable to be detained . . . under this Part of this Act of any power to order his discharge, any registered medical practitioner authorised by or on behalf of the nearest relative of the patient may, at any reasonable time, visit the patient and examine him in private.

(2) Any registered medical practitioner authorised for the purposes of subsection (1) above to visit and examine a patient may require the production of and inspect any records relating to the detention or treatment of the patient in any hospital.

These provisions enable the nearest relative to obtain independent medical advice upon the question of the patient's discharge and the medical adviser, who must be a registered doctor, is given power to demand access to the patient to examine him in private and to have access to all records relating to the patient's detention and treatment. These powers are also available to doctors appointed by the Secretary of State and Health Authorities in connection with their powers to order a patient's discharge but it is probably the nearest relative connection that has most relevance for the approved social worker.

2.2.12 The procedure to be used by the nearest relative in exercising his power to order the discharge of a patient and the restrictions on that power are set out in section 25:

Section 25 (1) An order for the discharge of a patient who is liable to be detained in a hospital shall not be made by his nearest relative except after giving not less than 72 hours' notice in writing to the managers of the hospital; and if, within 72 hours after such notice has been given, the responsible medical officer furnishes to the managers a report certifying that in the opinion of that officer the patient, if discharged, would be likely to act in a manner dangerous to other persons or to himself

(a) any order for the discharge of the patient made by that relative in pursuance of the notice shall be of no effect; and

(b) no further order for the discharge of the patient shall be made by that relative during the period of six months beginning with the date of the report.

(2) In any case where a report under subsection (1) above is furnished in respect of a patient who is liable to be detained in pursuance of an application for treatment the managers shall cause the nearest relative of the patient to be informed.

If the nearest relative wishes to discharge the patient, the approved social worker may consider providing the appropriate form (Form 34) and, if requested, assisting in its completion. Regulation 3(3) provides that notices and orders for discharge must be served either by delivery at the hospital to an officer authorised by the managers to receive it, or by sending it by pre-paid post to the managers at the hospital. If the responsible medical officer considers that the patient is likely to be a danger to himself or others if discharged he may report his view (using Form 36) to the hospital managers within 72 hours of the nearest relative's order for discharge. The effects of the issue of Form 36 are:

(a) the order for discharge is nullified;

(b) the nearest relative may not order the patient's discharge at any time within the next six months;

(c) if the patient concerned is detained for *treatment*, the nearest relative must be informed without delay. This is because the nearest relative has a right to apply to a Mental Health Review Tribunal within 28 days of the issue of Form 36. The nearest relative does not have this right if the patient was detained for *assessment*.

From the above it can be seen that the approved social worker is acting as an information channel and must, therefore, be aware of the nearest relative's rights where the patient is detained for treatment. It will be equally important for the nearest relative to be advised of the patient's right to apply for his own discharge if he is detained for assessment.

2.2.13 A final comment on section 2 is to be found in the DHSS

Guide which states that 'it is envisaged that many patients will complete their treatment in hospital within a period of detention under section 2 and can then be discharged. Others may stay as informal patients or, if they can satisfy the conditions, they can be detained under section 3 for longer term treatment.'

2.3 Admission for treatment (Forms 8 to 10, 1983 Regulations)

2.3.1 **Section 3** (1) A patient may be admitted to a hospital and detained there for the period allowed by the following provisions of this Act in pursuance of an application (in this Act referred to as 'an application for admission for treatment') made in accordance with this section.

(2) An application for admission for treatment may be made in respect of a patient on the grounds that—

(a) he is suffering from mental illness, severe mental impairment, psychopathic disorder or mental impairment and his mental disorder is of a nature or degree which makes it appropriate for him to receive medical treatment in a hospital; and

(b) in the case of psychopathic disorder or mental impairment, such treatment is likely to alleviate or prevent a deterioration of his condition; and

(c) it is necessary for the health or safety of the patient or for the protection of other persons that he should receive such treatment and it cannot be provided unless he is detained under this section.

This new section contains changes in the grounds for longer-term detention. The intention behind the changes is an attempt to ensure that this power is only used for the purposes of treatment of patients suffering from mental disorders which can benefit from treatment. In relation to section 3(2)(a), the links with section 1 will be noted, and the question must be asked, 'As an alternative to hospital admission, could the patient be treated in the community?' Section 3(2)(b) contains a new provision for those suffering from psychopathic disorder or mental impairment. In addition to the removal of age limits mentioned above, (Part 1, para 1.4.7) it provides that no such patients may be admitted under this power unless medical treatment is likely to alleviate or prevent a deterioration in their condition – the 'treatability test'. Section 3(2)(c) allows for the balancing of the health and safety of the patient against the protection of the community and contains within it the implication that the section should only be used if treatment cannot be provided in any other way, and where the patient is unwilling to stay as an informal patient. There are a number of difficulties with the grounds listed above:

(a) Section 3 (2) is an attempt to ensure that compulsory admission for treatment is a matter of last resort. Treatment as an informal patient, and, preferably, treatment in the community is to be preferred. This can only occur if sufficient resources are made available in the community.

(b) Will 'treatability' become confused with 'curability'? The test wisely says nothing in relation to curability but confusion may arise resulting in fewer psychopathic or mentally impaired patients being treated. The Mental Health Act Commission should closely monitor this issue.

(c) In relation to the 'balancing formula' set out in section 3(2)(c), detention must be necessary 'for the protection of other persons'; but the question is, 'from what must they be protected?' The Act does not answer this question. We submit that the phrase 'the protection of other persons' is intended to cover patients who, if discharged from detention in hospital, would be likely to commit acts of violence to persons in the community. It should not be used to justify the detention of patients who, if released, whilst likely to be a nuisance to others are otherwise quite harmless.

2.3.2 Who may make an application?

As seen in section 11(1) and (2) above an application can only be made by an approved social worker or the nearest relative. However a number of points arise in relation to an application for treatment:

(a) In most cases, good practice assumes that the approved social worker will not immediately consider the use of the admission for treatment provisions, unless there is a recent history of one or more admissions for assessment. During the Amendment Bill debates it was suggested that it should not be possible to make an admission for treatment unless a prior admission for assessment has been made. This suggestion failed to become law on the basis that the great majority of admissions for treatment would be based on preceding assessments.

(b) **Section 11**(4) provides:

Neither an application for admission for treatment nor a guardianship application shall be made by an approved social worker if the nearest relative of the patient has notified that social worker, or the local social services authority by whom that social worker is appointed that he objects to the application and, without prejudice to the foregoing provision, no such application shall be made by such social worker except after consultation with the person (if any) appearing to be the nearest relative of the patient unless it appears to that social worker that in the circumstances such consultation is not reasonably practicable or would involve unreasonable delay.

If the nearest relative objects, an approved social worker cannot proceed with an application for treatment. The way forward is by one of two routes – either

(i) an application to the county court to displace the objecting nearest relative under section 29 of the Act (see para 2.7.7 below) or

(ii) an application for admission for assessment which the nearest relative has no power to prevent (though there is still a statutory requirement for the social worker to consult section 11(3)).

We would have grave doubts about the propriety of the latter course of action if it were to be taken purely to override the nearest relative's wishes. It would only be justified if the approved social worker was genuinely convinced that the nearest relative's objection was invalid and to save the nearest relative from the anxiety and expense of a county court action under section 29. This course of action might also be justified if a current period of detention for assessment was about to expire and there was no time to apply to the county court, although this situation would be better covered by a report by the patient's medical practitioner under section 5 or by the exercise of the nurses' holding power under section 5(4) if the patient is about to leave.

(c) It is assumed that the approved social worker has a reasonable degree of knowledge of matters concerning medical treatment. The term 'medical treatment' is defined in the Act as including 'nursing, and also includes care, habilitation and rehabilitation under medical supervision.' Knowledge of resources is also implicit in this definition.

2.3.3   Who may make a medical recommendation?

Section 3 (3) An application for admission for treatment shall be founded on the written recommendations in the prescribed form of two registered medical practitioners, including in each case a statement that in the opinion of the practitioner the conditions set out in subsection (2) above are complied with; and each such recommendation shall include—
 (a) such particulars as may be prescribed of the grounds for that
  opinion so far as it relates to the conditions set out in paragraphs
  (a) and (b) of that subsection; and (b) a statement of the reasons
  for that opinion so far as it relates to the conditions set out in

paragraph (c) of that subsection, specifying whether other methods of dealing with the patient are available and, if so, why they are not appropriate.

The comments made above (para 2.2.3) in relation to section 12 apply here also, although it will be noticed that section 3(3) and section 3(6) are more stringent, particularly as the medical opinion must state whether other methods of dealing with the patient are available and, if so, why they are not appropriate. This is in keeping with the emphasis on the fact that compulsory detention for treatment should be a last resort.

2.3.4 What is the duration of authority to compulsorily detain patients for treatment?

Section 20 (1) Subject to the following provisions of this Part of this Act, a patient admitted to hospital in pursuance of an application for admission for treatment . . . may be detained in a hospital . . . for a period not exceeeding six months beginning with the day on which he was so admitted . . . but shall not be detained . . . for any longer period unless the authority for his detention . . . is renewed under this section.

(2) Authority for the detention . . . of a patient may, unless the patient has previously been discharged, be renewed:

(a) from the expiration of the period referred to in subsection (1) above for a further period of six months;
(b) from the expiration of any period of renewal under paragraph (a) above, for a further period of one year, and so on for periods of one year at a time.

The intention in the White Paper and Parliament was to halve the existing time periods for detention under the 1959 Act. These time periods were:

initial period of detention	– 1 year
first renewal period	– 1 year
subsequent renewal periods	– 2 years

The stated intention is accomplished by section 20(1) and (2) of the 1983 Act and the time periods are now respectively:

initial period of detention	– 6 months
first renewal period	– 6 months
subsequent renewal periods	– 1 year.

The effect of this is to exactly double the number of opportunities for an application to be made to a Mental Health Review Tribunal. The intentions behind this are clear, and, together with the availability of legal aid, it is bound to create another increase in the case load of the Tribunals. The implications for local social services authorities should also be clear – an up-to-date social circumstances report is required each time the case comes up for review.

2.3.5 **Section 20** (3) Within the period of two months ending on the day on which a patient who is liable to be detained in pursuance of an application for admission for treatment would cease under this section to be so liable in default of the renewal of the authority for his detention, it shall be the duty of the responsible medical officer—
    (a) to examine the patient; and
    (b) if it appears to him that the conditions set out in subsection (4) below are satisfied, to furnish to the managers of the hospital where the patient is detained a report to that effect in the prescribed form;
and where such a report is furnished in respect of a patient the managers shall, unless they discharge the patient, cause him to be informed.

The responsible medical officer is required to examine a patient detained for treatment during the two months before authority to detain expires. If the responsible medical officer considers that the patient should continue to be detained he must report his opinion to the hospital managers on Form 30. This form will then be lodged with the patient's admission documents and the patient must be informed that the report has been issued unless the managers intend to discharge the patient (an unlikely event if the responsible medical officer has recommended the patient's continued detention). The patient's right to apply to a Mental Health Review Tribunal for his discharge will start to run from the date the report is lodged until the end of the renewed period of detention.

2.3.6 Before the report can be lodged certain safeguards are built into the Act:

Section 20 (4) The conditions referred to in subsection (3) above are that—
    (a) the patient is suffering from mental illness, severe mental impairment, psychopathic disorder or mental impairment and his mental disorder is of a nature or degree which makes it appropriate for him to receive medical treatment in a hospital; and
    (b) such treatment is likely to alleviate or prevent a deterioration of his condition; and
    (c) it is necessary for the health or safety of the patient or for the protection of other persons that he should receive such treatment and that it cannot be provided unless he continues to be detained; but, in the case of mental illness or severe mental impairment, it shall be an alternative to the condition specified in paragraph (b) above that the patient, if discharged, is unlikely to be able to care

for himself, to obtain the care which he needs or to guard himself against serious exploitation.

(5) Before furnishing a report under subsection (3) above the responsible medical officer shall consult one or more persons who have been professionally concerned with the patient's medical treatment.

The safeguards or conditions for renewal of authority to detain a patient are substantially the same as the grounds in section 3 for an application for treatment. In effect the responsible medical officer must consider the patient's case as if it was a new application for admission for treatment under section 3. The alternative ground for renewing authority to detain a patient suffering from mental illness or severe mental impairment should be noted.

These conditions are a substantial change from the grounds for renewal in the 1959 Act. Under that Act the responsible medical officer did not have to consider whether the patient was still suffering from mental disorder – the only safeguard was that renewal could only take place if it appeared to the responsible medical officer that 'it is necessary in the interests of the patient's health or safety or for the protection of other persons that the patient should continue to be liable to be detained . . .'. Form 30 requires the responsible medical officer to state the reasons why treatment cannot be given except under detention and to 'indicate whether other methods of care or treatment (eg out-patient treatment or local social services authority services) are available and if so why they are not appropriate, and why informal admission is not appropriate.'

Before submitting his report the responsible medical officer must consult with 'persons who have been professionally concerned with the patient's medical treatment.' Whilst this does not place the responsible medical officer under a duty to consult with an approved social worker about the availability of community based resources for the patient's care outside hospital it would seem that in practice the terms of Form 30 make such consultation essential. In its original form the 1982 Amendment Bill did not contain subsection (5) or any requirement for the responsible medical officer to consult before issuing his report. During the Parliamentary debates on the 1982 Amendment Bill several attempts were made to place the responsible medical officer under a duty to consult. In the Lords Baroness Faithfull moved an amendment which required the responsible medical officer to

consult an approved social worker who will interview the patient and satisfy himself that detention in hospital is the most appropriate means of ensuring that the patient continues to receive the care and treatment he needs and the responsible medical officer and the approved social worker shall furnish to the managers of the hospital where the patient is liable to be detained reports to the above effect on the prescribed form.

In the Commons Mr Stan Thorne moved an amendment which required the responsible medical officer

to consult members of other professions in relation to the medical treatment of patients detained under the Principal Act or this Act in accordance with such regulations as the Secretary of State shall have made concerning the conduct and recording of such consultations and to receive from each of them a report in writing stating their opinions as to whether the conditions set out in subsection 3A of this section are satisfied.

These amendments failed because the Government resisted them mainly on the ground that the decision to renew is that of the responsible medical officer and rests on his clinical judgement; therefore his authority to renew must be unrestricted. However the Government did state that 'It is good practice that the responsible medical officer should take account of advice from a social worker in considering alternatives to detention before he makes his report', and undertook to introduce an appropriate amendment to the Bill. This was done by including subsection 5. This subsection does not fully meet the intentions of the amendments described above as the responsible medical officer can comply with it by consulting doctors who have been concerned with the patient's treatment and need not consult with an approved social worker.

If responsible medical officers do follow the practice of consultation recommended by the Government this will prove a useful indicator for approved social workers and their employing authorities of the number of renewals which are occurring through lack of resources in the community. It is clear that the provision of extensive alternative community based resources is central to the objects of the legislation and it is here that the approved social worker and the local social services authority can be most effective in bringing to the attention of the Mental Health Act Commission the incidence of renewals based on a lack of community resources.

2.3.7 Automatic referrals to Mental Health Review Tribunals

The provisions of section 20 presuppose that the patient (or his nearest relative) will make application for review during the relevant time periods if they so wish (remembering that they must be informed as to their rights in this regard – section 132). What if no referrals are made, perhaps for some years? Periodic hospital reviews must take place under the Act but this is an internal process (although subject to the scrutiny of the Mental Health Act Commission). This is not the same as an *automatic* application to a Mental Health Review Tribunal within the relevant time periods. The Act covers this point in section 68.

Section 68 (1) Where a patient who is admitted to a hospital in pursuance of an application for admission for treatment . . . does not exercise his right to apply to a Mental Health Review Tribunal under section 66(1) by virtue of his case falling within paragraph (b) . . . the managers of the hospital shall at the expiration of the period for making such an application refer the patient's case to such a tribunal unless an application or reference in respect of the patient has then been made under section 66(1) above by virtue of his case falling within paragraph (d), (g), or (h) of that section or under section 67(1) above.

(2) If the authority for the detention of a patient in a hospital is renewed under section 20 above and a period of three years (or, if the patient has not attained the age of sixteen years, one year) has elapsed since his case was last considered by a Mental Health Review Tribunal, whether on his own application or otherwise, the managers of the hospital shall refer his case to such a tribunal.

The combined effect of these subsections is that if a patient, his nearest relative or the Secretary of State do not apply to a Mental Health Review Tribunal within the initial period of the patient's detention for treatment, the hospital *must* refer the case to a Mental Health Review Tribunal at the time of the first renewal of detention (ie after the first six months of detention). The hospital must refer the case again to a Mental Health Review Tribunal if no further application is made in the subsequent three years (one year if the patient is under 16).

The process of applying to a Mental Health Review Tribunal could become a routine exercise if the patient is unable to call independent medical evidence in support of his application to be discharged. Such evidence could take several forms including a challenge to the hospital's medical evidence in support of the patient's continued detention, or the presentation of independent psychiatric opinion on behalf of the patient as to the patient's mental state and his ability to cope with life outside hospital. To help the patient in bringing such evidence there is provision in section 68(3) for the production of *any* records relating to the patient's detention and treatment in hospital. The records may only be produced to a doctor appointed by or on behalf of the patient and the doctor is also given power to visit and examine the patient in private.

> **Section 68** (5) For the purposes of subsection (1) above a person who applies to a tribunal but subsequently withdraws his application shall be treated as not having exercised his right to apply and where a person withdraws his application on a date after the expiration of the period mentioned in that subsection, the managers shall refer the patient's case as soon as possible after that date.

One of the most difficult decisions for patients and their advisers to take under the 1959 Act was when to exercise their single opportunity to apply to a Mental Health Review Tribunal during any period of detention. Even if an application was subsequently withdrawn before the hearing the right to make a further application during the same period of detention was lost. If an application was made and the strength of the medical evidence supplied by the hospital showed that the tribunal was unlikely to order the patient's discharge there was no point in making a tactical withdrawal with a view to applying again later when perhaps the patient's condition had improved sufficiently to increase the chances of success in the tribunal. Patients now have an opportunity to probe the hospital's case and withdraw their application if the evidence is too strongly in favour of continuation of detention without losing the right to apply again later in the same period of detention. The White Paper confidently stated that these provisions 'will ensure that patients who lack the ability or initiative to make an application to a Tribunal also have the safeguard of an independent review of their case.'

What will be the position of the patient who is content to remain in hospital and receive his treatment there? The hospital has no choice but to refer all cases in the circumstances set out in subsection (2) and the patient has no control over the referral procedure. So we may see the ironic situation where patients and their advisers argue against discharge and in favour of continued detention.

2.4   Admission for assessment in cases of emergency (Forms 5-7, 1983 Regulations)

2.4.1   Introduction

The power of emergency admissions is used more than any other admission power. In 1979 nearly 8,400 patients were admitted under this power. That was greater than the number admitted under any of the other powers. That was never intended, and the Bill shortens the time limits between examination and admission from three days to 24 hours, to help ensure that the power is used only in cases of genuine emergency. (Norman Fowler, Secretary of State for Social Services, Commons, March 1982.)

The Bill intends 'that section 29 is only used in a genuine emergency' (p 6, para 16 White Paper). However these changes which are mainly cosmetic, will not ensure this. They will not prevent the major abuses attached to the varying use of this section in different parts of the country to compulsorily admit patients who are not strict emergencies. (Prof M Rolf Olsen, Special Standing Committee, Commons April 1982.)

In 1979 45% of the 18,721 compulsory admissions were admitted [under section 29]. This is unacceptable. The Bill does not recognise that section 29 deprives a patient of his primary safeguard – a psychiatric and social work opinion – and risks the continuance of psychiatric practice based on what is convenient for the doctor rather than what is necessary for patients' rights and wellbeing. The British Association of Social Workers has long argued that the use of section 29 be reserved for the strict emergency. Moreover the majority of cases should pass through a 24-hour crisis service manned by an approved psychiatrist and an approved social worker. (BASW's evidence to Special Standing Committee, Commons, April 1982.)

As can be seen from the above extracts section 29 of the 1959 Act from which section 4 is substantially derived was subject to a great deal of criticism mainly on the grounds that it was used too often to admit patients for observation. Those responsible for the enactment of the 1959 legislation had not expected nor intended that section 29 would become the most common route to compulsory admission. It cannot be denied that section 29 was heavily used but the evidence that it was being misused was less convincing. The main evidence of misuse seems to date back to 1966 when Doctors Barton and Hander published their study of all admissions to a single hospital under section 29 over a three-year period. They concluded that only 72 out of 182 admissions were justified under section 29. This led to a national estimate that about 5,000 people throughout England and Wales were being wrongly admitted every year under section 29. At the same time the Ministry of Health carried out an enquiry to discover why section 29 was being used so often and the findings of this enquiry are referred to in the 1976 Review at paragraph 2.8. In summary these were:

(a) Widespread ignorance amongst medical and social work staff of the Act's requirements. In particular there was lack of appreciation that section 25 (admission for observation) should normally be used unless in an emergency.

(b) Emphasis in the 1959 Act on informal treatment had led to a practice of not admitting patients until a crisis developed. Also lack of community based resources hindered crisis prevention work in the community.

(c) A feeling existed amongst practitioners that the section 29 procedure was less traumatic for the patient because of its simpler procedure and short-term nature. This was allied to administrative convenience.

(d) Approved doctors were rarely used due to the reluctance of GPs and consultants to involve second opinions.

(e) A reluctance of hospital consultants to make home visits existed.

(f) There was pressure on mental welfare officers from both GPs and hospitals for them to make section 29 applications.

The 1976 review concluded that there was good reason for section 29 being used more frequently than the framers of the 1959 Act had expected, a conclusion which is difficult to understand given the findings of the Ministry of Health inquiry described above. The conclusion is based entirely on the view that the increased emphasis on informal treatment has led to patients being left undetained until a crisis is reached and then emergency admission is required. Yet at least two of the Ministry's findings show that administrative convenience was an important factor in the use of section 29. The 1976 Review claims that the abuses which were identfied have been curtailed by the issue of a Chief Medical Officer's letter in October 1966 'explaining the intended use of the two sections and emphasising the importance of keeping the use of the section 29 power to a minimum.'

None of the criticisms we have looked at so far actually question whether there is a need for an emergency admission procedure at all although the point was raised indirectly by BASW in its evidence to the Commons Committee. This was in its reference to a 24-hour crisis service. Supporters of the establishment of such a service (also known as crisis intervention centres) on a national basis argued that if such centres were developed there would be no need for patients to be admitted to hospital on an emergency basis – crises would be dealt with in the community by a multi-disciplinary crisis intervention team. If a hospital admission was eventually required then this could presumably take place under section 25 or 26 of the 1959 Act.

Reference to the development of crisis intervention centres had been made in the White Paper 'Better Services for the Mentally Ill' but both Reviews of the 1959 Act concluded that the resource implications of such centres particularly in terms of skilled staff meant there was no prospect of their being established on a national basis in the foreseeable future. Complete removal of power to admit patients on an emergency basis was ruled out on two grounds: resource implications preventing the establishment of crisis intervention services nationally, and the fact that they could never replace emergency admission procedures in rural areas. But the 1978 Review did accept that there was a need to amend section 29 to permit admission under detention to establishments other than hospitals, such as places of assessment, if crisis intervention centres ever did develop into a national service. An attempt by David Ennals was made in the Commons Committee to include crisis intervention centres as establishments to which patients could be admitted under section 29 but it was defeated by the Government. The Government opposed it mainly on the grounds that the concept was still in its early stages of development and therefore not yet capable of precise definition:

> There are now 20 crisis intervention centres in operation. No two are the same, and because there is no reason for it to have the information the DHSS does not have complete records on the subject. Some of the centres are community based. Some are hospital based. Some are based in day centres. Others are voluntary organisations . . . Some send a team to see prospective patients. In other cases patients come to see the team. There is no reason why the centres should be the same . . . this is very much an area of experimentation . . . There certainly did not seem to be a need for each area to have a crisis intervention centre. (Mr Geoffrey Finsberg, Special Standing Committee, Commons, May 1982).

2.4.2 We have looked at the debate upon the need for revisions to emergency admission powers in some detail. What was the end result?

Section 4 (1) In any case of urgent necessity, an application for admission for assessment may be made in respect of a patient in accordance with the following provisions of this section, and any application so made is in this Act referred to as 'an emergency application'.

(2) An emergency application may be made either by an approved social worker or by the nearest relative of the patient; and every such application shall include a statement that it is of urgent necessity for the

patient to be admitted and detained under section 2 above, and that compliance with the provisions of this Part of this Act relating to applications under that section would involve undesirable delay.

Admissions are limited to cases of 'urgent necessity', a phrase which is not new – it appeared in section 29 of the 1959 Act. It may well prove difficult to justify to the Mental Health Act Commission a high rate of emergency admissions particularly in an area which has alternative community based services such as a crisis intervention centre.

An important change lies in subsection 2: now only an approved social worker and a *nearest* relative can apply – before any relative could apply as well as a mental welfare officer.

Section 4 (3) An emergency application shall be sufficient in the first instance if founded on one of the medical recommendations required by section 2 above, given, if practicable, by a practitioner who has previous acquaintance with the patient and otherwise complying with the requirements of section 12 below so far as applicable to a single recommendation, and verifying the statement referred to in subsection (2) above.

2.4.3 Emergency applications need be supported by only one medical recommendation. If possible this should be given by a doctor who knows the patient such as his GP or a consultant psychiatrist who has treated him in the past. The criticism of the 1959 Act by BASW that patients could be admitted without the benefit of a psychiatric opinion has not been met in the 1983 Act – it is still possible for a medical recommendation to be given by a doctor without experience or expertise in the diagnosis or treatment of mental disorder. It is also not essential for the recommending doctor to have any prior knowledge of the patient or his medical history.

The applicant must have seen the patient within the previous 24 hours and the medical examination must also have taken place within the 24 hours prior to the patient's admission to hospital. If the latter requirements are not met then authority to take and convey the patient to hospital is lost; see section 6(1)(b).

The medical examination of the patient, the interview by the approved social worker and the conveyance of the patient all must take place within 24 hours. This represents a change from the 1959 Act which allowed a period of 3 days for this 'emergency' procedure. Admissions outside the time limits will be insufficient authority to detain the patient and may lead to an action by the patient for damages for false imprisonment. More likely however is that the Mental Health Act Commission will monitor emergency admission procedures closely to ensure that what are admittedly tight time limits are complied with.

2.4.4 A further attempt to tighten up emergency admission procedures lies in a new requirement that the recommending doctor must state (on Form 7 – the emergency medical recommendation) the reasons why, in his opinion, an emergency exists, approximately how many hours' delay would be caused if an application under section 2 was to be made and the fact that in his opinion such delay might result in harm to:

(a) the patient,
(b) those caring for him or
(c) others.

2.4.5   **Section 4** (4) An emergency application shall cease to have effect on the expiration of a period of 72 hours from the time when the patient is admitted to the hospital unless—
  (a) the second medical recommendation required by section 2 above is given and received by the managers within that period; and
  (b) that recommendation and the recommendation referred to in subsection (3) above together comply with all the requirements of section 12 below (other than the requirement as to the time of the signature of the second recommendation).

The patient can only be detained in hospital under an emergency application for 72 hours. This period can be extended to 28 days if the second medical recommendation required for admissions for assessment under section 2 is given within the 72-hour period.

2.5   Applications in respect of patients already in hospital

2.5.1   **Section 5** (1) An application for the admission of a patient to hospital may be made under this Part of this Act notwithstanding that the patient is already an in-patient in that hospital or, in the case of an application for treatment that the patient is for the time being liable to be detained in the hospital in pursuance of an application for admission for assessment; and where an application is so made the patient shall be treated for the purposes of this Part of this Act as if he had been admitted to the hospital at the time when that application was received by the managers.

This section permits applications to be made for the compulsory detention of informal patients (section 131) either for assessment or treatment. The section also permits an application for detention to be made in respect of a patient currently detained for assessment under section 2. One of the situations which the section seeks to deal with was described in the following terms in Parliament:

> The need to detain patients who are already voluntarily in hospital can cause difficulties. The patient may be in a distressed state and be quite unable to recognise the wisdom of staying in hospital, at least until the crisis passes. The [1959] Act already provides that in such cases the doctor responsible for the patient can authorise his detention for up to 3 days. But the doctor may not always be there in an emergency. (Lord Elton, Lords December 1981).

2.5.2 The solution to this problem is proposed is section 5(2) and (3):

> **Section 5** (2) If, in the case of a patient who is an in-patient in a hospital, it appears to the registered medical practitioner in charge of the treatment of the patient than an application ought to be made under this Part of this Act for the admission of the patient to hospital, he may furnish to the managers a report in writing to that effect; and in any such case the patient may be detained in the hospital for a period of 72 hours from the time when the report is so furnished.
>
> (3) The registered medical practitioner in charge of the treatment of a patient in a hospital may nominate one (but not more than one) other registered medical practitioner on the staff of the hospital to act for him under subsection (2) above in his absence.

The doctor in charge of the patient's treatment is given power to report to the hospital that in his opinion an application to detain the patient (for assessment or treatment) should be made either by the nearest relative or an approved social worker and as soon as that report is made (it must be made on Form 12) the patient becomes subject to a 72-hour detention period. This power is not new but there are 2 changes from the 1959 Act: the period of detention was 3 days and the doctor is now required on Form 12 to state the reasons why informal treatment 'is not or is no longer appropriate'. These changes are important – the first reduces the potential period of detention by describing it in hours which will run from the exact time of day that the report is made and the second requires the doctor to set down in writing the reasons for issuing the report and which may eventually be examined by the Mental Health Act Commission.

At Amendment Bill stage, an amendment was proposed which would have required the doctor to have personally examined the patient within 24 hours immediately before the making of the report but this amendment was not accepted because it might have led to daily cursory examinations which would not have benefited the patient nor made the best use of the consultant's time.

2.5.3 Two matters remain to be considered concerning section 5(2). First, who is the doctor in charge of the patient's treatment and second, which patients are covered by the term 'in-patient'?

The doctor will usually be the consultant psychiatrist in charge of the patient's treatment but the power to issue a report is not limited to patients receiving treatment for mental disorder. The DHSS Guide gives guidance on this matter:

> It may occasionally be necessary to make a report under section 5(2) in respect of a patient who is not in a psychiatric hospital or the psychiatric wing of a general hospital. Where a patient is receiving psychiatric treatment (even though he may also be receiving non-psychiatric treatment) the doctor in charge of the treatment for the purposes of section 5(2) will be the consultant or senior psychiatrist concerned. But where an in-patient is not receiving psychiatric treatment, the doctor who is in charge of the treatment the patient is receiving would have power to furnish the report. Where such a report is made by a non-psychiatrist, a senior psychiatrist should see the patient as soon as possible to determine whether the patient should be detained further.

Although the requirement in the last sentence of the quotation is obviously good practice the power to detain the patient starts as soon as the doctor issues the report and not when this second opinion has been given.

'In-patient' is not defined in the Act although it has a generally accepted meaning – a patient who has been admitted to a hospital ward. Unfortunately admission procedures vary throughout the country and a definition would have helped to identify the precise point at which patients become subject to the detention powers based on the report. This is not an academic point: we have come across cases of patients in casualty departments being detained under section 5(2) and subsequently transferred to a psychiatric hospital. In our view this procedure is wrong as casualty patients are not generally considered to have been admitted to hospital and therefore are not 'in-patients'. The correct procedure should be for an approved social worker to be called to consider making an application for admission or, if the casualty patient is accompanied by a (nearest) relative, for the relative to be asked to complete the necessary form for admission to hospital.

2.5.4 Section 5 (3) is new. The power to issue a report could not be delegated under the 1959 Act; now it can be delegated to a nominated doctor on the staff of the hospital in which the patient is being treated. Why introduce this power to delegate? Simply because the power to issue a report under section 5(2) (formerly section 30(2) of the 1959 Act) was being abused. Often the doctor in charge of the patient's treatment was not available in emergencies. The solution to this problem was that stocks of the appropriate forms were being held in wards signed in blank by the appropriate doctor, ready for use in an emergency. The problem was discussed at length in the Special Standing Committee and the following extract from the Committee's proceedings illustrates the issues involved:

> *Mr Geoffrey Finsberg:* What is important is that the power to detain a patient already in hospital is properly used . . . There have been genuine practical difficulties . . . It is possible that the doctor in charge of a patient may not be available at the critical time . . . the consultant is the responsible medical officer. He might be ill, tending another patient, away for a day on leave. We have tried to provide a form of cover in law . . .
>
> *Mr Christopher Price:* What has happened in the past twenty years when the responsible medical officer was away?
>
> *Mr Finsberg:* There have been practices that we are trying to stop. As originally drafted section 5(2) did not limit the power to delegate to only one doctor and set no requirements as to the status and qualifications of the delegatee. Members of the Commons Committee expressed concern over these points particularly the status and qualifications.
>
> *Mr Terry Davis:* May I draw the Minister's attention to the fact that it is not just a question of the status of the other medical practitioner? It is also a question of his qualifications. As the Bill stands it would in theory, be possible for a responsible medical officer to nominate a general practitioner who happens to be on the staff of the hospital.
>
> *Mr Finsberg:* We have to be certain that the person chosen would be appropriately qualified and experienced. We shall try to find a way to give force to what I have tried to say.

2.5.5 In the end the Bill as originally drafted was amended in two respects – the power to nominate was limited to one other doctor, and that doctor must be a registered medical practitioner on the hospital staff (but not necessarily an 'approved doctor' under section 12(2) of the Act).

Finally, who may be the one nominated doctor? The Act merely refers to a registered medical practitioner on the staff of the hospital. It is clear that the doctor in charge of the patient's treatment will have to nominate one particular doctor. It is the level of qualification of the nominated doctor which remains uncertain. Some guidance upon what the Government hoped would happen is contained in the speech of Lord Cullen speaking in the Lords debate:

> . . .the nominated deputy is likely to be a junior doctor in [the consultant's] team, and will, therefore, already be familiar with the patient and his medical history. The nominated deputy may, however, be any other medical practitioner on the staff of the hospital – for example, another consultant. As a matter of good practice, the doctor in charge of the patient's treatment would discuss the patient's case with another doctor whom he is nominating as his deputy and might invite the deputy to examine the patient.

2.5.6   Section 5(4) If, in the case of a patient who is receiving treatment for mental disorder as an in-patient in a hospital, it appears to a nurse of the prescribed class—

(a) that the patient is suffering from mental disorder to such a degree that it is necessary for his health or safety or for the protection of others for him to be immediately restrained from leaving the hospital; and

(b) that it is not practicable to secure the immediate attendance of a practitioner for the purpose of furnishing a report under subsection (2) above,

the nurse may record that fact in writing; and in that event the patient may be detained in the hospital for a period of six hours from the time when that fact is so recorded or until the earlier arrival at the place where the patient is detained of a practitioner having power to furnish a report under that subsection.

(5) a record made under subsection (4) above shall be delivered by the nurse (or by a person authorised by the nurse in that behalf) to the managers of the hospital as soon as possible after it is made; and where a record is made under that subsection the period mentioned in subsection (2) above shall begin at the time when it is made.

2.5.7 The 1976 Review sought views on a proposal that experienced registered mental nurses should be given power to issue reports under section 30(2) of the 1959 Act (now section 5(2)) to remove the anxieties and problems experienced by nursing staff when they were required to deal with uncooperative and often violent informal patients in the absence of the doctor in charge of their treatment. This proposal received little support and was discarded by the 1978 Review mainly because of medical opinion that to give nursing staff such a power would involve them in a medical decision and therefore would be inappropriate. There was, however, general support for the alternative proposal in the 1976 Review to give certain nursing staff a limited holding power as set out in subsections (4) and (5) above.

The power clarifies the legal position of nursing staff when dealing with unco-operative and violent patients. The legal uncertainties had been referred to in the COHSE booklet *The Management of Violent or Potentially Violent Patients* (1977) which stated that whilst the law probably permitted staff to restrain informal patients in an emergency their power to deal with potential emergencies was not clear.

Two points require immediate attention:
(1) The holding power applies only to an informal patient who is already being treated for mental disorder – it does not apply to patients who are being assessed.
(2) The power is only available to a nurse 'of the prescribed class'. The prescribed class is set out in The Mental Health (Nurses) Order 1983 which states that such nurses are first level nurses trained either in the nursing of persons suffering from mental illness or in the nursing of persons suffering from mental handicap and who are in both cases registered in the professional register kept under section 10 of the Nurses, Midwives and Health Visitors Act 1979. If the conditions in section 5(4) exist then the patient may be restrained provided the nurse completes Form 13. This power has been described as a nurse's holding power and it arises immediately upon completion of the Form (unlike most other powers under the Act which normally arise only after any necessary documentation has been delivered to the hospital managers) and lasts for 6 hours. The Regulations require that the managers should be notified of the expiry of the holding power by completion of Form 16. Note that the six-hour period is deducted from the 72-hour detention power in section 5(2) ie if a patient is held for six hours under the nurse's holding power with a view to a doctor completing a report under section 5(2) and the doctor eventually completes the report, only

66 hours remain for application for the patients's admission to be made.

2.5.8 The new provisions in section 5(3) and (4) have not been universally welcomed by nursing staff. The powers are stated to be discretionary, but what if a nurse decides as a matter of principle not to exercise the power, and a violent patient is allowed to leave the hospital and subsequently injures himself or others? Would the nurse be responsible for the patient's acts or safety after he left hospital? It is our view that the nurse's duty is limited to considering whether or not the patient is likely to harm himself or others if he is not detained. If (s)he has reasonable grounds for believing there will be no danger of harm to the patient or others (s)he is entitled to decide against using the holding power. The power is not to be used automatically on each occasion when an informal patient leaves a hospital.

It is unclear how often the holding power can be used in respect of the same patient. In its evidence to the Commons Committee, COHSE stated that the 1982 Amendment Bill 'should be amended to show clearly after what length of break a nurse may exercise the holding power again in relation to the same patient. The Confederation considers that a 30-minute break should be sufficient to enable the power to be used again.' The point was neither raised nor debated in Parliament but it raises an important issue in the exercise of the power. It is difficult to envisage situations arising where there is a genuine need to use the power more than once within a period of, say, six hours. A doctor should be available within such a period to consider whether a report should be issued especially now that a nominee may be available. If the proposed COHSE amendment had been made, nurses would have been able to hold patients for indefinite periods without a proper medical diagnosis of the patient's condition. This would be unacceptable in an Act purporting to increase patients' rights and would also have placed an unfair burden on nursing staff. The problem is that as the Act is silent upon the point the power may properly be exercised on a series of occasions. Would the nurse be accountable for such a practice? If so the supposed power becomes a duty to detain in relevant circumstances thereby raising the problem of the personal safety of the nurse.

2.5.9 **Section 5**(6) The reference in subsection (1) above to an in-patient does not include an in-patient who is liable to be detained in pursuance of an application under this Part of this Act and the references to subsections (2) and (4) above do not include an in-patient who is liable to be detained in a hospital under this Part of this Act.

Briefly, the powers in section 5 are only available in respect of informal patients. The section 5, 72-hour, holding power may be invoked for the purpose of determining whether, according to medical opinion, an application to detain the patient for assessment or treatment should be made. It is merely a power of detention. If during or at the end of the time period a section 2 application is made and accepted, does the 72-hour period become subsumed within the subsequent 28 days? It is submitted that the correct legal interpretation is that the period of time during which the patient is 'held' under section 5 does not become included within the 28 days but rather is *additional to it*. The spirit of the Act would not necessarily encourage this, and it should be noted that the section 5 provisions (including the time period) would cease immediately an application under section 2 or 3 is received and accepted by the hospital. Seventy-two hours is, therefore, a maximum not a minimum.

2.6   The effect of an application for admission

2.6.1   Section 6 (1) An application for the admission of a patient to a hospital under this Part of this Act, duly completed in accordance with the provisions of this Part of this Act, shall be sufficient authority for the applicant, or any person authorised by the applicant, to take the patient and convey him to the hospital at any time within the following period, that is to say—

(a) in the case of an application other than an emergency application, the period of 14 days beginning with the date on which the patient was last examined by a registered medical practitioner before giving a medical recommendation for the purposes of the application;

(b) in the case of an emergency application, the period of 24 hours beginning at the time when the patient was examined by the practitioner giving the medical recommendation which is referred to in section 4(3) above, or at the time when the application is made, whichever is the earlier.

(2) Where a patient is admitted within the said period to the hospital specified in such an application as is mentioned in subsection (1) above, or, being within that hospital, is treated by virtue of section 5 above as if he had been so admitted, the application shall be sufficient authority for the managers to detain the patient in the hospital in accordance with the provisions of this Act.

(3) Any application for the admission of a patient under this Part of this Act which appears to be duly made and to be so founded on the necessary medical recommendations may be acted upon without further proof of the signature or qualification of the person by whom the application or any such medical recommendation is made or given or of any matter of fact or opinion stated in it.

(4) Where a patient is admitted to a hospital in pursuance of an application for admission for treatment, any previous application under this Part of this Act by virtue of which he was liable to be detained in a hospital or subject to guardianship shall cease to have effect.

2.6.2 Some of the detail of this section has already been referred to above but there are some further points in need of clarification.

The application for admission and the necessary medical recommendations confer legal authority on the applicant or any one authorised by him to take the patient to the hospital named in the application. This legal authority lasts for 14 days or 24 hours depending on the type of application.

If the hospital admits the patient under the authority of the application, then the hospital obtains authority to detain the patient for the periods set out in section 20 of the Act. It is important to remember that hospitals have no statutory obligation to admit patients even if all the statutory requirements have been satisfied. Put another way neither the applicant nor the patient have the right to demand admission to a hospital. So it is a wise precaution for the applicant to check with the hospital named in the application (if this has not already been done by the GP or other recommending doctor) that a hospital bed is available for the patient. The patient cannot be admitted to any hospital other than that named in the application. The Act places Regional Health Authorities under a duty to notify Local Social Services Authorities of hospitals which can take emergency admissions but this duty is limited to notification and does not extend to provision of beds. The DHSS Guide states:

> This duty will be met if the (Regional Health) Authority makes arrangements for social services authorities to be kept aware of psychiatric catchment areas for particular hospitals within the Region, with suitable notes explaining, for example, where the catchment area for elderly patients differs from that of younger patients.

2.6.3 The applicant will be expected to ensure that the application form and supporting medical recommendations are properly completed (otherwise his authority to take and convey the patient will not exist). It will also be the hospital's responsibility to check the forms as they form the hospital's authority to detain the patient. Subsection (3) is relevant here – if there are no apparent errors on the face of the form (ie it 'appears to be duly made') then the hospital may act upon the application without any further checking. However if there are obvious errors such as missing signatures, expired time limits or conflicting medical recommendations then the hospital cannot rely on subsection (3) or section 15 (rectification of applications and recommendations, see below) as justification for accepting a defective application. The position is clearly set out in the DHSS Guide.

Faults which invalidate the application

52. Documents cannot be rectified under section 15 unless they are documents which can properly be regarded as applications or medical recommendations within the meaning of the Act. A document cannot be regarded as an application or medical recommendation if it is not signed at all or is signed by a person who is not empowered to do so under the Act. This means that a check should be made to confirm that an application is signed by the patient's nearest relative or the acting nearest relative or an approved social worker; and that each medical recommendation is signed by a practitioner who is not excluded under section 12. In doing so the officer scrutinizing the form may take statements at face value; for example he need not check that the doctor who states he is a registered medical practitioner is registered (Regulation 3(4)). Another fault which would invalidate the application completely would be if the two medical recommendations did not specify at least one form of mental disorder in common.

53. If any fault of this sort is discovered there is no authority for the patient's detention. Authority can only be obtained through a new application. If the patient is already in hospital he can only be detained if the medical practitioner in charge of his treatment (or his nominee) issues a report under section 5 of the Act. Any new application must, of course, be accompanied by medical recommendations which comply with the Act, but this does not exclude the possibility of one of the two existing medical recommedations being used if the time limits and other provisions of the Act can still be complied with (sections 11, 12 & 6).

Errors which may be amended under Section 15

54. Section 15 allows an application or medical recommendation which is found to be in any respect incorrect or defective to be amended by the person who signed it, with the consent of the managers of the hospital, within the period of 14 days from the date of the patient's admission. Faults which may be capable of amendment under this section include the leaving blank of any spaces on the form which should have

been filled in (other than the signature) or failure to delete one or more alternatives in places where only one can be correct. The patient's forenames and surname should agree in all the places where they appear on the application and supporting recommendations.

55. Any document found to contain faults of this sort should be returned to the person who signed it for amendment. When the amended document is returned to the hospital it should again be scrutinized to check that it is now in the proper form. Consent to the amendment should then be given by a senior officer of the hospital or mental nursing home who has been authorised to consent to amendments on behalf of the managers (Regulation 4(2)). In the case of mental nursing homes, the managers, if two or more in number, may authorise one of their number to consent to amendments. These officers can also issue notices under section 15(2). Similarly a local social services authority may authorise in writing an officer to carry out these functions (Regulation 5(2)). The consent should be recorded in writing and could take the form of an endorsement on the document itself. If this is all done within a period of 14 days starting on the date on which the patient was admitted (or the date when the documents were received if the patient was already in hospital when the application was made) the documents are deemed to have had effect as though originally made as amended.

In summary, whilst it is important for the applicant to ensure that all the forms are properly completed, if he succeeds in taking and conveying a patient under a defective application, and the application is obviously defective, the hospital cannot rely on the defective application or on section 6(3) to justify detaining the patient. It is important for admitting hospitals to make their own arrangements to scrutinize all forms relating to compulsory admission as they will be open to inspection by the Mental Health Act Commission.

2.6.4 What if the patient refuses to co-operate with the applicant in the arrangements for his admission to hospital? The applicant's powers in such a situation are set out in sections 137 and 138:

Section 137 (1) Any person required or authorized by or by virtue of this Act to be conveyed to any place or to be kept in custody or detained in a place of safety or at any place to which he is taken under section 42(6) above shall, while being so conveyed, detained or kept, as the case may be, be deemed to be in legal custody.

(2) A constable or any other person required or authorised by or by virtue of this Act to take any person into custody, or to convey or detain any person shall, for the purposes of taking him into custody or conveying or detaining him, have all the powers, authorities, protection and privileges which a constable has within the area for which he acts as constable.

(3) In this section 'convey' includes any other expression denoting removal from one place to another.

Section 138 (1) If any person who is in legal custody by virtue of section 137 above escapes, he may, subject to the provisions of this section, be retaken—

(a) in any case, by the person who had his custody immediately before the escape, or by any constable or approved social worker;

The following points emerge from these provisions:

(a) As soon as the application supported by the appropriate medical recommendation(s) has been properly completed the patient is deemed to be in the applicant's legal custody;
(b) The applicant gains all the powers of a policeman;
(c) If the patient escapes from the applicant's custody he can be retaken;
(d) The powers in sections 137 and 138 last for 24 hours or 14 days depending on whether the application is an emergency application under section 4 or an application under sections 2 or 3.

2.6.5 What 'powers, authorities, protection and privileges' does a constable have?

The police possess few powers which are not held by ordinary members of the public and there has been a traditional reluctance to give them increased authority. It is important to bear this in mind when considering section 137 and the apparently wide powers it appears to give to applicants.

The powers to be considered do not arise unless the application form and supporting medical recommendation(s) have been fully completed and signed by the applicant and the recommending doctor(s) respectively. These powers cannot be used to enable the forms to be completed and signed.

(a) *Powers of entry*

The police have no general power to enter premises without a warrant (with two exceptions dealt with below) and therefore an applicant cannot enter premises for the purpose of taking a patient to hospital under an application for admission. Faced with a situation where an application has been completed and a patient, his relatives or any one else refuse entry to the applicant, the correct procedure is to apply to a JP for a warrant under section 135 (see para 2.9.2 following) to search for and remove the patient. The two exceptions referred to earlier are that the police have a common law power to enter premises:

(i) when they are in immediate pursuit of an escaped prisoner, and
(ii) to save life and limb and prevent serious damage to property.

So if a patient escapes from the applicant's legal custody it would appear that the applicant may enter premises (using such force as is reasonably necessary) to retake the patient under section 137(1)(a). But there is no case law on this point and we would suggest that entry under these circumstances should be made as a last resort. The only conceivable situations where an applicant should properly force entry to premises are:

(i) where authority under an application is about to expire and there is no time to make an application under section 135 and
(ii) where the patient has entered premises and is causing or threatening serious injury to himself or others and the emergency does not allow the normal powers of the Act to be invoked.

In all other situations section 135 should be used. Note also section 115, para 10.7.

(b) *Powers of arrest*

Arrest is the beginning of imprisonment and therefore the courts have laid down safeguards for persons who are arrested by the police. Normally there must be 'seizure or touching of a person's body with view to his restraint' but words alone will be enough if they are intended to bring to a person's attention that he is under arrest and he submits to the restraint of his freedom. Also the arrested person must be informed of the reason for his arrest unless it is obvious from the circumstances.

The Act gives no specific power of arrest to applicants so it would be useful to look at police powers of arrest to discover whether section 137 gives such a power to applicants. The most relevant police power would appear to be the power to arrest persons who are wilfully obstructing the police in the execution of their duty (Police Act 1964, section 51). An approved social worker is given duties to make an application (section 13) and to take and convey a patient (section 6), therefore any one who prevents an approved social worker from carrying out those duties is guilty of obstructing the approved social worker in the execution of his duties and is liable to arrest. Unfortunately the position is not as clear as we have implied. The following extract from *Mental Health Services* (A. H. Edwards; Shaw and Sons, 1976), the leading work on the 1959 Act, illustrates the problem in this area:

> the mental welfare officer's duty, where it exists, is primarily to make an application for the purpose of the Mental Health Act and not to make an arrest, the exercise of the statutory power to arrest would normally arise only where compliance with the provisions of the Act makes it necessary to exercise that power. If such action is necessary, reasonable force would appear to be justifiable, having regard to the circumstances.

This confirms the view that whilst a power of arrest is implied by section 137 it, like all the powers implied by section 137 and discussed above only arise when an approved social worker is seeking to take and convey a patient under section 6 to hospital. If an application under the Act has not been properly completed any approved social worker seeking to exercise the powers described above and below would be acting unlawfully and the consequences of this are well illustrated by the case described at para 2.2.5.

(c) *Use of force*

The police are permitted to use such force as is reasonably necessary to carry out a lawful arrest (Criminal Law Act 1967, section 3). Whilst there is no doubt that in law this right is also possessed by approved social workers by virtue of section 137 it is our view that the use of force by an approved social worker to carry out his duties under the Act is wholly inappropriate. If a situation develops where an approved social worker expects that he will need to use force in respect of a compulsory admission to hospital he should withdraw and seek police assistance.

Three final points in relation to sections 137 and 138 remain:

   (i) A police constable has a right to call upon bystanders to assist him in the execution of his duty and if they refuse to help they may be guilty of an offence.

  (ii) The police have power to search persons detained in their custody and to remove any item or weapon which a prisoner (patient) could use to escape or to injure himself.

 (iii) There is no geographical limit to the extent of the powers implied by section 137 even though such a limit is suggested by the words 'which a constable has within the area for which he acts as constable.' The suggestion is that constables are limited to operate within the area of their force; since 1964 however members of police forces have had all the powers and privileges of a constable throughout England and Wales (Police Act 1964, section 19).

2.7   The role of relatives

2.7.1   There has been considerable debate as to whether relatives should continue to fulfil any significant role in the compulsory detention of patients in hospital. According to the 1978 Review few representations were received which favoured the removal of the nearest relative's right to make admissions whilst retaining the right to order discharge. The only change recommended in the 1978 Review was to limit the power to make emergency applications to nearest relatives as opposed to any relative, as was the position under the 1959 Act. The reason for this preservation of the status quo was given to be that some relatives may wish to have a role in the admission process and therefore it would be wrong to exclude them.

If however approved social workers were to be required to display a greater degree of professionalism and expertise in mental health work, would there be any need to retain the nearest relative's powers under the 1983 Act? In particular, should the law continue to permit the nearest relative to block applications for admission for treatment?

The point was made most strongly by Professor Olsen in his evidence to the Commons Special Standing Committee:

> The clear implication of the Bill is that compulsory admission to hospital should only be prescribed and undertaken by specially trained, experienced people who have understanding of mental disorder and knowledge of the alternative treatment and care facilities which are available . . . yet the Bill proposes that the nearest relative, without any training and who may not know of the resources available; who is often powerless to challenge a recommendation for compulsory admission; and who themselves may be in need of support and guidance, should continue to exercise this function.

> Of course relatives do have obligations and rights which must be protected. This would be best afforded by an amendment which would give those relatives most responsible for a patient's care the right to request that an approved social worker should investigate the case for

compulsory admission. If the social worker is unable to support the application, he must record his reasons and make them known to the relative.

> . . . it is often difficult for a relative to resist a recommendation by a GP, let us say, at 3 o'clock in the morning. The GP may say, 'Perhaps you would like to sign the order and we will effect admission.' Relatives usually have limited knowledge of mental disorders and the resources available to them.

In the Lords, Baroness Faithfull made two attempts to reduce the role of relatives in the admission process. Both were withdrawn in the face of Government opposition.

The object of the first amendment was to remove the nearest relative's power to make an application for admission of a patient to hospital for treatment. The justification for this amendment was not to protect patients 'against abuse from an evil member of the family' as it was put by Lord Donaldson but to place the responsibility for deciding upon the appropriateness of an admission upon an independent person. This would be an approved social worker who was not affected by the emotional and moral pressures of the crisis faced by the patient and his family. Equally important, the approved social worker would be fully trained in mental health practice with the mentally disordered and would have full knowledge of the resources available outside the hospital to help persons suffering from mental disorder. The Government's objection to this first amendment was based entirely upon the potential delay in arranging emergency admissions which might have occurred if the involvement of an approved social worker was mandatory, and for operational reasons an approved social worker was not available at the time of crisis. The need for an informed and professional view as to whether or not compulsory admission was appropriate was not recognised by the Government: its main concern, conversely, was to avoid delay in admitting patients. Other speakers in the debate were more concerned with the effect which removal of any family involvement in admissions would have on family responsibility and relationships.

Baroness Faithfull's second amendment was less controversial. It sought not to remove the relative's rights but to make an interview with the patient by an approved social worker and an approved doctor mandatory before a compulsory admission could be made. The interview would not be required where there were 'reasonable grounds for believing that there is an immediate risk of harm to [the patient] or to others or of damage to property, or that the patient is likely to abscond before he can be examined by an approved doctor.' The Government's reasons for opposing the amendment were that it was unnecessary as such safeguards against inappropriate admissions already existed in the 1959 Act, and again that the proposed procedure might lead to a delay in admissions in an emergency situation.

In the event, not only have the original nearest relative provisions been retained, but they have actually been strengthened.

2.7.2 Who is the nearest relative?

Section 26 (1) In this Part of this Act 'relative' means any of the following persons:
    (a) husband or wife;
    (b) son or daughter;
    (c) father or mother;
    (d) brother or sister;
    (e) grandparent;
    (f) grandchild;
    (g) uncle or aunt;
    (h) nephew or niece.

There is one change to the 1959 Act list – the father no longer takes precedence over the mother. But the position is not as simple as it appears from the statutory list:

Section 26 In deducing relationships for the purposes of this section, any relationship of the half-blood shall be treated as a relationship of the whole blood, and an illegitimate person shall be treated as the legitimate child of his mother.
    (3) In this Part of this Act, subject to the provisions of this section and to the following provisions of this Part of this Act, the 'nearest relative' means the person first described in subsection (1) above who is for the time being surviving, relatives of the whole blood being preferred to relatives of the same description of the half-blood and the elder or eldest being preferred to the other or others of those relatives, regardless of sex.

These provisions are not new. Whilst subsection (1) lays down a clear order of precedence for relatives of mentally disordered persons, disputes can still occur where two or more relatives exist in the same paragraph on the list. Also subsection (1) does not deal with the position of illegitimate and half-relatives. Questions such as:

(a) Does a patient's illegitimate daughter take precedence over his parents? or

(b) Which of a patient's three daughters can claim to be his nearest relative? are not answered in the list in subsection (1). The answers can be found in subsections (2) and (3) and are:

(a) Yes, a patient's illegitimate daughter is his nearest relative even if his parents are still alive because illegitimate persons are treated as if they were legitimate, and

(b) The eldest daughter, because elder relatives take precedence over younger when they are both in the same paragraph in subsection (1).

> **Section 26** (4) Subject to the provisions of this section and to the following provisions of this Part of this Act, where the patient ordinarily resides with or is cared for by one or more of his relatives (or, if he is for the time being an in-patient in a hospital, he last ordinarily resided with or was cared for by one or more of his relatives) his nearest relative shall be determined—
>
> (a) by giving preference to that relative or those relatives over the other or others; and
>
> (b) as between two or more such relatives, in accordance with subsection (3) above.

This is new. Its effect is that preference in the list in subsection (1) must be given where applicable to a relative with whom the patient has usually lived or by whom he has been cared for. The relationship between this subsection and subsection (7) is discussed below. Where the patient has usually lived with or been cared for by more than one relative, preference must be given to the older relative and to full blood relatives.

What does 'cared for' mean? The words are not defined but we would suggest it covers any regular contact with the patient on a daily, weekly or even a monthly basis. The patient's individual needs must be looked at to decide whether he is being cared for by a relative – if the support he is receiving enables him to live a relatively independent life then this support will amount to his being 'cared for'. The support can range from washing and cooking for the patient to regular visits to ensure he is looking after himself properly.

2.7.3 **Section 26** (5) Where the person who, under subsection (3) or (4) above, would be the nearest relative of a patient—

(a) in the case of a patient ordinarily resident in the United Kingdom, the Channel Islands or the Isle of Man, is not so resident; or

(b) is the husband or wife of the patient, but is permanently separated from the patient, either by agreement or under the order of a

court, or has deserted or has been deserted by the patient for a
period which has not come to an end; or
(c) is a person other than the husband, wife, father or mother of the
patient, and is for the time being under 18 years of age; or
(d) is a person against whom an order divesting him of authority over
the patient has been made under section 38 of the Sexual Offences
Act 1956 (which relates to incest with a person under eighteen)
and has not been rescinded,
the nearest relative of the patient shall be ascertained as if that person
were dead.

This subsection commits statutory 'murder' upon several categories
of potential nearest relatives so that they are disregarded for the
purposes of the rules laid down in subsections (3) and (4) (but not
for the purposes of the list in subsection (1)). The relatives covered
are quite clearly laid down. The most important part of this
subsection is that it only applies to persons who are claiming to be a
patient's nearest relative because they are the eldest or whole blood
relatives or living with or caring for the patient. Some examples will
show how subsection (5) works:

(a) An unmarried patient living alone in the UK has a father living
in France and a sister living in the UK. Who is the patient's
nearest relative?
Answer: The patient's father. It does not matter that his
father is living in France – he claims to be the nearest relative
because he is higher on the list in subsection (1) and not because
he is relying on the rules in subsections (3) and (4).
(b) An unmarried patient lives alone in the UK and his only living
relatives are three brothers. The eldest brother lives in
Australia, the second eldest and the youngest brothers live in
the UK.
Answer: The second eldest brother is the nearest relative –
the eldest brother being disqualified under subsection (5).
(c) A patient and his wife are separated by a court order. Can the
wife still claim against their son to be the nearest relative?
Answer: Yes – she is the nearest relative because she is higher
on the list in subsection (1) and not because of any of the rules in
subsections (3) and (4).

2.7.4 **Section 26** (6) In this section 'husband' and 'wife' include a person
who is living with the patient as the patient's husband or wife as the case
may be (or, if the patient is for the time being an in-patient in a hospital,
was so living until the patient was admitted), and has been or had been so
living for a period of not less than six months; but a person shall not be

treated by virtue of this subsection as the nearest relative of a married patient unless the husband or wife of the patient is disregarded by virtue of paragraph (b) of subsection (5) above.

This, the so-called 'cohabitation' provision, is not new in that exactly similar wording appeared in section 49 of the 1959 Act. It was subject to criticism during the Commons Committee stage of the Amendment Bill because of its limited application, namely to couples living together as man and wife. The parties to the relationship had to be of the opposite sex and, therefore, two male or two female friends living together were excluded from the benefits of the subsection. Pressure for change was strong from all sides of the Committee especially as the Government had already opened the door slightly by giving statutory recognition to relatives living with or caring for patients in subsection (4). The Government opposed further change on the ground that it would 'weaken family relationships and ties' but were defeated and subsection (7) was inserted during the Commons Committee stage.

2.7.5 **Section 26** (7) A person, other than a relative, with whom the patient ordinarily resides (or, if the patient is for the time being an inpatient in a hospital, last ordinarily resided before he was admitted), and with whom he has or had been ordinarily residing for a period of not less than five years, shall be treated for the purposes of this Part of this Act as if he were a relative but—

    (a) shall be treated for the purposes of subsection (3) above as if mentioned last in subsection (1) above; and

    (b) shall not be treated by virtue of this subsection as the nearest relative of a married patient unless the husband or wife of the patient is disregarded by virtue of paragraph (b) of subsection (5) above.

As stated this is an entirely new provision which did not appear in the original Amendment Bill but is an amendment inserted during the Commons Committee stage upon which the Government was defeated. In its original form the amendment sought to include the word 'co-habitee' with 'husband and wife' in subsection (1) paragraph (a) (the statutory list of priority). The Government accepted its defeat and redrafted the amendment into its present form. The amendment gives an opportunity for non-relatives to claim nearest relative status based simply upon the fact of at least 5 years residence with the patient. The apparent effect is to place such persons at the end of the statutory list in subsection (1). The position, however, is not quite that simple because subsection (7) must be read in conjunction with subsection (4) although there are no cross-references between the subsections. In our view the combined effect of subsections (4) and (7) is that any person who has lived with a patient for five years will automatically take precedence over any blood relatives on the statutory list in subsection (1). Only if a blood relative is also living with the patient or caring for the patient can he or she defeat a claim to be the nearest relative put forward by a person who has lived with the patient for five years.

What does 'with whom the patient ordinarily resides' mean? There is no definition in the Act and whilst each case will depend upon its own facts the following points should always be taken into account when deciding the matter:

(a) Are the person and the patient sharing the same roof?
(b) Is it their intention that this will be a permanent arrangement at least for the foreseeable future?
(c) Temporary periods spent apart may be disregarded provided the intention to remain resident together continues.
(d) The person and the patient need not have a sexual relationship to fall within this subsection; friendship is sufficient.

2.7.6   Nearest relatives of children

Sections 27 and 28 of the Act make special provision for the nearest relatives of children subject to:

(a) Resolutions to assume parental rights under section 3 of the Child Care Act 1980 – here the nearest relative is the local authority which has assumed parental rights. If only one parent's rights have been taken the other parent remains as nearest relative.
(b) Care orders made under the Children and Young Persons Act 1969 – here the nearest relative is the care authority.
(c) Guardianship of Minors orders – the nearest relative will be the guardian named in the order.
(d) Custody orders in matrimonial proceedings – the nearest relative will be the parent given custody by the order.
(e) Wills in which the parents appoint guardians of their children – the nearest relative will be the person named as guardian in the will.

2.7.7   Removing the nearest relative

The important status given to the nearest relative can be lost if the county court appoints an acting nearest relative under section 29.

Section 29 (1) The county court may, upon application made in accordance with the provisions of this section in respect of a patient, by order direct that the functions of the nearest relative of the patient under this Part of this Act and sections 66 and 69 below shall, during the continuance in force of the order, be exercisable by the applicant, or by any other person specified in the application, being a person who, in the opinion of the court, is a proper person to act as the patient's nearest relative and is willing to do so.

The effect of this section is clear and requires little further comment. Notice that the functions of a nearest relative which can be exercised by a person appointed under section 29 are specified:

(a) to apply for the patient's admission to hospital for assessment under sections 2 and 4 or for treatment under section 3.
(b) to apply for the patient to be received into guardianship under section 7.
(c) to order the patient's discharge from hospital under section 23.
(d) to apply for the patient's discharge to a Mental Health Review Tribunal either under section 66 (civil patients) or section 68 (criminal patients).

Notice also that the applicant under section 29 can specify that someone other than the applicant may be appointed to act as the nearest relative.

2.7.8   Who can apply under section 29?

The persons who can apply are specified in section 29 (2):

Section 29 (2) An order under this section may be made on the application of—
(a) any relative of the patient;
(b) any other person with whom the patient is residing (or, if the patient is then an in-patient in a hospital, was last residing before he was admitted); or
(c) an approved social worker;
but in relation to an application made by such a social worker, subsection(1) above shall have effect as if for the words 'the applicant' there were substituted the words 'the local social services authority'.

The grounds for making an order under section 29 are set out in subsection (3):

Section 29 (3) An application for an order under this section may be made upon any of the following grounds, that is to say—
(a) that the patient has no nearest relative within the meaning of this Act, or that it is not reasonably practicable to ascertain whether he

has such a relative, or who that relative is;
(b) that the nearest relative of the patient is incapable of acting as such by reason of mental disorder or other illness;
(c) that the nearest relative of the patient unreasonably objects to the making of an application for admission for treatment or a guardianship application in respect of the patient; or
(d) that the nearest relative of the patient has exercised without due regard to the welfare of the patient or the interests of the public his power to discharge the patient from hospital or guardianship under this Part of this Act, or is likely to do so.

An important effect of an application under section 29 is that it prolongs any period of a patient's detention beyond the normal expiry date until the application has been finally considered by the county court and any appeal has been heard. Under the 1959 Act all acting nearest relative appointments were of indefinite duration. Now, under the 1983 Act, the county court has power to make an appointment for a limited period which could prove useful where the patient has children under 18 who are willing to undertake the responsibilities of a nearest relative when they become adults but cannot do so immediately because they are under age. The county court is given power in subsection (5) to appoint acting nearest relatives for a period specified in the order and this power could be used to appoint a distant adult relative until the children are 18.

2.8 The role of the approved social worker

2.8.1 So far we have only examined specific aspects of the approved social worker's role: applications for admission to hospital or for reception into guardianship. This section has three wider objectives:

(a) To relate the wider perceived role of the approved social worker to the more limited statutory duties given to approved social workers by the Act.
(b) To identify and discuss the problems an approved social worker may encounter in fulfilling his statutory duties.
(c) To offer some guidance upon the problems identified in (b) above.

2.8.2 But first a few preliminary observations upon three paradoxes in the 1983 Act:

(a) One of the major objects of the 1983 Act is to increase the standing of approved social workers in the eyes of other professionals working with the mentally disordered. Yet the approved social worker can still be by-passed by relatives if he refuses to apply for the admission of a patient to hospital. Also, as has been shown in paragraph 2.7, the number of potential relatives who can apply for a person's admission to hospital has been increased.

(b) The approved social worker's role is not clearly identified in the 1983 Act. An attempt to do this in the Lords was opposed by the Government on two grounds:

(i) the amendments proposed were actually achieved by proposed Government amendments to section 54 of the 1959 Act (now section 13 of the 1983 Act), and

(ii) some of the points contained in the proposed amendments were matters of good practice and as such were not appropriate for legislation but should be covered by guidance. Yet in its final form section 13 of the 1983 Act does contain points which are matters of good practice, eg the duty to interview the patient in a suitable manner.

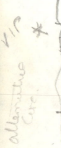

(c) The approved social worker, the person whose responsibility it is to decide whether a patient requires treatment in hospital or the community, has no statutory power or duty to control the allocation of community resources within his employing authority's area. The main objective of the 1983 Act is that treatment should always be given in the least restrictive environment possible and this will not be achieved unless the necessary alternative placements in the community are available. Who other than the approved social worker is better placed to identify and press for allocation of resources that are required within his employing authority's area to fulfil the stated objectives of the 1983 Act?

2.8.3 What do social workers think their role in mental health work should be? This question must be answered before we can consider whether the 1983 Act goes far enough in specifying the approved social worker's duties. It is our experience that social workers display great uncertainty over their role in mental health work. This is confirmed by what little published research exists on the subject. A Scottish study in 1978 'Social Workers as Mental Health Officers' by the Scottish Office is of particular interest. Whilst Scottish Mental Health legislation differs from its counterpart in England and Wales the framework is similar and it places similar duties on Scottish social workers. Therefore it is reasonable to expect that the views of Scottish workers are representative of their English and Welsh colleagues.

Some social workers saw their role in very limited terms – to carry out the legal formalities and act as a 'kind of psychiatric policeman or removal man' or a 'medical auxiliary'; others thought they were acting as a protector of the client (patient) to speak for him whilst he was unable to do so. Others felt that the role was much wider:

> ... seeking to modify the social circumstances of the patient to alleviate as far as possible stress on the patient, his relatives and others in order to create an environment as supportive as possible for all concerned. This was seen as part of an effort to offer a preventative service as the ultimate goal of the service. Several members of the group surveyed felt that it would be possible to remove the need for formal admission entirely in many cases if it were possible to provide adequate supervision to families which included a mentally disordered member. As a further extension of this focus, some saw an important dimension of the work of the mental health officer being a concern to help the community as a whole to better understand mental health problems and procedures.

In the face of such divergent views on the proper role of the approved social worker it is difficult if not impossible to set down a role which will be acceptable to all.

2.8.4   The 1983 Act deliberately refrains from specifying the role of an approved social worker in any detail and therefore the approved social worker is entitled to look to his employing authority for guidance upon a proper role to adopt. The obvious objection to local authorities laying down the role is that the 1983 Act places responsibility upon individual approved social workers to carry out the duties given to them and not upon their employing authorities. The extent to which an employing authority can seek to influence its approved social workers' activities must be limited in comparison with other areas of social work such as care of children or the elderly.

Is the answer, then, for local authorities to leave role definition and responsibility for carrying it out entirely to its approved social workers because of the personal nature of the duties in the 1983 Act? To do so, in our opinion, would fail to attack the problems experienced by mental welfare officers under the 1959 Act particularly since the formation of generic social services departments in 1970.

Since the establishment in 1970 of social services departments with responsibility for a wide range of clients it has been the usual practice for local authorities to appoint mental welfare officers from the ranks of their generic social work staff. Often such staff have had little or no interest or experience in mental health work. This has led to difficult and sometimes non-existent working relationships with medical staff concerned with the care and treatment of mental disorder. A major difficulty for medical staff has been to appreciate the wider responsibilities of social workers performing mental welfare officer's work and to understand their new role. Unless he is part of a specialist team, a mental welfare officer's case-load will contain only a small number of mentally disordered clients and therefore his opportunities to gain experience in mental health work are reduced. This has led to a reduction in the status of mental health workers in the eyes of the medical staff. The re-introduction of specialist mental health workers by creating approved social worker posts is an ideal opportunity for local authorities to define in general terms the role approved social workers will be expected to perform in mental health work.

A clear definition of the approved social worker's role will also help the development of better relationships with patients' relatives who are often unsure at a time of extreme crisis of the functions of the various personnel involved in compulsory admissions, eg social workers, police, GPs, consultant psychiatrists.

It is the local authority which allocates resources for mental health services within its area. Any programme which it develops will have little chance of success unless it is drawn up in consultation with its mental health workers. As part of its programme for mental health services the local authority should set out the parameters within which its approved social workers should operate by defining their role. The importance of consulting with approved social workers in drawing up a programme cannot be overstated. As has been stated already it is the approved social worker who is best placed to identify specific local needs.

2.8.5   What role should be laid down for approved social workers by their employing authorities? A good starting point is that proposed for insertion in the 1982 Amendment Bill by Baroness Faithfull:

The role of the approved social worker of a social services department is:

(a) to make application for admission or guardianship where required;

(b) to investigate the patient's social situation and to identify in consultation with others involved, the extent to which social and environmental pressures have contributed to his observed behaviour and to interview the patient;

(c) to use his professional skills to help resolve any social, relationship or environmental difficulties which have contributed to the crisis, and to mobilise community resources appropriately;

(d) to be familiar with legal requirements and to ensure that they are complied with;

(e) to form his own opinions, following an interview with the patient, with those closest to him, and with others involved, as to whether compulsory admission is necessary having regard to any alternative methods of resolving the crisis, and of securing necessary care or treatment;

(f) to ensure that care and treatment is offered in the least restrictive conditions possible;

(g) to work in partnership with the medical profession; and

(h) to be trained at an approved Mental Health Training Centre.

2.8.6   We would suggest that the following matters should also be included in the approved social worker's role:

(a) adviser to patient and relatives;

(b) obligation to visit the patient and his relatives during the patient's treatment process, whether or not the patient has been admitted to hospital;

(c) liaison with medical staff and hospital social workers;

(d) power to apply to a Mental Health Review Tribunal for a patient's discharge;

(e) power to override a nearest relative's objection to an application for admission to hospital.

2.8.7   Having examined in detail a variety of tasks which should make up the role of approved social workers, we can now look at the statutory role assigned to them under the Act:

Section 13 (1) It shall be the duty of an approved social worker to make an application for admission to hospital or a guardianship application in respect of a patient within the area of the local social services authority by which that officer is appointed in any case where he is satisfied that such an application ought to be made and is of the opinion, having regard to any wishes expressed by relatives of the patient or any other relevant circumstances, that it is necessary or proper for the application to be made by him.

(2) Before making an application for the admission of a patient to hospital an approved social worker shall interview the patient in a

suitable manner and satisfy himself that detention in a hospital is in all the circumstances of the case the most appropriate way of providing the care and medical treatment of which the patient stands in need.

The approved social worker is placed under a statutory duty to make applications for admission to hospital or reception into guardianship. This duty can be broken down into several elements which operate in conjunction with other parts of the 1983 Act:

(a) The patient must be within the area of the approved social worker's employing authority.

(b) The approved social worker must satisfy himself that the patient's condition justifies the making of an application either by the nearest relative or himself.

(c) If the approved social worker is satisfied that an application should be made he should then decide whether it is right for him to make the application. In making this decision the approved social worker should take into account the wishes of the patient's relatives or any other circumstances relevant to the case.

(d) The approved social worker must interview the patient 'in a suitable manner'. These words are intended to cover patients who are blind, deaf, dumb or unable to understand English. In such circumstances an approved social worker should use the services of an appropriate interpreter to carry out the interview.

(e) Where admission of the patient to hospital is contemplated the approved social worker must be satisfied that the care and medical treatment needed by the patient can only be provided in hospital. If approved social workers are to carry out this part of their duties properly they must be fully aware of all alternative placements within the community such as hostels for the mentally disordered, day centres, boarding-out schemes, etc and this information should be supplied to them by their employing authority.

(f) The approved social worker must discover who is the patient's nearest relative.

(g) The approved social worker must consult with the patient's nearest relative before or within a reasonable time of an application for assessment being made – section 11(3).

(h) The approved social worker must not make an application to hospital for treatment if the nearest relative has objected.

(i) Once an application for admission to hospital has been made by an approved social worker the duty to take and convey the patient to hospital arises under section 6 (see paragraph 2.6).

The approved social worker's duties in section 13 are supported by powers of entry and inspection in section 115 (see para 10.7).

It is also the approved social worker's duty to ensure that the application is properly completed if he is the applicant. This is entirely the approved social worker's responsibility for the hospital can rely on section 6(3) to cover itself if there are any latent defects in the application or the supporting medical recommendations (see paragraph 2.2.9).

2.8.8 Guidance concerning the issues an approved social worker must take into account when considering a patient's case is given by the DHSS Guide:

> 38. Section 13(2) requires the approved social worker to interview the patient 'in a suitable manner' – ie taking into account any hearing or linguistic difficulties the patient may have. He must also satisfy himself that detention in hospital is the most appropriate way of providing the care and medical treatment the patient needs. He is required to consider 'all the circumstances' of the case: these will include the past history of the patient's mental disorder, his present condition and the social, familial, and personal factors bearing on it, the wishes of the patient and his relatives, and medical opinion. To do this he will need to consult with all those professionally involved in the case (for example the doctor or a community psychiatric nurse). In order to assess the available options the approved social worker will have to inform himself as to the availability and suitability or other means of giving the patient care and medical treatment, such as treatment as an informal patient, day care, out patient treatment, community psychiatric nursing support, crisis intervention centres, primary health care support, local authority social services provision, and support from friends, relatives and voluntary organisations.

Further aspects of the approved social worker's duties are to be found in section 13(3) and (4), following.

2.8.9 **Section 13** (3) An application under this section by an approved social worker may be made outside the area of the local social services authority by which he is appointed.

It is now clear that an approved social worker may operate outside his appointing authority's area. There was no equivalent provision in the 1959 Act.

Mental welfare officers often experienced some anxiety when asked to make an application outside their appointing authority's area (usually in a psychiatric hospital situated in a neighbouring local authority's area). This was and will continue to be a quite common occurrence where the neighbouring local authority(ies) do not provide a 24-hour standby service and where the local psychiatric hospital's catchment area does not coincide with local authority boundaries. Ministry of Health guidance on this point in 1965 was that a mental welfare officer could properly act outside his employing authority's area provided that the terms of his appointment were not limited to the area of his employing authority.

An opportunity to clarify the position of approved social workers in such circumstances has been taken in subsection (3). It should be noted that the approved social worker is not under a mandatory duty to make applications outside his area – the mandatory duty only arises where a patient is within his employing authority's area. Outside of that area he has a discretion to act and may decline to make an application if he feels it would be more appropriate for the application to be made by an approved social worker appointed by the local authority in whose area the patient is located. Although subsection (3) makes it clear that approved social workers can operate outside the boundaries of their appointing authorities, confusion will be avoided if, in future, appointments of approved social workers are not limited by reference to their employing authorities' boundaries.

2.8.10 **Section 13** (4) It shall be the duty of a local services authority, if so required by the nearest relative of a patient residing within their area, to direct an approved social worker as soon as practicable to take the patient's case into consideration under subsection (1) above with a view to making an application for his admission to hospital; and if in any such case that approved social worker decides not to make an application he shall inform the nearest relative of his reasons in writing.

This subsection has operational implications for local authorities in respect of the manner in which nearest relatives may issue their request for the local authority to direct its approved social worker to consider a case. Does the request need to be in writing? Can a non-approved social worker be given delegated authority to direct approved social workers to consider a case after a request has been received? How are repeated and unjustified requests from the nearest relative to be handled? How detailed must be the reasons for refusing to make an application? None of these questions are answered by the Act but some guidance can be offered:

(a) There is no requirement for the requests to be in writing so a local authority cannot refuse to act upon a verbal request provided it appears genuine. A local authority may be justified in requesting proof of a relative's status if a verbal request is made (and often if a written request is made) especially if it has no previous knowledge of the patient or his family.

(b) How the local authority handles requests internally under subsection (4) is left entirely to its own discretion. It is important that local authorities lay down a clear procedure for directing their approved social workers to consider cases. This procedure should designate staff who are authorised to receive requests from nearest relatives under subsection (4) and specify the manner in which the direction should be made to the approved social worker who is to consider the case.

(c) It is significant that unlike other procedures under the Act, there is no statutory form prescribed in which the approved social worker can give reasons for not making an application for admission. This, combined with the emphasis in the Act upon a moving away from routine procedures, suggests that some detail should be included in the communication to the nearest relative. It will not be acceptable to give standard reasons; each case should be communicated on an individual basis.

2.8.11 Although the 1983 Act gives approved social workers a limited role, guidance in DHSS Circular LAC (83) 7 suggests that they have a wider role to play in mental health work:

Duties of Approved Social Workers

12. Approved social workers should have a wider role than reacting to requests for admission to hospital, making the necessary arrangements and ensuring compliance with the law. They should have the specialist knowledge and skills to make appropriate decisions in respect of both clients and their relatives and to gain the confidence of colleagues in the health service with whom they are required to collaborate. They must be familiar with the day to day working of an integrated mental service and be able to assess what other services may be required from the social services department and elsewhere and know how to mobilise them. They should have access to, consultation with and supervision from qualified and experienced senior officers. Their role is to prevent the necessity for compulsory admission to hospital as well as to make application where they decide this is appropriate.

2.8.12 The uneasy relationships which can exist between medical and social work staff have already been referred to. The Act provides no immediate solution to these problems, although it is to be hoped that the higher standards that social workers will have to achieve to attain approved social worker status will eventually lead to an enhanced status for social workers in the eyes of their medical colleagues.

The possibility of conflict between doctors and approved social workers is built into the Act. In theory, their roles appear quite separate – the doctor examines the patient, makes a medical diagnosis and completes an appropriate medical recommendation, whilst the approved social worker decides on social work principles whether or not the patient should be admitted to hospital. In practice, however, there is a substantial overlap in the roles of the doctor and the approved social worker and it is in this area of overlap that disputes can occur. In Form 10, the medical recommendations for admission for treatment under section 3, the doctors state that the patient's mental disorder 'makes it appropriate for him to receive medical treatment in a hospital' and that treatment 'cannot be provided unless he is detained under section 3 of the Act . . .'. Form 9, the application by the approved social worker for admission for treatment under the same section, requires the approved social worker to state that he is 'satisfied that detention in a hospital is in all the circumstances of the case the most appropriate way of providing the care and medical treatment of which the patient stands in need.' Conflict between the doctor and approved social worker is inevitable where the doctor signs the medical recommendation and the approved social worker refuses to make an application because the patient is prepared to be admitted to hospital on a voluntary basis or because the approved social worker is aware of local authority hostel accommodation in which the patient can be accommodated and treated.

Here the duty of the approved social worker is to ask the question, 'Why can treatment not be given in a less restrictive environment than a hospital?' He is not challenging the doctor's diagnosis by asking this question but the doctor's statement that treatment cannot be provided unless the patient is detained. Such situations of conflict are not rare and are particularly likely to arise where the recommending doctor is not 'approved' but is a GP whose ability and experience in the diagnosis and treatment of mental disorder may be limited. By refusing to make an application an approved social worker is challenging part of the doctor's judgement and his role under the Act requires him to do so.

2.8.13 All that can be said in conclusion on this point is that the the statutory role of the approved social worker requires him to be satisfied as to the need for the hospitalisation of the patient before making an application, and if this means that the approved social worker must challenge the doctor's medical recommendation so far as it relates to where the patient should receive his treatment, then such a challenge must be made. The consequences of merely 'rubber-stamping' a medical recommendation are illustrated in a case decided in 1960, *Buxton v Jayne,* which we look at in detail at paragraph 2.8.17. The case was one of the few where a patient was given leave to bring an action against a mental welfare officer who made an application to admit her to hospital where there was little or no evidence that she was suffering from mental disorder.

2.8.14 A further area causing problems in practice is the position of hospital based social workers. There has been long-standing concern over the practice of authorising such social workers as mental welfare officers particularly if they are expected to make applications for admission to the hospital in which they are based. The argument against such social workers making applications under the 1959 and 1983 Acts is that they could conceivably come under the influence and direction of the consultant psychiatrist with whom they work in the hospital. This could lead to collusion if the hospital social worker makes an application supported by a medical recommendation from 'his' consultant psychiatrist. The Act prohibits (except in limited circumstances) the giving of both medical recommendations by doctors on the staff of the same hospital but does not prohibit either hospital social workers being appointed as approved social workers or applications being made by hospital social workers based in the admitting hospital. In 1974 the DHSS issued a letter of guidance entitled 'Admission to hospital under the provisions of Part IV of the Mental Health Act 1959'. This letter stated:

> The Department has received representations from some hospital social workers who are unhappy about proposals to appoint them, following their transfer to local authority employment on 1 April 1974, as mental welfare officers . . . They feel that it might be difficult for them to express a truly independent opinion if they are called upon to make an application for compulsory admission in hospital if a doctor with whom they work has made one of the medical recommendations on which the application must be founded and that even where they feel confident that

they can take an independent view the patient or his relatives may feel that they are subject to control or influence by the hospital doctor and therefore not truly independent . . .

. . . [There are] no restrictions upon a local authority in its choice of an officer to act as a mental welfare officer . . . and we recognise that hospital social workers may have considerable expertise in the social aspects of mental illness and that it may be felt appropriate to appoint some as mental welfare officers. In most cases the mental welfare officer will be in agreement with the medical recommendations, but it must be remembered that the officers' powers in section 27 of the Mental Health Act and his duty in section 54(1) would not have been enacted by Parliament if it had been intended that medical opinion alone should authorise detention under Part IV of the Act.

It is important therefore that a person performing the duties of a mental welfare officer not only should be but should appear to be in a position in which he or she can exercise a completely independent judgement when assuming the responsibility of making an application for the compulsory admission and detention of a patient, whether for observation or treatment.

We think therefore that it should be made clear to each hospital social worker who is appointed as a mental welfare officer that if in any case she feels that she cannot act truly independently, or if she feels that it might be thought by the patient or his relatives that she could not do so, she should seek advice from her superior officer as to whether it would be advisable for another officer to act in her stead.

2.8.15 The solution to the dilemma must lie with the individual approved social worker as the Act lays responsibility on him to satisfy himself 'that it is necessary or proper for the application to be made by him.' Whilst his employing authority may approve him as an approved social worker and offer guidance and support on undertaking his duties it cannot take upon itself the responsibility of deciding whether or not to make an application in any particular case. This responsibility lies entirely with the individual approved social worker. If an approved social worker based in a hospital feels he cannot give an objective consideration to a particular case, he should decline to make the application and refer the case to another approved social worker not connected with the admitting hospital. It is essential that local authorities lay down clear guidelines for their approved social workers based in hospitals on how to deal with this problem and that such approved social workers familiarise themselves with such guidance. The hospital staff who work with hospital based approved social workers should also have access to this guidance so that they are aware of the procedures to be adopted and the reasons for them.

2.8.16 **Section 14** Where a patient is admitted to a hospital in pursuance of an application (other than an emergency application) made under this Part of this Act by his nearest relative, the managers of the hospital shall as soon as practicable give notice of that fact to the local social services authority for the area in which the patient resided immediately before his admission; and that authority shall as soon as practicable arrange for a social worker oftheir social services department to interview the patient and provide the managers with a report on his social circumstances.

This section is also new. It was not in the Government's original 1982 Amendment Bill but is the result of pressure during the Commons Committee stage of the Bill's progress through Parliament. An amendment which was in principle similar to section 14 was moved but it contained three important differences:

(a) It included patients admitted under section 29 (now section 4)
(b) It gave an approved social worker the power to 'consider the most appropriate way of providing care and medical treatment'
(c) The hospital managers had to refer all cases to an approved social worker within 24 hours of admission.

The amendment was not pressed after a Government undertaking to introduce an appropriate clause in the Bill. The Government clause which was introduced was section 14.

The object of the original amendment was to ensure that approved social workers were involved in the process of compulsory admissions to hospital. This went too far for the Government (and presumably for the medical fraternity) by including approved social workers in the treatment plan and in requiring cases to be referred within 24 hours. The eventual outcome was section 14 as printed.

The section deals with the situation where the patient is admitted without the involvement of an approved social worker, ie where a nearest relative applies. Once the patient is admitted the hospital must inform the local authority. There is no time limit within which this must be done other than the somewhat vague 'as soon as practicable'. Upon this happening the local authority is then under a duty, again vague in terms of time limit, to arrange for the patient to be interviewed by a *social worker,* not necessarily an approved social worker. The purpose of this interview is to provide the hospital with a report on the patient's 'social circumstances'. The Act gives no guidance upon what should be contained in this report nor is the term social circumstances defined. Furthermore there is no indication as to what action the hospital should take on receipt of the report, eg if the report recommends that the patient could be treated in the community. Some guidance upon the content can be gained from the Mental Health Review Tribunal Rules 1983 where the term social circumstances occurs in the context of reports to be submitted to the Tribunal in proceedings for the discharge of a patient from hospital. There the social circumstances should refer to the following matters:

(a) the patient's home and family circumstances including the attitude of the patient's nearest relative or the person acting as the nearest relative;

(b) the opportunities for employment or occupation and the housing facilities which would be available to the patient if discharged;

(c) the availability of community support and relevant medical facilities;

(d) the financial circumstances of the patient.

The DHSS Guide states that the matters referred to in paragraph 2.8.8 above should be included in a social report issued under section 14 of the 1983 Act.

There are two potential areas of difficulty with this section:

(a) The efficiency factor. How quickly will hospitals pass on the information to local authorities? This is particularly relevant in the context of a possible early application to a tribunal from a patient detained for assessment.

(b) The identity factor. The section refers to the local authority for the area in which the patient lived before admission. In most cases this will be clear, but problems can be anticipated with patients who have no fixed address or who are temporarily resident in a local authority's area. It will be necessary for local authorities to enter into agreed arrangements with their local psychiatric hospitals to ensure that the preparation of the report is not held up by disputes as to which local authority is responsible to arrange for the social circumstances report.

2.8.17 Immunity from legal proceedings – background

I have a totally unbounded admiration for the dedication of people who, in exhausting circumstances, day after day, week after week, year after year, give of themselves to the disordered, and sometimes aggressive people whom they serve and whom, willy-nilly sometimes they must detain. I believe that they deserve and must have protection from the sort of litigation which can endlessly get them into court and against which they can protect themselves only by being always accompanied, like St. Paul, a great cloud of witnesses.

Staff involved in the care and treatment of mentally disordered persons have traditionally enjoyed freedom from legal action arising from their work. This tradition is carried on in the 1983 Act in a slightly modified form by section 139 and the above words of Lord Elton speaking in the Lords debates on the 1982 Amendment Bill attempt to justify the substantial protection enjoyed by medical and social work staff against legal proceedings by patients.

The equivalent section in the 1959 Act, section 141, was strongly criticised by MIND on the grounds that it was wider than necessary to give staff the protection they required. This was illustrated by a case in 1975 where a conviction of a male nurse at Broadmoor for assaulting a patient was quashed on the ground that the patient had not obtained the High Court's permission to bring the prosecution. The patient contended that the alleged assault was not an act in pursuance of the 1959 Act. The court rejected that contention on the ground that acts done for the purpose of controlling patients were protected under section 141 (the assault having been committed in the course of ushering the patient back to the ward).

The 1978 Review suggested that staff were becoming increasingly uncertain of their legal position in a number of situations and reforms such as the nurses' holding power and the consent to treatment provisions were intended to remove such uncertainties. Yet it was still necessary to have a 'long-stop' provision which would 'reassure staff that they will not be involved unnecessarily in ill-founded court cases'. This 'long-stop' provision would be a modified version of section 141. The proposed modifications were:

(a) to remove the need for the High Court's permission for criminal proceedings and transfer responsibility to the Director of Public Prosecutions; and
(b) to require litigants to show a prima facie case rather than 'substantial grounds' for permission to bring an action from the High Court. These modifications have been made and protection for staff is contained in section 139 of the 1983 Act.

The Law

Section 139 (1) No person shall be liable, whether on the ground of want

81

of jurisdiction or on any other ground, to any civil or criminal proceedings to which he would have been liable apart from this section in respect of any act purporting to be done in pursuance of this Act or any regulations or rules made under this Act, or in pursuance of anything done in, the discharge of functions conferred by any other enactment on the authority having jurisdiction under Part VII of this Act, unless the act was done in bad faith or without reasonable care.

(2) No civil proceedings shall be brought against any person in any court in respect of any such act without the leave of the High Court; and no criminal proceedings shall be brought against any person in any court in respect of any such act except by or with the consent of the Director of Public Prosecutions.

(3) This section does not apply to any proceedings for an offence under this Act being proceedings which, under any other provision of this Act, can be instituted only by or with the consent of the Director of Public Prosecutions.

In paragraph 4.3 we look at the provisions of the Act which emphasise the patient's sense of isolation when in hospital. Section 139 is probably the most serious infringement in the Act of the usual rights he enjoys when not detained in hospital. It is based upon an unproven assumption that 'Patients under the Mental Health Act may generally be inherently likely to harass those concerned with them by groundless charges and litigation, and may therefore have to suffer modification of the general right of free access to the courts' (Lord Simon). There is little evidence that mentally disordered patients are more likely to bring 'groundless charges and litigation' The 1976 Review stated that very few applications had been made for permission to start cases under the equivalent section in the 1959 Act;

Year	No of applications
1970	4
1971	1
1972	3
1973	7
1974	4
1975	5

but it was not known if this was due to solicitors advising against proceedings because of the heavy burden involved in satisfying the requirements of the old section. MIND pointed out in their criticism of the old section that some groups of patients such as paranoid schizophrenics and patients in special hospitals may be more likely to bring legal proceedings than others such as mentally handicapped patients or patients suffering from depression. Both the old and the new sections fail to recognise this and impose unacceptable restrictions on all patients.

It is also worth noting that all courts have inherent powers to control frivolous or vexatious litigation so the need for this extra protection for staff is questionable. This is particularly so if we look at the cases where patients have sought permission to start a case. The earlier attitude of the courts to patients as litigants is illustrated by the typically graphic words of Lord Justice Denning in a case in 1957:

> This seems to be one of the very cases which Parliament had in mind when they said that an action such as this should not be brought without the leave of the court. It is an unfortunate feature of mental illness that those afflicted by it do not realise the need for their being under the care and control of others. They resent it, much as a small child or a dumb animal resents being given medicine for its own good, and they are apt to turn round and claw and scratch the hand that gives it.

A more sympathetic view of the patient's position is given by Lord Simon nearly 20 years later in 1975 when in a qualification to the statement quoted earlier he says:

> But they are, on the other hand, a class of citizen which experience has shown to be peculiarly vulnerable . . . the operation of section 141 should be kept under close scrutiny by Parliament and the Department of Health and Social Security.

There are limits to the protection given by section 139 and this is illustrated by a case in 1960. The case involved the grounds for compulsory admission to hospital in the Lunacy Act 1890. Under this Act a duly authorised officer had power to admit a patient if he had reasonable grounds for believing that the patient was a person of unsound mind and a proper person to be sent to a mental hospital. In this case the patient was a lady who became emotionally upset following family troubles. Her GP called in a duly authorised officer who tried to persuade her to go to hospital for treatment on a voluntary basis. She refused so the duly authorised officer made an application for her compulsory admission. The patient was eventually discharged after four days in hospital when a JP refused to make a reception order. The patient started proceedings against the duly authorised officer alleging that he had acted without reasonable care in removing her to hospital. The patient needed the permission of the High Court to start the proceedings and this could only be given if there were substantial grounds for the patient's contention that the duly authorised officer had acted without reasonable care. The High Court granted the patient permission to start the proceedings because the duly authorised officer was unable to state that he believed her to be of unsound mind when he applied for her admission to hospital. In effect he had merely agreed with the GP that she should be admitted to hospital. The evidence of the duly authorised officer is of interest: he stated that when he visited the patient in her home she was 'shouting and screaming to such an extent that it was quite impossible to carry on a normal conversation with her. She was very obviously greatly disturbed and acting in a quite abnormal manner and was highly excited.' Referring to her removal to hospital he stated: 'It was quite clear to me that for her own protection this was the only sensible and proper step as [she] could there be looked after, whereas at home she clearly could no longer be looked after properly. I thought that she was in real danger unless she were removed to somewhere where proper care could be given to her.' The GP stated: 'I formed the clear opinion that [she] required observation and psychiatric treatment and skilled attention which clearly she could not get if she remained at home.'

Although this case concerns mental health legislation which is nearly 100 years old, the issues involved are still relevant today and the message for the approved social worker is clear – the 1983 Act requires him to satisfy himself that a patient's mental condition warrants detention in hospital and if he is not so satisfied he should not make an application. If he does, and a patient brings an action for negligence, it seems that the approved social worker will not be protected by section 139.

In conclusion the following points should be noted on the terms of section 139:

(a) The section is not limited to proceedings by a patient – it applies to proceedings brought by any person in respect of action under the 1983 Act.
(b) The grounds for bringing proceedings are bad faith, ie malice or fraud, and lack of reasonable care, ie negligence.
(c) Civil proceedings require the permission of the High Court, criminal proceedings require the permission of the DPP.
(d) The Secretary of State and Health Authorities are excluded from the protection of the section but not, it seems, local authorities.
(e) It has been held in a case in 1977 that the equivalent section in

the 1959 Act did not apply to an informal patient. The 1978 Review stated that this point was not free from doubt and it was intended to clarify the position in the 1983 Act. As the section contains no reference to informal patients it must be assumed that the 1977 case still applies.

2.8.18 Conclusion

We have deliberately dwelt at length on the role of the approved social worker because the Act gives approved social workers a key position in the care and treatment of mentally disordered people. The intention of the Act is that approved social workers will be fully equipped in terms of training, experience and competence to fulfil this role (a topic considered later in Part 12) and it will require a change in the attitude of medical staff engaged in the treatment of mental disorder if the objectives of the Act are to be realised. The situation is aptly summed up in the following quotation from Baroness Faithfull:

> . . . approved social workers. and indeed the social work service, should take a partnership responsibility with the doctors in dealing with admissions and . . . in the first instance, the social worker should be enabled to see what were the community facilities and to ensure that the patient's needs were met.

Whilst the Act does not give approved social workers the wider role we think they should perform, it does give them almost total control over admissions and they should exercise this power, supported fully by their employing local authorities, in order to ensure that patients are not admitted to hospital unnecessarily.

2.9 The role of the police

2.9.1 Introduction

We now come to section 135 and 136 of the Act which gives the police powers to remove certain persons to places of safety for medical examination. These powers should not be confused with those in section 137 which gives persons authorised under the Act all the powers of a police constable *once an application has been made* (considered at paragraph 2.6) nor should they simply be viewed as powers for the police to admit patients to hospital. The purpose of sections 135 and 136 is limited to the removal of persons suspected to be suffering from mental disorder to a place where they can be examined to discover whether or not the grounds for an application for admission exist.

During the two Reviews of the 1959 Act there was some discussion as to whether or not the powers should be dropped from the Act. Section 135 had been little used (only 13 times during 1976) and there was a wide variation throughout the country in the use of section 136, ranging from 1 in every 1,000 admissions in cities such as Leeds, Sheffield and Manchester to 34 in every 1,000 admissions in the SW Metropolitan Police Area. MIND pressed for the following changes to section 136.

(a) That the original recommendation of the Percy Committee be enacted. This was that police power to remove a person from a public place should only apply if a person is behaving in such a manner as to render him liable to arrest under ordinary police powers of arrest.
(b) In addition to (a) above a further test should apply – dangerous behaviour by the person liable to be removed.
(c) The period of detention should be reduced from 72 hours to 24 hours.

At the same time BASW argued for the eventual phasing out of the section 136 power on the grounds that it would eventually become unnecessary when crisis intervention services were developed.

During the Reviews there was some dispute as to the accuracy of the national figures for the use of the powers in sections 135 and 136. Some areas always listed the use of these powers prior to hospital admissions direct from police stations. Other areas did not indicate when sections 135 and 136 had been used prior to a hospital admission.

2.9.2 Another area of concern was how suitable a police station was as a place of safety in which to examine a person prior to hospital admission. The 1959 Act definition of 'place of safety' included a variety of premises, but it was the usual practice of the police to bring persons suspected of suffering from a mental disorder to a police station for examination, usually by the police surgeon. It was not normal practice to take persons direct to hospital, mainly because of the hospitals' reluctance to admit persons who had not been medically examined and diagnosed as suffering from a mental disorder. The police are in a difficult position here – they have a duty to remove persons if the grounds exist but where can they take them other than to a police station if the hospital will not admit them? The objection to a police station is that the person is likely to become even more disturbed at the prospect of being taken to a police station which could lead to unnecessary admission to hospital. An attempt to resolve this problem was put forward in the 1976 Review, which aimed to revise the definition of 'place of safety' so that it would not include a police station unless there was no other suitable place to which the patient could be taken. The Government eventually decided that whilst this would be a useful improvement it would be better achieved by guidance rather than by altering the Act. This has been done in paragraph 291 of the DHSS Guide which states:

> Only in exceptional circumstances should a police station be used as a place of safety. If a police station is used, the patient should remain there for no longer than a few hours while an approved social worker makes the necessary arrangements for his removal elsewhere, either informally or under Part II of the Act.

Section 135 (1) If it appears to a justice of the peace, on information on oath laid by an approved social worker, that there is reasonable cause to suspect that a person believed to be suffering from mental disorder—

(a) has been, or is being, ill-treated, neglected or kept otherwise than under proper control, in any place within the jurisdiction of the justice, or

(b) being unable to care for himself, is living alone in any such place, the justice may issue a warrant authorising any constable named in the warrant to enter, if need be by force, any premises specified in the warrant in which that person is believed to be, and, if thought fit, to remove him to a place of safety with a view to the making of an application in respect of him under Part II of this Act, or of other arrangements for his treatment or care.

(2) If it appears to a justice of the peace, on information on oath laid by any constable or other person who is authorised by or under this Act or under section 83 of the Mental Health (Scotland) Act 1960 to take a patient to any place, or to take into custody or retake a patient who is liable under this Act or under the said section 83 to be so taken or retaken—

(a) that there is reasonable cause to believe that the patient is to be found on premises within the jurisdiction of the justice; and

(b) that admission to the premises has been refused or that a refusal of such admission is apprehended, the justice may issue a warrant authorising any constable named in the warrant to enter the premises, if need be by force, and remove the patient.

(3) A patient who is removed to a place of safety in the execution of a warrant issued under this section may be detained there for a period not exceeding 72 hours.

(4) In the execution of a warrant issued under subsection (1) above, the constable to whom it is addressed shall be accompanied by an approved social worker and by a registered medical practitioner, and in the execution of a warrant issued under subsection (2) above the constable to whom it is addressed may be accompanied—

  (a) by a registered medical practitioner
  (b) by any person authorised by or under this Act or under section 83 of the Mental Health (Scotland) Act 1960 to take or retake the patient.

(5) It shall not be necessary in any information or warrant under subsection (1) above to name the patient concerned.

(6) In this section 'place of safety' means residential accommodation provided by a local social services authority under Part III of the National Assistance Act 1948 or under paragraph 2 of Schedule 8 to the National Health Service Act 1977, a hospital as defined by this Act, a police station, a mental nursing home or residential home for mentally disordered persons or any other suitable place the occupier of which is willing temporarily to receive the patient.

2.9.3   There are two separate powers in this section. Subsection (1) is to be used where the approved social worker suspects that a person suffering from mental disorder is in premises in the circumstances described in paragraphs (a) or (b) and the approved social worker wishes to gain access to the patient so that he can be interviewed and examined by a doctor. Subsection (2) is used when a patient has escaped from custody whilst being taken to hospital or when a patient has escaped from compulsory detention in hospital.

The following points should be noted in respect of subsection (1):

(a) A patient who is unable to care for himself must be living alone. This requirement does not apply where the patient is being ill-treated, etc. This is a defect in the powers as the powers are not available if a patient who is unable to care for himself is living with another person who is not attending to the patient's needs and who may or may not also be suffering from mental disorder.
(b) The approved social worker makes the application but the warrant is issued to a named constable who is entitled to use force if necessary to execute the warrant. The police constable *must* be accompanied by an approved social worker and a doctor.
(c) The purpose of removal is to enable consideration to be given to whether or not an application for compulsory admission to hospital should be made *or* whether other arrangements should be made for the patient's care and treatment.

We are aware of the reluctance of doctors to be involved in the section 135 process but it is a mandatory requirement that the police constable should be accompanied by both an approved social worker and a doctor. If this does not happen then the warrant is improperly executed and those actually involved in the process could be liable to proceedings by the patient for wrongful imprisonment. This is not a mere procedural requirement and an approved social worker faced with a situation where a doctor will not be present at the execution of a warrant would be unwise to attend. The warrant is effective for 72 hours which should provide adequate time in which to make alternative arrangements if a doctor fails to attend.

With regard to subsection (2) the following points should be noted:

(a) Power to apply for a warrant is not limited to approved social workers. It is also available to police officers, nearest relatives (who will be authorised under the Act to take the patient to a hospital if they have signed an application under Part II) and guardians to compel a patient to comply with directions issued under their powers in section 8(1) of the Act.

(b) It is not mandatory for the police officer to whom the warrant is issued to be accompanied by any person when he executes the warrant.

2.9.4   What is the role of those accompanying the police constable?

The object of subsection (1) is to enable an approved social worker and a doctor to gain access to the patient to discover whether he needs to be admitted to hospital, either compulsorily or informally, and also to discover whether the patient's needs can be met outside hospital. To do this the Act gives power to a *police constable*, and not an approved social worker or doctor, to enter premises where the patient is assumed to be, using force if necessary. The doctor and approved social worker must also enter at the same time as the police constable. Control always remains with the police constable, and if he does not consider that it is appropriate to remove the patient, his decision is final and all present must leave with the police constable. The danger of remaining if the police officer leaves is clear from the case of *Townley v Rushworth* (see paragraph 2.2.5) which, although not on this point, shows that the courts will steadfastly uphold the rights of private individuals to be left in their homes even if those seeking to intrude are acting from the best possible motives. To remain in private property once the purposes of the warrant have been served is a trespass. Where the police constable, the approved social worker and the doctor cannot agree as to what should be done once entry has been made the approved social worker and the doctor should leave. If the doctor has examined the patient and both he and the approved social worker are satisfied that the patient should be removed to hospital then the approved social worker should complete Form 6 so that the patient can be admitted to hospital. Entry to the premises to remove the patient would be by means of a warrant under subsection (2).

2.9.5   **Section 136** (1) If a constable finds in a place to which the public has access a person who appears to him to be suffering from mental disorder and to be in immediate need of care and control, the constable may, if he thinks it necessary to do so in the interests of that person or for the protection of other persons, remove that person to a place of safety within the meaning of section 135 above.

(2) A person removed to a place of safety under this section may be detained there for a period not exceeding 72 hours for the purpose of enabling him to be examined by a registered medical practitioner and to be interviewed by an approved social worker and of making any necessary arrangements for his treatment or care.

The powers in section 135 are used where the patient is in private property and for that reason contain the requirement that any forced entry to such property should be sanctioned by a JP. No such requirement exists if the patient is in a public place. Here the police have a power to remove the patient upon their own initiative to a place of safety for examination and decision upon whether or not an application under Part II of the Act should be made. An attempt in the House of Lords to reduce the period of 72 hours to 24 hours failed.

There is no definition in the 1983 Act of 'a public place' which is a possible area of abuse. There is a natural preference to use this power as it does not require a warrant. Whilst this is primarily a matter for the police it is useful to note the words of a judge in a case in 1965 concerning the meaning of 'a public place':

. . . 'a public place' is a place to which the public can, and do, have access . . . it matters not whether they come to that place at the invitation of the occupier or whether they come to it merely with his permission; . . . it matters not whether some payment or, indeed, the performance of some small formality such as the signing of a visitors' book, is required before they are allowed access.

For some case studies relating to this Part, see para **11.2.2** *in Part 11 following.*

3 Guardianship

3.1 Introduction

3.1.1 A very small number of mentally disordered people who do not require treatment in hospital, either informally or formally, nevertheless need close supervision and some control in the community as a consequence of their mental disorder. These include people who are able to cope provided that they take their medication regularly, but who fail to do so, and those who neglect themselves to the point of seriously endangering their health. (White Paper, 1981).

The 1976 Review included statistics on the use of guardianship: in 1960 in England and Wales 1,133 persons had been subject to guardianship and in 1974 the number was 159. But neither of the Reviews gave convincing reasons for the lack of use of this apparently useful power. All that was said was that some local authorities used it relatively often and others not at all:

> The figures show marked regional variations. An analysis of the 1973 totals shows that 24 out of 46 old style county councils had guardianship cases and, of those, 2 councils accounted for 28 cases out of a total of 95. Of the 79 county boroughs, 25 had cases but 3 of them accounted for 23 cases out of a total of 70. Out of 33 new London Boroughs only 7 had cases and 1 of these accounted for 13 out of a total of 26 cases (para 5.2 of the 1976 Review).

We would suggest that the following reasons account for the very patchy use of guardianship powers:

(a) It is costly to resource. It resembles a supervision order in child care proceedings with the same difficulties concerning provision of adequate supervision.

(b) Uncertainty over the extent of the guardianship powers. Under the 1959 Act a guardian had 'all such powers as would be exercisable by . . . him in relation to the patient if . . . he were the father of the patient and the patient were under the age of 14 years'. Such draconian and outdated powers were rightly considered to conflict with modern principles of good social work practice and thus to be avoided unless the circumstances were exceptional.

3.1.2　However the availability of guardianship powers seemed likely to further the principles of the 1959 Act which preferred patients to be treated outside of hospital if at all possible. In appropriate cases guardianship should have proved useful to enable a social worker or relative to assist a mentally disordered person to cope on his own either at home or in a hostel.

It will be seen that whilst uncertainty over the extent of the powers has been removed the question of resources has not been tackled and it is because of this that the new powers are unlikely to be used any more than the old. Before looking at the new guardianship sections in detail it will be helpful to consider the various options that were open to the Government for reform. There were four and these were described in paragraphs 4.14 to 4.20 of the 1978 Review:

(a) to retain guardianship in its present form with revisions to the criteria for applications;
(b) to create the concept of community care orders as proposed by BASW in *Mental Health Crisis Services – A New Philosophy* (BASW Publications: 1977);
(c) to reduce guardianship powers to the minimum required to ensure that medical treatment, social support, training etc can be undertaken;
(d) short-term guardianship (28 days) as an additional power to long-term guardianship.

It was noted in the 1978 Review that if option (c) were adopted some patients who had little or no understanding may require additional protective powers such as power for a guardian to consent to treatment or arrange admission to hospital which would lead to two different sets of powers for two groups of patients. Finally BASW's recommendation that local authorities should be placed under a statutory duty to act as guardian where no-one else was available was not accepted by the Government. Of the four options explored, BASW's idea of a community care order is the most interesting.

What would it entail? BASW suggested that 'power under a community care order should be comparable to that of the existing power over a detained patient on leave from hospital' (para 4-9 of the 1978 Review). This was the responsible medical officer's power under section 39 of the 1959 Act (now section 17 of the 1983 Act) to impose conditions in the interest of the patient or to protect others. Under the community care order a local authority would 'have responsibility to provide care for and control to persons made subject to Community Care Orders and . . . this responsibility should be exercised on the authority's behalf only by social workers approved for the purpose as having the requisite training and experience.' BASW's main point was that community care should be voluntary and only as a last resort should compulsion be used to provide care and control for those who need it. But at present the only alternative is compulsory detention in hospital; community care orders would be an alternative to hospitalisation in such circumstances. The same problem occurs in respect of after-care for detained patients who could be discharged if there were powers available to supervise them in the community. The 1978 Review admitted that there were defects in section 39 which were being overcome by misuse of the powers in that section. Leave of absence could not last longer than six months, so patients who needed a longer 'trial period' on leave than six months were brought back to hospital for a token overnight stay to avoid the power to detain from lapsing. Mental Health Review Tribunals were relcutant to order the discharge of patients as there was no way in which the patient could be compulsorily supervised. The community care order would resolve these problems.

MIND was also keen to promote the greater use of guardianship:

> Guardianship is a powerful tool, which can be a viable and beneficial alternative to hospital admission. It would obviate the need for expanding Tribunal powers . . . The use of guardianship orders is in practice quite rare. They could in many more instances be a viable and beneficial alternative to admission for treatment, and should be used more frequently by the medical profession as a means of assuring community-based treatment. (Larry O. Gostin, *A Human Condition* (MIND: 1975) Vol 1 p 64.)

Which option was finally chosen by the Government? Unfortunately, in our opinion, the opportunity to overhaul guardianship powers and produce a viable alternative to hospital was not taken.

3.2 Grounds for applications

3.2.1 **Section 7**(1) A patient who has attained the age of 16 years may be received into guardianship, for the period allowed by the following provisions of this Act, in pursuance of an application (in this Act referred to as 'a guardianship application') made in accordance with this section.

(2) A guardianship application may be made in respect of a patient on the grounds that—

(a) he is suffering from mental disorder, being mental illness, severe mental impairment, psychopathic disorder or mental impairment and his mental disorder is of a nature or degree which warrants his reception into guardianship under this section; and

(b) it is necessary in the interests of the welfare of the patient or for the protection of other persons that the patient should be so received.

3.2.2 To avoid overlap/duplication with child care powers it is clearly stated that guardianship powers are only available if the patient is 16 or over; under the 1959 Act, in theory at least, it was possible to place a person of any age under guardianship. As a child of 16 to 18 years may be a ward of court, section 33 of the 1983 Act implies that the High Court's permission must be obtained before an application is made to place a ward under guardianship, which is not a new requirement. Similarly it is good practice to obtain the consent of the High Court or a county court where a child is in care by virtue of a care order made in matrimonial or custody proceedings under the Matrimonial Causes Act 1973 or the Guardianship of Minors Act 1971.

The effect of subsection (1) is, therefore, to require local authorities to care for mentally disorderd children under 16 using child care powers, eg the Child Care Act 1980 and the Children and Young Persons Act 1969. The following points should be noted concerning the grounds:

3.2.3 The patient must be suffering from one of the four categories of mental disorder set out in section 1 (but note that 'any other disorder or disability of mind' is not a ground for guardianship applications).

3.2.4 The patient's condition must warrant reception into guardianship.

3.2.5 Reception into guardianship must be in the patient's interests or to protect others.

3.2.6 This is a substantial change from the grounds in the 1959 Act. Now a person of any age suffering from psychopathic disorder or mental impairment (subnormality) may be received into guardianship; before only patients under 21 suffering from those conditions could be the subject of a guardianship application. A further change is that the application must be in the interests of the patient's welfare whereas before it was sufficient if the application was in the patient's interests.

3.3 Who may make applications?

Either the nearest relative or an approved social worker; section 11(1) (see para 2.2.2). The applicant must have seen the patient within 14 days prior to the application. The nearest relative may block an application by an approved social worker by objecting (section 11(4)). Although the duty to inform nearest relatives in section 11(3) only applies to admissions for assessment and not to guardianship applications, section 11(4) requires an approved social worker to consult with the nearest relative, if practicable, before a guardianship application is made.

3.4 Medical recommendations

3.4.1 As in the case of hospital admissions two medical recommendations in the prescribed form (Forms 19 and 20) are needed. It should be remembered that sections 11(7) and 12 apply to medical recommendations in support of guardianship applications. So one recommendation *must* be given by an 'approved doctor' and should be given by a doctor who has had some previous contact with the patient. Since it is unlikely that guardianship applications will ever be made in the emergency situations that can arise in respect of hospital admissions it is to be expected that these requirements should always be complied with – the 'other' recommendation should be given by the patient's GP or consultant psychiatrist. The other requirements as to recommendations are:

3.4.2 the recommending doctors each personally examine the patient either jointly or within five days of each other;
3.4.3 whilst each recommendation may specify several forms of mental disorder at least one form of disorder must be common to both recommendations;
3.4.4 the restrictions upon persons who may not give medical recommendations set out is section 12(5) also apply to guardianship applications (see para 10.6, below).

95

3.5 Procedure for making a guardianship application

3.5.1 **Section 7** (5) The person named as guardian in a guardianship application may be either a local social services authority or any other person (including the applicant himself); but a guardianship application in which a person other than a local social services authority is named as guardian shall be of no effect unless it is accepted on behalf of that person by the local social services authority for the area in which he resides, and shall be accompanied by a statement in writing by that person that he is willing to act as guardian.

3.5.2 The procedure is clearly set out in subsection (5). Note that the local social services authority is not under a mandatory duty to accept a guardianship application – the DHSS Guide is misleading here as it states at paragraph 47: 'The guardianship application, and the guardian, if a private individual must be accepted by this authority', meaning that the application is not effective until accepted by the local social services authority, and not that the authority has no choice but to accept the application. It follows that BASW's recommendation (see para 3.1.2) has not been accepted by the Government. Local social services authorities are still free to accept or refuse applications and the 1983 Act lays no duty on them to give reasons for their decisions. Neither does the Act give any criteria upon which authorities must base their decisions.

So can an authority decide as a matter of policy never to accept an application for a patient to be received into its guardianship? At first sight this approach would appear to be open to it. But authorities are bound by the general law relating to public bodies which requires them to act in a responsible manner and to consider each application on its merits and not merely to apply a rigid and inflexible predetermined policy. Thus if an application is properly made in accordance with the procedure laid down in the Act and the patient is within the criteria for guardianship the local social services authority to whom the application is properly addressed must consider it and come to a reasoned decision.

The right to refuse applications together with the failure of the Act and Government to encourage local authorities to devote any resources to community provision probably means that there will not be any great increase in the number of guardianship cases under the new provisions.

3.6   Effect of an application

3.6.1   **Section 8**(1) Where a guardianship application, duly made under the provisions of this Part of this Act and forwarded to the local social services authority within the period allowed by subsection (2) below is accepted by that authority, the application shall, subject to regulations made by the Secretary of State, confer on the authority or person named in the application as guardian, to the exclusion of any other person.—

   (a) the power to require the patient to reside at a place specified by the authority or person named as guardian;

   (b) the power to require the patient to attend at places and times so specified for the purpose of medical treatment, occupation, education or training;

   (c) the power to require access to the patient to be given, at any place where the patient is residing, to any registered medical practitioner, approved social worker or other person so specified.

3.6.2   (5) Where a patient is received into guardianship in pursuance of a guardianship application, any previous application under this Part of this Act by virtue of which he was subject to guardianship or liable to be detained in a hospital shall cease to have effect.

It will be seen that whilst the powers of a guardian have been substantially revised the opportunity to create community care orders has not been taken. The result is a combination of options (a) and (c) referred to earlier at para 3.1.2. whilst options (b) and (d) have been discarded. An attempt to amend the 1982 Amendment Bill was made by Mr Terry Davis in the Commons Committee to 'add to the existing guardianship powers a short-term guardianship power'. This was rejected by the Government and defeated in the Committee. The reasons were based mainly on their reluctance to increase powers of compulsion in the Amendment Bill and because in their view the new power would, if enacted, be used to compel persons to attend crisis intervention centres. We have already seen how opposed the Government was to the idea of crisis intervention centres on the grounds that they were experimental in nature. This line was continued in opposition to Mr Davis's amendment. Selected extracts from the speech of Mr Kenneth Clarke, the Minister of Health, illustrate the Government's misgivings over the Amendment and also their philosophy of guardianship:

   During the relatively restricted period the guardian – either the local authority or someone nominated will be able to direct a person to various places of residence. BASW seem to have in mind particularly that someone could be directed to go to a crisis intervention centre rather than to a hospital. That would be a startling change in the nature of guardianship compared with anything contemplated before and would perhaps not be an altogether welcome improvement. Guardianship has always been regarded as a long-term arrangement to enable a patient suffering from mental impairment or mental illness to cope in the community. It deals with patients who need some supervision and control if they are to cope in the community or to be protected against exploitation by others. The majority of the few cases of guardianship that have occurred appear to involve people suffering from mental impairment. One assumes they are subject to the guidance and control of a guardian to stop them sleeping rough and spending their money unwisely or to stop people taking advantage of them. Such guardianship is designed and used to provide a long-term protection to such patients.

If the amendment were accepted, short-term powers of direction would be given perhaps to a guardian to cause someone to reside in a specific place. It would be a new restriction on people's civil liberties if local authorities' social service departments had presented to them the ability to take, for 28 days, power to direct that someone should live in a certain place or not do this, that or the other.

If the . . . idea is that they should go to a crisis intervention centre, so far as I am aware these centres do not operate for patients who are there under legal compulsion. I wish to hear far more satisfactory evidence that assessment and treatment at a crisis intervention centre could, in practice, be carried out successfully for patients who are so ill that they potentially justify detention or guardianship, and for unwilling attenders at the centre who are there under legal compulsion imposed as a result of a guardian having taken short-term powers. I do not think that any of them operate that way now, but it is by no means clear that they could operate satisfactorily in such conditions.

Thus the idea of short-term guardianship was rejected on the rather unsatisfactory ground that it would be used to place patients in crisis intervention centres and there was no experience of how effective such centres could be in dealing with compulsorily restricted patients which is not surprising as there was no power in the 1959 Act to compulsorily detain a patient anywhere other than in hospital.

3.6.3 In the event the 'essential powers' approach (option (c)) was favoured and adopted by the Government. The undefined powers of a father over a 14-year-old child are now limited to three specific powers which, taken together, strongly resemble a supervision order in child care legislation:

(a) The power to specify the place of residence. Used in conjunction with other local authority powers to provide residential accommodation such as Part III of the National Assistance Act 1948 or National Health Service Act 1977, section 21. Where the local authority is named as guardian the power may be useful to guard against exploitation or ill-treatment of a patient. However it should be remembered that guardianship is not a power to detain patients and we would question whether it should be used to compel a person to live in local authority accommodation. And if its use is limited to patients who are willing to comply with a guardian's directions the obvious question arises as to why compulsory powers are needed in respect of a patient who is prepared to co-operate with the local authority.

(b) The power to require attendance at specified places. This power is appropriate to ensure that the patient attends a doctor's surgery, a clinic, an out-patient's department of a hospital, a day centre or a sheltered workshop. There are limits as to what can be specified and these are considered at para 3.6.1.

(c) The power to require access to the patient. Such a power could be particularly useful for patients living in private lodgings or boarding-out schemes for the mentally ill/handicapped arranged by the local authority. It can be used to ensure that the patient is being properly looked after in his lodgings and will usually be directed to the landlady of the boarding house where the patient lives. Such schemes depend greatly upon co-operation between local authority, patient and landlady but there will be situations where the landlady will derive assistance from a document issued by the local authority guardian under this power which lists those persons who must be allowed to visit the patient. The local authority may hold the view that certain relatives or friends of the patient should not be permitted to see him because in the past they have not acted in the patient's best interests or have had an adverse effect on the patient's mental condition. Power to name persons who are to be allowed to see the patient can be used in a negative way by excluding such relatives or friends from a list of persons drawn up under this power. The power is closely linked to the approved social worker's powers in section 115 (see paragraph 10.7) and the offences set out in section 129 (see paragraph 10.2) and also with the responsible local social services authority's duty to arrange for the patient to be visited at least once every three months under Regulation 13.

3.7 Continuation and termination of guardianship

3.7.1 **Section 20** (1) Subject to the following provisions of this Part of this

Act . . . a patient placed under guardianship in pursuance of a guardianship application, may be . . . kept under guardianship for a period not exceeding six months beginning with . . . the day on which the guardianship application was accepted . . . but shall not be so . . . kept for any longer period unless the authority for his . . . guardianship is renewed under this section.

(2) Authority for the . . . guardianship of a patient may, unless the patient has previously been discharged, be renewed—
  (a) from the expiration of the period referred to in subsection (1) above, for a further period of six months;
  (b) from the expiration of any further period of renewal under paragraph (a) above, for a further period of one year,
and so on for periods of one year at a time . . .

(6) Within the period of two months ending on the day on which a patient who is subject to guardianship under this Part of this Act would cease under this section to be so liable in default of the renewal of the authority for his guardianship, it shall be the duty of the appropriate medical officer—
  (a) to examine the patient; and
  (b) if it appears to him that the conditions set out in subsection (7) below are satisfied, to furnish to the guardian, and, where the guardian is a person other than a local social services authority, to the responsible local social services authority a report to that effect in the prescribed form;
and where such a report is furnished in respect of a patient, the local social services authority shall, unless they discharge the patient, cause him to be informed.

(7) The conditions referred to in subsection (6) above are that—
  (a) the patient is suffering from mental illness, severe mental impairment, psychopathic disorder or mental impairment and his mental disorder is of a nature or degree which warrants his reception into guardianship; and
  (b) it is necessary in the interests of the welfare of the patient or for the protection of other persons that the patient should remain under guardianship.

(8) Where a report is duly furnished under subsection . . . (6) above, the authority for the . . . guardianship of the patient shall be thereby renewed for the period prescribed in that case by subsection (2) above.

3.7.2 The initial period of guardianship is, as in applications for admission for treatment, six months from the date the local authority accepts the application, renewable for another six months and thereafter annually. The procedure for renewal is also exactly similar to that for renewal of admissions for treatment with one minor variation for patients under private guardianship. The appropriate medical officer (who is the patient's nominated medical attendant in private guardianships or in the case of local authority guardianships the medical officer authorised to act by the local authority) must within the last two months of the period of guardianship give the guardian (and the local authority in private guardianships) a report that in his opinion the grounds for guardianship in section 20(7) still exist. Once this report is in the hands of the local authority or private guardian, authority to keep the patient under guardianship is renewed. Unless the local authority decides to discharge the patient it must tell him that the guardianship has been renewed.

3.7.3 The patient may apply for discharge from guardianship to a Mental Health Review Tribunal once every six months – section 66(2)(c) (see para 6.2) and by section 23 (see para 2.2.10) the patient may be discharged from guardianship at any time by the medical officer authorised to act for the local social services authority, the local social services authority itself or the patient's nearest relative. Note that the nearest relative's power to order the patient's discharge from guardianship cannot be blocked by the medical officer the local social services authority. The only control over the nearest relative's power to discharge from guardianship is to displace him under section 29 (see paragraph 2.7.7).

3.8   Defects in guardianship

In our view the revised guardianship powers are unlikely to lead to a significant increase in their use because the inherent defects which applied to the old guardianship powers – lack of resources and mandatory obligations upon local authorities to provide community based care – have not been attacked at all in the 1983 Act. There is a serious implication for local authority resources if patients are to be properly cared for in the community. At present only a relatively small number of mentally disordered patients can live in the community because the powers to protect and where necessary control seriously mentally ill or impaired patients are not available. The alternative for such patients is hospital unless they are fortunate enough to have relatives who are able and willing to take on the heavy burden of full-time care of a patient at home.

The failings of the 1959 Act powers were not merely the apparently unlimited and ill-defined powers given to guardians, they were the failure of local authorities to take patients into guardianship and to provide sufficient accommodation in the community in which patients could live a normal and useful life outside of hospital. Local authorities were and still are under no positive duty to receive patients into their guardianship – we have seen that BASW's proposal to give such a duty to local authorities was rejected and also that local authorities' discretion as to whether or not an application should be accepted is virtually unfettered. Whilst it is to be hoped that the Mental Health Act Commission will monitor this area, its major monitoring role relates to hospital admissions and the care and treatment of patients whilst in hospital rather than upon the use, or non-use of guardianship powers.

There are however some encouraging signs. More use is being made of schemes for the fostering or boarding-out of patients in private accommodation and it is hoped that local authorities will use the revised guardianship powers to support such schemes. Unfortunately the number of patients who can benefit from these schemes is likely to remain small and guardianship powers are not appropriate to help the mentally ill or severely mentally impaired who will probably remain in hospital.

For a case study relating to this Part, see para **11.2.3** *in Part 11 following.*

4 The patient in hospital

4.1 Introduction

4.1.1 This Part is concerned with the rights of patients who are admitted to hospital suffering from mental disorder. It concerns both compulsorily detained and informal patients. Its importance for the approved social worker may not be immediately apparent. The limited statutory role of approved social workers under the Act suggests that what happens to the patient after admission to hospital is of no concern to approved social workers. We would challenge that view for the following reasons:

(a) In the absence of either a system of advocacy for patients, or a system of patients' advisers (two proposals which were put forward by MIND during the Reviews of the 1959 Act), it is to be expected that patients and their relatives will naturally turn to approved social workers for advice upon their new rights in hospital. This will be particularly true for hospital-based social workers whose work inevitably brings them into close contact with patients and their relatives during their time in hospital.

(b) Although there is little evidence that this is occurring at present, we would expect hospitals to turn to hospital-based social workers for assistance in carrying out their duties to keep patients informed of their rights.

(c) The latest proposals for the training of approved social workers require a detailed knowledge of not only Part II of the 1983 Act but also 'Detailed working knowledge of the Mental Health Act 1983 and understanding of the background to the changes introduced to protect the interests of patients subject to compulsory care in hospital or elsewhere.'

4.1.2 Section 132 of the 1983 Act (referred to at para 2.2.8) places a duty on hospitals to ensure that patients know and understand their rights. This must be done in writing (leaflets for this purpose have been produced by the DHSS) and orally using hospital administrative staff or possibly hospital social workers. The patient's rights are:
(a) to be informed of the section under which he or she is detained and of the implications of such detention;
(b) to apply to a Mental Health Review Tribunal for his or her discharge from hospital;
(c) to be told who can discharge him or her and how;
(d) to be informed of the consent to treatment provisions in the 1983 Act;
(e) to be informed of the contents of the Code of Practice;
(f) to receive and send correspondence to certain persons or organisations without restriction;
(g) possibly to be informed of his or her electoral rights.

4.1.3 Before considering patients' rights in depth, two points should be made:
(a) It is not necessary for patients suffering from mental disorder to be accommodated in a psychiatric hospital. The 1983 Act permits patients to be detained in establishments ranging from NHS hospitals (including special hospitals) to mental nursing homes. The latter are private institutions which may be run for profit and which provide nursing or other medical treatment for mentally disordered patients. They are controlled through a registration system operated by District Health Authorities on behalf of the Secretary of State (see the Nursing and Mental Nursing Homes Regulations 1981).
(b) NHS hospitals are run by managers. This means the District Health Authority for the area in which the hospital lies, except in the case of special hospitals, where the managers are the Secretary of State for Social Services. The managers of Mental Nursing Homes are the registered proprietors. Most of the obligations to keep patients informed of their rights are placed upon managers.

4.1.4 The 1983 Act will probably be most remembered for the debate which it stimulated upon the need to create and safeguard patients' rights in hospital and much of the pressure for change in the 1970s centred around the controversial issue of consent to treatment.

4.2 Consent to treatment

4.2.1 Introduction

The main issues in the debate were :

(a) Did the law permit doctors to give treatment to detained patients without their consent?
(b) Should the law permit treatment to be given to detained patients without their consent?
(c) Did the position of informal patients in this matter differ from that of detained patients?
(d) Should decisions upon whether or not a patient is capable of giving an informed consent and upon whether or not treatment should be imposed upon a patient be taken by doctors alone?

4.2.2 The DHSS view, based upon legal advice, was stated in the 1978 Review: 'Where the purpose of detention is treatment, the 1959 Act gives the Responsible Medical Officer implied authority to treat a patient in relation to his mental disorder, if necessary without the consent of the patient or any other person.' This view was limited to patients detained under section 26 of the 1959 Act (ie for treatment). The position regarding patients detained for observation under sections 25 and 29 of the 1959 Act was less clear. This situation has been resolved by replacing the power to detain for observation with a power to detain for assessment or for assessment followed by treatment. The DHSS view was not shared by others involved in the care and treatment of detained patients and it was usual practice to obtain the consent of both the patient and his nearest relative before treatment was given. Also despite the DHSS's stated view on the subject doctors were advised 'to obtain if possible the consent of both the patient and the nearest relative . . . before beginning a form of treatment *which involves any appreciable risk*' (emphasis added). The core of the problem was that the legal position had never been tested in the courts. The opportunity to remove this uncertainty was taken by introducing the consent to treatment provisions which set out the types of treatment requiring consent and/or a second opinion. The justification for the imposition of treatment without consent was that the very reason for the patient's detention was to enable him to receive treatment for his mental disorder, therefore it was illogical to allow him to remain untreated whilst under detention in hospital.

4.2.3 The legal position regarding imposing treatment upon informal patients without consent was far clearer. It was unlawful for a doctor to do so except, perhaps, to save a patient's life. This follows naturally from the voluntary nature of his admission – he is always free to discharge himself as long as he retains his voluntary status. It was not the Government's intention to change the position of informal patients concerning consent to treatment and the provisions as originally drafted did not include informal patients. However an amendment was won during the Amendment Bill's passage through Parliament and the Government was defeated on this point. We shall look at the informal patient's rights concerning consent to treatment later at paragraph 4.2.16.

4.2.4 The consent to treatment provisions are complicated but their consideration can be simplified by dividing them into five parts:

(1) treatment covered by the 1983 Act
(2) treatment not covered by the 1983 Act
(3) patients who are the subject of the consent to treatment provisions
(4) procedures involved in consent to treatment
(5) informal patients

4.2.5 Treatment covered by the consent provisions

The type or types of treatment which the doctor proposes to administer to the patient govern whether or not the treatment can be administered without consent or with a second opinion. The 1983 Act divides treatment into the most serious and irreversible forms which cannot be given without the patient's consent and the less serious forms which can be given without consent provided an independent second opinion is obtained. The forms of treatment are specified in the 1983 Act and the 1983 Regulations and further forms may be specified by the Mental Health Act Commission in the proposed Code of Practice.

Treatment requiring consent and a second opinion

Section 57 (1) This section applies to the following forms of medical treatment for mental disorder—
    (a) any surgical operation for destroying brain tissue or for destroying

the functioning of the brain tissue; and
(b) such other forms of treatment as may be specified for the purposes of this section by regulations made by the Secretary of State.

At the time of writing the two forms of treatment to which this section applies are:

(a) psychosurgery (section 57(1) (a)) and
(b) surgical implantation of hormones for the purpose of reducing male sexual drive. This form of treatment has been specified by the Secretary of State under his power in section 57(1)(b) and can be found in Regulation 16.

Treatment requiring consent or a second opinion

Section 57 treatments are rare but the same cannot be said of treatment covered by section 58. It covers treatment which is routine in nature. For the first time an Act of Parliament *expressly* permits the treatment of patients without their consent.

> **Section 58** (1) This section applies to the following forms of medical treatment for mental disorder—
> (a) such forms of treatment as may be specified for the purposes of this section by regulations made by the Secretary of State; ECT
> (b) the administration of medicine to a patient by any means (not being a form of treatment specified under paragraph (a) above or section 57 above) at any time during a period for which he is liable to be detained as a patient to whom this Part of this Act applies if three months or more have elapsed since the first occasion in the period when medicine was administered to him by any means for his mental disorder.

In addition to the administration of medicine the 1983 Regulations have specified ECT as a form of treatment covered by section 58. Four points should be noted about section 58:

(1) As with section 57 it only applies to treatment for mental disorder.
(2) It does not come into effect in relation to medicine until the medicine has been given for three months. There may be problems over calculating this three-month period – see below.
(3) There is no provision for section 58 treatments to be covered by the Code of Practice which is a surprising omission;
(4) Reclassification may start the three-month period running again.

During the first three months that medicine is given to a patient it will not be a treatment covered by section 58 and the safeguards in the section have no application – they only come into effect at the end of the three-month period. The problem referred to above in calculating this period may arise because there is no link between 'the first occasion . . . when medicine was administered . . .' and the date and status of the patient's first admission to hospital. This does not provide for situations (which are not unusual) where a patient's status changes during the three-month period – the only requirement being that the patient must be liable to be detained at the time the medicine is administered. What will be the position in the following contexts?

(a) Patient is admitted on 1 June as informal patient. His mental disorder is diagnosed and a course of drug treatment starts on 3 June. During this course of treatment the patient attempts to discharge himself on several occasions but is persuaded on each occasion to remain in hospital. His admission is converted to an admission for treatment under section 3 on 8 July. When does section 58 (1) (b) come into operation? The answer in our view must be 3 September if the course of drug treatment has been given continuously since 3 June and not, as might be expected, 8 October (ie three months after the section 3 admission.)

(b) The patient is admitted on 1 June under section 2. At the end of the 28-day period the patient is 'sectioned up' on to a treatment order. From the outset, the patient has consistently refused to consent to any form of treatment. It is proposed to administer one or more treatments falling within the provisions of section 58(1)(b). Can such treatments be administered during the first three months following admission?

Clearly, there are important implications here for the approved social worker when making an assessment. If previous history has shown that the patient has resisted treatment before, what is the point of making the application if proposed treatment cannot be given for a period of three months?

There are two schools of thought on this issue:

(i) the common law school would hold that as the provisions of section 58(1)(b) do not operate during the first three months, treatment can only be given either where the patient consents, which is not the case in our example, or where it is immediately necessary to save the patient's life (the common law rule identical to that relating to physical disorder);

(ii) the statutory school, to which the authors subscribe, which recognises the difficulties which would be placed on both the social work and medical professions should the above view be correct.

It is submitted that the provisions of section 63 provide the answer to the problem:

> The consent of a patient shall not be required for any medical treatment given to him for the mental disorder for which he is suffering, not being treatment falling within section 57 or 58 above, if the treatment is given by or under the direction of the responsible medical officer.

During the first three months the provisions of section 58(1)(b) do not apply to the treatment proposed, and section 63 would thus appear to apply, ie treatment can be given during this period irrespective of the absence of the patient's consent.

It would be useful for all concerned if the Code of Practice could clarify this issue.

4.2.6 Further treatment which is not covered by the consent to treatment safeguards

Section 62 deals with the matter of urgent treatment for mental disorder:

> **Section 62** (1) Sections 57 and 58 above shall not apply to any treatment—
> (a) which is immediately necessary to save the patient's life; or
> (b) which (not being irreversible) is immediately necessary to prevent a serious deterioration of his condition; or
> (c) which (not being irreversible or hazardous) is immediately necessary to alleviate serious suffering by the patient; or
> (d) which (not being irreversible or hazardous) is immediately necessary and represents the minimum interference necessary to prevent the patient from behaving violently or being a danger to himself or to others.

The safeguards in sections 57 and 58 are expressly stated in those sections to be subject to the urgent treatment provisions contained in section 62. The section does not create separate categories of treatment from those contained in 57 and 58 – it merely provides that if the patient requires treatment of the types specified in 57 or 58 *and any of the circumstances described in section 63 exist*, the treatment can be given without the patient's consent or a second opinion. This is of great significance (see para 4.2.15 following). Furthermore, the safeguards only apply to the treatments specified in the 1983 Act, this being the effect of section 63.

The importance of section 62 lies in the wide and unfettered discretion it gives to the doctor in charge of the patient's treatment. The doctor is given virtually unlimited power to ignore the consent to treatment safeguards. In our opinion, the scope of section 62 is too wide, and this is particularly the case in respect of paragraphs (c) and (d). The apparent safeguard that the treatment must not be 'irreversible or hazardous' is defined in such vague terms in subsection (3) as to leave matters entirely to the discretion of the doctor:

> **Section 62** (3)   For the purposes of this section treatment is irreversible if it has unfavourable irreversible physical or psychological consequences and hazardous if it entails significant physical hazard.

It is to be hoped that the Mental Health Act Commission will investigate all cases where section 62 is used to justify by-passing the consent to treatment procedures, and that the proposed Code of Practice will give practical guidelines upon the treatments and situations where section 62 properly applies.

4.2.7   Patients who are subject to the consent to treatment provisions

> **Section 56** (1) This Part of this Act applies to a patient liable to be detained under this Act except—
>
> (a) a patient who is liable to be detained by virtue of an emergency application and in respect of whom the second medical recommendation referred to in section 4 (4) (a) above has not been given and received;
>
> (b) a patient who is liable to be detained by virtue of section 5 (2) or (4) or section 35 above or section 135 or 136 below or by virtue of a direction under section 37 (4) above; and
>
> (c) a patient who has been conditionally discharged under section 42 (2) above or section 73 or 74 below and has not been recalled to hospital

The effect of the exclusions in paragraphs (a), (b) and (c) is to remove all patients subject to short-term detention powers (usually no longer than 72 hours) from the consent to treatment provisions. This is logical because the powers referred to in these paragraphs are not powers to detain for treatment; eg section 136 is a power to remove a patient from a public place to a place of safety 'for the purpose of enabling him to be examined by a registered medical practitioner and to be interviewed by an approved social worker and of making any necessary arrangements for his treatment and care'.

The position regarding patients detained under these excluded powers as regards consent to treatment is that the common law rules apply.

The use of the words 'liable to be detained' is significant for patients granted leave of absence under section 17 of the 1983 Act (see paragraph 4.6.4) because they remain liable to be detained and, therefore, benefit from the safeguards in sections 57 and 58. As such patients are often granted leave on condition that they continue to take their prescribed medication, section 58(1)(b) will be of most relevance to them.

4.2.8   Consent to treatment procedures

Subject to section 62, which has been dealt with in paragraph 4.2.6, the procedures involved are set down in sections 57 and 58:

Treatment requiring consent and a second opinion

> **Section 57**(2)   Subject to section 62 below, a patient shall not be given any form of treatment to which this section applies unless he has consented to it and—
>> (a) a registered medical practitioner appointed for the purposes of this Part of this Act (not being the responsible medical officer) and two other persons appointed for the purposes of this paragraph by the Secretary of State (not being registered medical practitioners) have certified in writing that the patient is capable of understanding the nature, purpose and likely effects of the treatment in question and has consented to it; and
>> (b) the registered medical practitioner referred to in paragraph (a) above has certified in writing that, having regard to the likelihood of the treatment alleviating or preventing a deterioration of the patient's condition, the treatment should be given.

Two parallel and related procedures are involved. The 1983 Act places great importance both upon the patient's consent and upon his competence to consent. Decisions in regard to that competence cannot be taken by the doctor in charge of the patient's treatment alone.

The patient must consent. If he does not or cannot consent, the specified form of treatment cannot be given. If the patient does consent, then a team of three independent assessors must visit the hospital and certify using Form 37 that the patient has genuinely consented to the treatment. Of the three, one must be a psychiatrist whilst the other two must not be doctors. All three must be members of, or appointed by, the Mental Health Act Commission. To date, the personnel involved have tended to be a psychiatrist, a lawyer and a nurse, but there is nothing to prevent one of the two non-doctors being a social worker member of the Mental Health Act Commission.

The independent psychiatrist must certify that having regard to the 'treatability test' the treatment should be given. Although section 57 does not state that the psychiatrist must examine the patient before issuing the certification required, we would expect such an examination to take place as a matter of course.

> **Section 57** (3) Before giving a certificate under subsection (2)(b) above the registered medical practitioner concerned shall consult two other persons who have been professionally concerned with the patient's medical treatment, and of those persons one shall be a nurse and the other shall be neither a nurse nor a registered medical practitioner.

Thus, persons involved in the consultation process must include a nurse and someone who is neither a nurse nor a doctor. The DHSS Memorandum suggests that the third party could be a psychologist, social worker or other therapist.

4.2.9 What is the purpose of the consultation process?

If the patient does not consent then the responsible medical officer cannot administer a section 57 treatment. The patient's consent must be such that he understands the nature, purpose and likely effects of the treatment proposed. The decision as to whether the patient's consent complies with these criteria is not that of the responsible medical officer but of an independent doctor and two non-doctors. If they do not give the certificate required by section 57 then the matter is at an end and the treatment cannot be given. It is only if they do certify that the patient's consent complies with section 57 that a consultation process comes into operation. Before giving his second opinion the independent doctor must consult with two persons who have been concerned with the patient's treatment. The independent doctor is not bound by the views of the persons with whom he consults, but the requirement to consult with staff who have direct personal knowledge of the patient's case should ensure that the independent doctor bases his opinion upon a fuller knowledge of the patient's case than he would have if there was no duty to consult. It is at the point of consultation during the section 57 procedure that a non-medical view upon the patient's needs can be introduced and it is here that an opportunity arises for the hospital-based social worker to introduce a wider perspective regarding the patient's treatment.

Treatment requiring consent or a second opinion

4.2.10   **Section 58** (3) Subject to section 62 below, a patient shall not be given any form of treatment to which this section applies unless—
   (a) he has consented to that treatment and either the responsible medical officer or a registered medical practitioner appointed for the purposes of this Part of this Act by the Secretary of State has certified in writing that the patient is capable of understanding its nature, purpose and likely effect and has consented to it; or . . .

The first step for the responsible medical officer is to decide whether the patient can give a valid consent to the treatment he is receiving or electro- convulsive therapy which he is about to receive. If the responsible medical officer is satisfied that the patient can give a valid consent he must obtain the patient's consent (there is no statutory form in which this may be indicated and it may presumably be given orally) and also he must certify using Form 38 that the patient is capable of giving a valid consent. Once this certificate has been signed by the responsible medical officer he may administer any section 58 treatment to the patient. If the responsible medical officer has any doubts as to the patient's capability to give a valid consent he may still proceed with the treatment proposed provided one of two alternative statutory procedures is followed. The first alternative is for the responsible medical officer to call upon an independent doctor appointed by the Mental Health Act Commission to certify that the patient is capable of giving a valid consent. The second alternative is set out in section 58 (3)(b) and (4).

4.2.11   **Section 58** (3) (b) A registered medical practitioner appointed as aforesaid (not being the responsible medical officer) has certified in writing that the patient is not capable of understanding the nature, purpose and likely efffects of that treatment or has not consented to it but that, having regard to the likelihood of its alleviating or preventing a deterioration in his condition, the treatment should be given.
   (4) Before giving a certificate under subsection (3) (b) above the registered medical practitioner concerned shall consult two other persons who have been professionally concerned with the patient's medical treatment and of those persons one shall be a nurse and the other shall be neither a nurse nor a registered medical practitioner.

These provisions apply where:

(a) the patient has refused consent, or

(b) the patient withdraws consent, or

(c) the patient is unable to give a valid consent.

In such circumstances, if the responsible medical officer continues to hold the opinion that the patient should receive the proposed treatment, he must contact the Mental Health Act Commission and request that a doctor be appointed to give the second opinion required under section 58 (3) (b). This procedure is less involved than that for second opinions given under section 57 in that the opinion of the Mental Health Act Commission's appointed doctor is sufficient and there is no need to involve two non-doctors appointed by the Mental Health Act Commission. However, the Mental Health Act Commission's doctor must still consult on a limited basis upon the treatability test.

The Mental Health Act Commission's doctor must visit and examine the patient and consult with the persons referred to in subsection (4). Form 39 in the Regulations enables the Mental Health Act Commission's doctor to set out his decision.

Finally, it should be remembered that the provisions of section 58 do not apply to informal patients. If they refuse treatment, whether covered by section 58 or not, then it cannot be given unless it is of an emergency nature.

4.2.12   Plans of treatment

Section 59.   Any consent or certificate under section 57 or 58 above may relate to a plan of treatment under which the patient is to be given (whether within a specified time or otherwise) one or more of the forms of treatment to which that section applies.

In addition to allowing patients to consent to individual treatments the Act also provides for a patient to consent to a plan of treatment. Such a plan may include within it several different types of treatment, eg ECT and drugs, and provided the various types are within the same general category, the patient's consent may relate to all types of proposed treatment. The use of a treatment plan, however, does not avoid the need for the procedures in sections 57 and 58 to be followed – it is merely a convenient administrative arrangement which reduces form–filling and consequent delays especially in relation to the less serious forms of treatment covered in section 58.

The Act does, by implication, limit the use of treatment plans to the forms of treatment within either section 57 or section 58. By this we mean that a patient may not consent to a single treatment plan which includes forms of treatment falling within both sections, eg hormonal implant and ECT could not be included within the same plan.

4.2.13 Withdrawal of consent

Section 60 (1) Where the consent of a patient to any treatment has been given for the purposes of section 57 or 58 above, the patient may, subject to section 62 below, at any time before the completion of the treatment withdraw his consent, and those sections shall then apply as if the remainder of the treatment were a separate form of treatment.

(2) Without prejudice to the application of subsection (1) above to any treatment given under the plan of treatment to which a patient has consented, a patient who has consented to such a plan may, subject to section 62 below, at any time withdraw his consent to further treatment or to further treatment of any description under the plan.

The effect of this section is to allow the patient to withdraw his consent at any time to any treatment covered by sections 57 and 58. The only qualification to this rule is that treatment may continue uninterupted after consent has been withdrawn if it is of an emergency nature and falls within section 62. Withdrawal of consent can relate to individual treatments or plans of treatment and once consent is withdrawn the treatment must stop immediately.

An obvious difficulty for the doctor in charge of the patient's treatment, faced with the withdrawal of consent, is to decide whether or not the patient's withdrawal is genuine and whether he fully appreciates the consequences of his treatment being stopped. It is easier to deal with this problem by separating section 57 treatment from treatment covered by section 58.

Under section 57 the patient's consent is essential and, therefore, the doctor faced with an apparent withdrawal of consent should certainly temporarily stop treatment unless to do so would endanger the patient's life. Where the treatment involved is covered by section 58 the doctor has more scope for continuing with the treatment. The doctor can either regard the withdrawal of consent as invalid because of the patient's inability to form a genuine intention, or he can treat the withdrawal of consent as valid and call upon the Mental Health Act Commission to provide a second opinion, thus removing the need for the patient's consent at all.

The problem of deciding whether or not the withdrawal of consent is freely made by the patient is not confined to cases where the patient initially consented to treatment. It is also relevant where treatment was given on the basis of a second opinion. At the time that treatment was first proposed the patient may not have been capable of making an informed and genuine decision on the question of treatment. But the nature of his mental disorder may be that the patient has lucid intervals when he can form reasonable judgements and during such an interval he may withdraw consent. In such circumstances can the patient's purported withdrawal of consent be effective so that the doctor must stop treatment? In our view, there is a situation where the answer to this question is 'yes' – namely where the patient's consent was dispensed with and a second opinion obtained on the grounds that he was unable to understand 'the nature, purpose and likely effects of the treatment in question.' If the treatment causes such an improvement in the patient's condition that he becomes able to understand the nature of the treatment then if the patient refuses to continue with the treatment he must be taken to have withdrawn his consent under section 60. There can be less doubt on this point where the patient initially consented to the treatment; withdrawal of consent cannot be ignored by the doctor.

We have seen that the 1983 Act places great importance upon the need for a genuine informed consent to treatment by the patient and introduces safeguards to ensure that such consents are freely given and with full understanding of the consequences. Unfortunately the same is not true of the withdrawal provisions. The section is apparently clear in its terms – if a patient withdraws consent then treatment must stop immediately. But how is a doctor to deal with a patient who gives and then withdraws his consent on a series of occasions, possibly in advance of the administration of the proposed treatment? If it is a section 58 treatment then the option of a second opinion is available but not if it is a section 57 treatment. Furthermore the Mental Health Act Commission's resources will not stand the demands of numerous second opinions being required for an individual patient. The point must come when the validity of a patient's withdrawal of consent must be questioned. The patient may withdraw his consent to a section 58 treatment (eg ECT) from a genuine fear of the treatment proposed but without understanding the consequences of his action, namely the end of his treatment.

Can the doctor ignore the patient's withdrawal of consent? We would suggest that he does so at his peril – a safer course of action is to arrange for the patient to be counselled by a person independent of the treatment process such as an approved social worker or hospital-based social worker. Although there is no statutory role for social workers the availability of such a counselling process for patients who vacillate between consent and withdrawal could help solve the doctor's problem.

4.2.14 Review of treatment

The safeguards in sections 57 and 58 are limited in that they occur before treatment is given and cannot be used to monitor how effective the treatment is for the patient. Further protection is provided for patients who are given:

(a) serious treatments covered by section 57, and
(b) less serious treatments covered by section 58 (but only if a patient has not consented and a second opinion has been given by a Mental Health Act Commission doctor).

> **Section 61** (1) Where a patient is given treatment in accordance with section 57(2) or 58(3)(b) above a report on the treatment and the patient's condition shall be given by the responsible medical officer to the Secretary of State—
> (a) on the next occasion on which the responsible medical officer furnishes a report in respect of the patient under section 20(3) above; and
> (b) at any other time if so required by the Secretary of State.
> (2) In relation to a patient who is subject to a restriction order or restriction direction subsection (1) shall have effect as if paragraph (a) required the report to be made—
> (a) in the case of treatment in the period of six months beginning with the date of the order or direction, at the end of that period;
> (b) in the case of treatment at any subsequent time, on the next occasion on which the responsible medical officer makes a report in respect of the patient under section 41(6) or 49(3) above.

The protection takes two forms:

(a) an automatic review of treatment and the patient's condition upon each renewal of authority to detain the patient (ie at intervals of six months, six months and then annually) and
(b) a review at any time at the discretion of the Mental Health Act Commission.

Three further points should be noted:

(a) The review of treatment provisions apply only to detained patients and not informal patients.
(b) The Secretary of State has delegated his functions under this section to the Mental Health Act Commission.
(c) Reviews of treatment given to restricted patients take place 6 months after the restriction order and then annually.

> **Section 61** (3) The Secretary of State may at any time give notice to the responsible medical officer directing that, subject to section 62 below, a certificate given in respect of a patient under section 57(2) or 58(3) (b) above shall not apply to treatment given to him after a date specified in the notice and sections 57 and 58 above shall then apply to any such treatment as if that certificate had not been given.

This subsection provides the final safeguard for the patient by giving the Mental Health Act Commission power to end the effect of any certificates under sections 57 or 58. This can be done by the Mental Health Act Commission giving notice to the relevant doctor that the certificate will be ineffective after a date specified in the notice. The power is widely drawn and, therefore, the notice may be given at any time – it need not await an automatic review or indeed a special review requested by the Mental Health Act Commission. If the Mental Health Act Commission receives information from any reliable source (including the patient) which indicates that treatment is not benefitting the patient it may act accordingly. The effect of the notice is that if the doctor wishes to continue treatment after the date specified in the notice he must carry out the section 57 or section 58 procedures.

4.2.15   The overriding power of the Reponsible Medical Officer

> **Section 62** (2) Sections 60 and 61(3) above shall not preclude the continuation of any treatment or of treatment under any plan pending compliance with section 57 or 58 above if the responsible medical officer considers that the discontinuance of the treatment or of treatment under the plan would cause serious suffering to the patient.

It has already been stated (paragraph 4.2.6) that section 62(1) reduces patients' rights by extending doctors' powers to give treatment in situations which extend beyond traditionally recognised emergencies. This is surprising in an Act which has as its main objective the increase and strengthening of patients' rights. The above arguments are even more applicable to subsection (2) which effectively nullifies the withdrawal of consent provisions.

The doctor is given power to continue treatment in spite of the patient having withdrawn his consent and, more controversially, even where the Mental Health Act Commission has issued a 'stop notice' in relation to treatment. The statutory safeguard is that to stop treatment would cause the patient 'serious suffering', and the DHSS Guide suggests that, in the case of section 58 treatments, the doctor must contact the Mental Health Act Commission for a second opinion if one has not already been obtained. If this practice, which has no statutory basis, is followed how can continuation of the treatment be said to be 'immediately necessary'? The DHSS Guide then appears to contradict itself by stating that, in cases where the treatment is not immediately necessary, or where it is proposed to continue treatment after the initial urgent administration, the Mental Health Act Commission should be contacted.

4.2.16   Informal patients

It was generally accepted under the 1959 Act that doctors had no power to administer treatment to informal patients without consent. For this reason it was not considered necessary to include informal patients within the consent to treatment provisions in the 1982 Amendment Bill. Pressure during its passage through Parliament led the Government to accept that the consent to treatment provisions should be extended to informal patients and that protection is contained in section 56(2).

Subject to the comments below, the position of informal patients is now considerably improved over that which previously existed at common law. Two statutory checks have been introduced:

(a) on the validity of any consent given by an informal patient to serious treatment under section 57, and
(b) on the benefit the informal patient will derive from the treatment.

The provisions relating to less serious treatments in section 58 do not apply to informal patients; therefore, treatment covered by this section cannot be given unless they consent. Furthermore, informal patients may consent to treatment plans and may withdraw their consent to any treatment whether or not it is covered by section 57 or section 58 .

The problem for informal patients is that the emergency treatment provisions in section 62 apply to them. So the criticism we have made of section 62, that it is wider than necessary to cover genuine emergencies, applies even more so to informal patients. One would not expect to find in an Act which purports to increase patients' rights that the rights of one particular group of patients are undermined. This will be the effect of applying section 62 to informal patients, particularly subsection (1)(a) and (d). Poor drafting aggravates the situation. Section 56(2) states that section 62 only applies to serious treatments covered by section 57. Taken literally this means that section 57 treatments can be imposed against the wishes of informal patients without consent in the situations laid down in section 62, but less serious treatments covered by section 58 can never be imposed without consent upon an informal patient except to save life. This was surely not the intention of Parliament.

4.3   Correspondence

4.3.1.   Introduction

The 1959 Act gave doctors wide powers to intercept mail to and from informal and detained patients. The grounds of interception were:

1 *Incoming mail*

(a) receipt would interfere with treatment; or
(b) cause unnecessary distress.

2 *Outgoing mail*

(a) addressee had given the hospital written notice that he did not want to receive mail from the patient; or
(b) the mail appeared to the doctor to be 'unreasonably offensive to the addressee' or;
(c) the mail was defamatory of others; or
(d) the mail was 'likely to prejudice the interests of the patient'.

The above provisions did not allow mail addressed to certain official bodies to be intercepted, eg the Minister of Health, MPs, Mental Health Review Tribunals or persons entitled to discharge the patient.

Much criticism was directed at such wide powers of interception and the arguments against the powers are well expressed in MIND's

A Human Condition Vol 1:

> Mental illness is often described as an impairment of the ability to communicate effectively. Yet the response of society, both historically and through modern psychiatric practice, has been to retard, rather than encourage the acquisition of linguistic skills. The all-encompassing . . . total character of the institution, exemplified by its physical distance from population centres, discourages normal social intercourse with the wider world. Further, there are more direct disincentives to the acquisition of communicative skills, which may take the form of restraints on the use of postal and telephone services . . .

MIND described the 1959 Act powers as 'censorship'. This is not strictly accurate since no power was given to alter the contents of patients' correspondence. It was an all or nothing power to withhold or prevent communications in their entire form. Other criticisms of the powers were made by MIND:

> The grounds upon which a responsible medical officer may prevent the dispatch of outgoing post are not within the realm of his medical expertise. No person is particularly qualified to decide for another what is 'offensive' or 'defamatory' and surely this judgement cannot be made by the doctor . . .

> Further the non-medical judgement which the responsible medical officer is authorised to make constitutes a prior restraint on free communication; that is, on the unilateral authority of the doctor, an individual's possible expressions are suppressed in advance of their actual occurrence.

> Some patients in mental hospitals (and especially those in special hospitals) fear 'the censor'. Patients who write to MIND for help sometimes ask that a duplicate reply be sent to one of their friends outside the hospital. In this way the letter sent to the patient can be compared with the one sent to the friend, in order to see whether the incoming letter has been censored. Other patients have refused to explain their problems in the post.

To sum up, MIND's criticisms were that:

(a) The very nature of mental illness requires patients to be given *more* not less opportunities to communicate with others and thus improve their communication skills;

(b) the powers given to doctors require them to exercise judgements on non-medical matters such as the right to free speech;

(c) the powers are viewed with apprehension and fear by patients who regard them as a form of censorship.

We would add two further criticisms to those put forward by MIND:

(a) the patient had no right to be informed that his mail was being interfered with;
(b) there was no independent supervision of the exercise of the powers by the doctors.

Further objections to the powers to interfere with mail were identified in the 1978 Review which pointed out that the powers were probably rather outdated in the light of changes in methods of communication, eg increased use of the telephone, and of changes in hospital practice – admissions were apparently shorter and more repeated. With the increasing use of out-patient and day-patient services the rigid distinction between in-patients and other patients was less relevant. Effective control over patients' correspondence was less easy to exercise. The 1978 Review also pointed out that although the 1959 Act powers were widely drawn, it was not possible under the Act to withhold mail 'on the grounds of security', although criminal law powers probably permitted hospitals and staff to prevent patients receiving or keeping dangerous articles. The need was for preventative powers, particularly in special hospitals, to deter patients from planning escapes or from obtaining articles to assist in an escape.

The 1981 White Paper stated that the 1982 Amendment Bill would 'considerably curtail the circumstances in which incoming or outgoing mail may be withheld, and will ensure that there is no scrutiny at all of the mail of informal patients.' The changes are set out in section 134 of the 1983 Act.

4.3.2   **Section 134** (1) A postal packet addressed to any person by a patient detained in a hospital under this Act and delivered by the patient for dispatch may be withheld from the Post Office—

(a) if that person has requested that communications addressed to him by the patient should be withheld; or
(b) subject to subsection (3) below, if the hospital is a special hospital and the managers of the hospital consider that the postal packet is likely—

(i) to cause distress to the person to whom it is addressed or to any person (not being a person on the staff of the hospital); or
(ii) to cause danger to any person;

and any request for the purposes of paragraph (a) above shall be made by a notice in writing given to the managers of the hospital, the registered medical practitioner in charge of the treatment of the patient or the Secretary of State.

(2) Subject to subsection (3) below, a postal packet addressed to a

patient detained in a special hospital may be withheld from the patient if, in the opinion of the managers of the hospital, it is necessary to do so in the interests of the safety of the patient or for the protection of other persons.

Powers to inspect and withhold outgoing mail have been kept in respect of some patients, but they have been considerably reduced. The principle change is that the powers no longer apply to informal patients. Where detained patients are affected, the powers are limited to situations where:

(a) An addressee has specifically requested in writing that mail from any detained patient should be withheld; or
(b) The patient is detained in a special hospital. Here both incoming and outgoing mail can be withheld on the grounds set out in subsections (1)(b) and (2).

The following points should be noted:

(a) Postal packets include letters, postcards, parcels and telegrams.
(b) The powers to intercept mail are now given to the hospital managers rather than the responsible medical officer.
(c) The managers may delegate their powers to specified hospital staff thus allowing some flexibility which was not available under the 1959 Act.

4.3.3 Mail which cannot be interfered with

Section 134 (3) Subsections (1)(b) and (2) do not apply to any postal packet addressed by a packet to, or sent to a patient by or on behalf of—

(a) any Minister of the Crown or member of either House of Parliament;
(b) the Master or any other officer of the Court of Protection or any of the Lord Chancellor's Visitors;
(c) the Parliamentary Commissioner for Administration, the Health Service Commissioner for England, the Health Service Commissioner for Wales or a Local Commissioner within the meaning of Part III of the Local Government Act 1974;
(d) a Mental Health Review Tribunal;
(e) health authority within the meaning of the National Health Service Act 1977, a local social services authority, a Community Health Council or a probation and after-care committee appointed under paragraph 2 of Schedule 3 to the Powers of Criminal Courts Acts 1973;
(f) the managers of the hospital in which the patient is detained;
(g) any legally qualified person instructed by the patient to act as his legal adviser; or
(h) the European Commission of Human Rights or the European Court of Human Rights.

A similar list was contained in the 1959 Act, but there are several differences between the two Acts that are worth noting:

(a) The Parliamentary categories in (a) and (b) have been extended; before only the Secretary of State for Social Services and MPs were included.

(b) The 1959 Act list did not include any Ombudsmen or the European institutions which were, of course, either not in existence or not relevant to the UK in 1959. However, no attempt had been made to extend the categories since 1959, although the power to do so was available.

(c) The 1959 Act list included anyone with power to discharge a patient. Surprisingly, this category is omitted from the 1983 Act.

(d) It is still open to a person included on the list referred to above to ask for mail addressed to him to be withheld under section 134 (1) (a). It is not clear whether this right is also available to bodies or office-holders on the list. Our view is that probably only local authorities (and health authorities) can ask for mail to be withheld since the word 'person' is defined in general law as including corporate bodies but not office-holders.

4.3.4   Procedure for opening, inspecting or withholding mail

1   *Inspection and opening*

The person involved must make a written statement containing the following information:

(a) that the packet has been opened and inspected;
(b) that nothing has been withheld;
(c) his name and the name of the hospital.

The statement must be placed in the packet which is then resealed.

2   *Withholding*

The person involved must record the following information in a register:

(a) that a packet or its contents have been withheld;
(b) the date of withholding;
(c) the grounds for withholding;
(d) a description of what has been withheld;
(e) his name.

A statement containing all the above information must be prepared and put in the packet which is then resealed.

3   *Notice to the patient*

(a) Outgoing mail. Within seven days of a packet being opened the patient must be notified that it has been interfered with.
(b) Incoming mail. Again notice must be given within seven days, and both the sender and the patient are entitled to notice.

The importance of this part of the procedure is that the notices must state the rights of the patient and the sender to request the Mental Health Act Commission to review any decision to interfere with post. Such a request must be made within six months of the notice, and the Mental Health Act Commission has power to overrule any decision to interfere with mail.

4.4   Telephones

Reference is made in the extracts from MIND's *A Human Condition* above (para 4.3.1) to 'restraints on the use of postal and telephone services'. There is no power in the 1983 Act to interfere with telephone calls nor was there in the 1959 Act. Specific powers to deal with mail were, and still are, needed because to interfere with post is an offence under the Post Office Act 1953.

Can a hospital prevent patients from making or receiving telephone calls? Unless such restrictions can be justified, either on the grounds that they are necessary to prevent a criminal offence by the patient, or to protect the patient from nnecessary suffering or distress, it is our view that the hospital has no general power to restrict or curtail telephone calls to or from patients.

4.5   Voting

Traditionally great importance has been given to the right to vote yet this is another area where mentally disordered persons have been discriminated against in a manner which emphasises their isolation from the community. Electoral law since 1949 has prohibited patients in psychiatric hospitals from registering as electors, thereby depriving them of voting rights in Parliamentary or local government elections. The prohibition is based on the type of institution in which the patient is resident and not the patient's mental capacity to vote. No attention was paid to this anomaly in either of the Reviews, and it only received passing reference in MIND's *A Human Condition*. Consequently the 1982 Amendment Bill contained no proposals to change the existing law, but attempts were made in both Houses to give all patients the right to register as electors. These attempts were opposed by the Government on no better ground than that it would not be appropriate to change electoral law in mental health legislation (although the 1959 Act had done so). This Government's approach to the problem was described by one MP as one of 'the 100 standard arguments for use in resisting amendments to Bills'. The Government eventually relented and introduced a limited reform. The existing electoral law was that anyone who was a patient in a psychiatric hospital or a mental nursing home was not treated as resident in the hospital or nursing home and was, therefore, not eligible for inclusion in the register of electors. Revised electoral law came into force on 1 April 1983. This provided that *informal patients* (detained patients still cannot be registered as electors) who are resident in mental illness or mental handicap hospitals on 10 October of each year (the qualifying date for electoral registration purposes) are given the opportunity to make a 'patient's declaration' which will entitle them to have their names included on the register in respect of an address outside of the hospital. This declaration must be made without assistance. The address to be given in the declaration is the address at which the patient would be resident if not in hospital. Patients who cannot give such an address are permitted to give an address at which they have lived at any time before admission. The declaration and requirement that it must be made without assistance are intended to provide an indication of the patient's capacity to vote, ie the patient must understand the information required to make the declaration and be able to communicate that information to the person who witnesses the declaration. This does not prevent hospital staff from answering queries or assisting blind or illiterate persons to complete the declaration. The witness to the declaration must be someone on the hospital staff authorised by the health authority.

4.6   Privacy

Has a patient a right of privacy? This is an important question in view of the stigma which still attaches to mental disorder, a stigma which is probably even greater if the patient is detained in hospital.

There are two aspects to this right – the right to keep the fact of admission to hospital from others (including relatives), and the right to privacy whilst in hospital. Clearly those professionally concerned with the treatment of the patient – doctors, nurses and approved social workers – must respect the confidential nature of their relationship with the patient, as must those more indirectly concerned with the patient's affairs, ie lawyers, doctors, and social workers appointed on behalf of the patient or the nearest relative. Does this provide sufficient protection for the patient's privacy? What if the patient does not want his relatives to know of his mental disorder? Unfortunately the Act contains a curious anomaly which ensures that relatives may not be kept uninformed even if the patient wishes it.

4.6.1 **Section 132** (4) The managers of a hospital or a mental nursing home in which a patient is detained as aforesaid shall, except where the patient otherwise requests, take such steps as are practicable to furnish the person (if any) appearing to them to be his nearest relative with a copy of any information giving to him in writing under subsections (1) and (2) above; and those steps shall be taken when the information is given to the patient or within a reasonable time thereafter.

Section 11 (3) Before or within a reasonable time after an application for the admission of a patient for assessment is made by an approved social worker, that social worker shall take such steps as are practicable to inform the person (if any) appearing to be the nearest relative of the patient that the application is to be or has been made and of the power of the nearest relative under section 23(2)(a) below.

(4) Neither an application for admission for treatment nor a guardianship application shall be made by an approved social worker if the nearest relative of the patient has notified that social worker, or the local social services authority by whom that social worker is appointed, that he objects to the application being made and, without prejudice to the foregoing provision, no such application shall be made by such a social worker except after consultation with the person (if any) appearing to be the nearest relative of the patient unless it appears to that social worker that in the circumstances such consultation is not reasonably practicable or would involve unreasonable delay.

The contradiction inherent in these two sections is obvious. Section 132 attempts to preserve confidentiality but the requirement to consult with or inform relatives in section 11 nullifies the effect of section 132. It is only if the patient is admitted informally that the matter can be kept from relatives. It is also interesting to note that the approved social worker has no clear power to interview patients

127

in private before an application is made, although the words 'in a suitable manner' in section 13 should prove sufficient authority for an approved social worker to require anyone present to withdraw whilst the interview is taking place.

Once the patient is in hospital his privacy is better protected. Most of the statutory provisions relating to visiting and examining the patient state that this may be done in private:

Section 24 (1) For the purpose of advising as to the exercise by the nearest relative of a patient who is liable to be detained or subject to guardianship under this Part of this Act of any power to order his discharge, any registered medical practitioner authorised by on behalf of the nearest relative of the patient may, at any reasonable time, visit the patient and examine him in private . . .

(4) Any person authorised for the purposes of subsection (3) above to visit a patient may require the production of and inspect any documents constituting or alleged to constitute the authority for the detention of the patient under this Part of this Act; and any person so authorised who is a registered medical practitioner, may examine the patient in private, and may require the production of and inspect any other records relating to the treatment of the patient in the home.

The Act also contains provisions to ensure privacy in county court proceedings and in Mental Health Review Tribunal proceedings (the latter are considered in detail at Part Six).

Investigations by the Mental Health Act Commission on behalf of the Secretary of State provide that the Commission may interview patients in private:

Section 120 (1) The Secretary of State shall keep under review the exercise of the powers and the discharge of the duties conferred or imposed by this Act so far as relating to the detention of patients or to patients liable to be detained under this Act and shall make arrangements for persons authorised by him in that behalf—

(a) to visit and interview in private patients detained under this Act in hospitals and mental nursing homes; and . . .

(4) For the purpose of any such review as is mentioned in subsection (1) above or of carrying out his functions under arrangements made under this section any person authorised in that behalf by the Secretary of State may at any reasonable time—

(a) visit and interview and, if he is a registered medical practitioner, examine in private any patient in a mental nursing home; and

4.6.2 There is increasing public pressure for individuals to be given the legal right to see whatever information public and private organisations hold on file concerning their private affairs. A series of Private Members' Bills have been introduced into Parliament which seek to establish public rights of attendance at a wider range of local authority meetings and to create specific rights for individuals to see internal departmental documents and personal files. Although the Bills have little chance of becoming law, we expect that the government will respond positively to this pressure by introducing legislation containing such rights. A further, more certain, right is the Data Protection Act which received the Royal Assent on 12 July 1984 and is expected to be fully implemented by 1987. This will give individuals rights of access to personal information held by public and private bodies and individuals provided that the information is held on computer. It is virtually certain that social work and medical records will be exempt from these access rights. Finally there is a DHSS Circular, LAC(83) 14, which instructs LAs to establish arrangements to allow clients access to their files. The circular applies to all social services files, whether held manually or on computer, but contains a list of five types of information which should not be revealed to a client:

(1) Where a file contains information about a third party and disclosure of this information would be harmful to the third party;
(2) Where information on a file has been supplied on the understanding that it will not be revealed to the client;
(3) Confidential professional judgements made by social work staff;
(4) Information about children and their parents;
(5) Information which would cause distress to the client if revealed to him or her.

A person who seeks the assistance of the courts in gaining access to his file will probably fail as did a client of Liverpool Social Services Department. Here the client proposed to sue Liverpool City Council for negligently handling his case whilst he was in their care. To proceed with this action he needed to see case notes and records on his file and was refused access to them by Liverpool. The client took his case to the Court of Appeal which, in 1980, refused to order Liverpool to hand over the records on the grounds that they were protected by a type of privilege similar to that which exists between clients and their lawyers. Since this case Liverpool have declared a policy of open access to their social services records but it too has various exceptions which are similar to those in the DHSS circular. The DHSS circular was an overhasty response by the DHSS to Liverpool's policy decision. It failed to take into account the imminent Data Protection legislation (all that was said concerning this was that further guidance would be issued on computer held records at a later date). A much more important criticism of the circular is that it is an inappropriate vehicle to contain such important client rights. Although it is expressed as being given to Local Social Services Authorities under Local Authorities Social Services Act 1970, section 7 (and which they must therefore follow) it is difficult to say how a client who is refused access to his file in contravention of the circular can enforce a right which is contained in a circular.

4.6.3 A further difficulty lies in the rights of councillors to information which they require in order to carry out their duties. This was considered by the House of Lords in 1983 in a case involving Birmingham City Council and one of its councillors who wished to see some confidential adoption records. The councillor was not a member of Birmingham's Social Services Committee. The councillor's right to see the records was challenged by the proposed adopters. The case was eventually decided in favour of the councillor in the House of Lords which laid down the following rules governing councillors' rights to information held by their local authority:

(a) councillors have a general right of access to all information held by their local authority which they need to carry out their duties;
(b) this general right extends to all information held by committees which they are members of but not automatically to information held by committees they are not members of;
(c) to gain access to information held by a committee of which a councillor is not a member the councillor must show he has a 'need to know';
(d) to satisfy the 'need to know' test a councillor must show he needs the information in order to carry out his duties as a councillor.

4.6.4 It will be obvious from the above that the position of clients regarding access to and control of their files is most confused. Some aspects are covered by existing or proposed legislation but the position as a whole is quite unsatisfactory and needs a comprehensive review. If and when such a review takes place we suggest that it should cover the following issues:

(a) how far should clients be able to control who (including councillors) has access to their personal files;
(b) what rights of access to personal files should clients possess;
(c) should the manner in which files are kept (ie manually or on computer) determine the client's rights of access;
(d) how far should client's rights of access be restricted in order to encourage sharing of information between agencies involved in their care and protection?

4.7 Leave of absence from hospital

Although this is not a right conferred upon the patient, a power is granted to the responsible medical officer to grant the patient leave of absence in circumstances set out in section 17:

Section 17 (1) The responsible medical officer may grant to any patient who is for the time being liable to be detained in a hospital under this Part of this Act leave to be absent from the hospital subject to such conditions (if any) as that officer considers necessary in the interests of the patient or for the protection of other persons.

(2) Leave of absence may be granted to a patient under this section either indefinitely or on specified occasions or for any specified period; and where leave is so granted for a specified period, that period may be extended by further leave granted in the absence of the patient.

(3) Where it appears to the responsible medical officer that it is necessary so to do in the interests of the patient or for the protection of other persons, he may, upon granting leave of absence under this section, direct that the patient remain in custody during his absence; and where leave of absence is so granted the patient may be kept in the custody of any officer on the staff of the hospital, or of any other person authorised in writing by the managers of the hospital, or if the patient is required in accordance with conditions imposed on the grant of leave of absence to reside in another hospital, of any officer on the staff of that other hospital.

(4) In any case where a patient is absent from a hospital in pursuance of leave of absence granted under this section, and it appears to the responsible medical officer that it is necessary so to do in the interests of the patient's health or safety or for the protection of other persons, that officer may, subject to subsection (5) below, by notice in writing given to the patient or to the person for the time being in charge of the patient, revoke the leave of absence and recall the patient to the hospital.

(5) A patient to whom leave of absence is granted under this section shall not be recalled under subsection (4) above after he has ceased to be liable to be detained under this Part of this Act; and without prejudice to any other provision of this Part of this Act any such patient shall cease to be so liable at the expiration of the period of six months beginning with the first day of his absence on leave unless either—

(a) he has returned to the hospital, or has been transferred to another hospital under the following provisions of this Act, before the expiration of that period; or

(b) he is absent without leave at the expiration of that period.

More important for the patient is section 18 which could be said to confer a right upon a patient:

Section 18 (1) Where a patient who is for the time being liable to be detained under this Part of this Act in a hospital—

(a) absents himself from the hospital without leave granted under section 17 above; or

(b) fails to return to the hospital on any occasion on which, or at the expiration of any period for which, leave of absence was granted to him under that section, or upon being recalled under that section; or

(c) absents himself without permission from any place where he is required to reside in accordance with conditions imposed on the grant of leave of absence under that section.

he may, subject to the provisions of this section, be taken into custody and returned to the hospital or place by any approved social worker, by any officer on the staff of the hospital, by any constable, or by any person authorised in writing by the managers of the hospital.

(2) Where the place referred to in paragrpah (c) of subsection (1) above is a hospital other than the one in which the patient is for the time being liable to be detained, the references in that subsection to an officer on the staff of the hospital and the managers of the hospital shall respectively include references to an officer on the staff of the first-mentioned hospital and the managers of that hospital.

(3) Where a patient who is for the time being subject to guardianship under this Part of this Act absents himself without the leave of the guardian from the place at which he is required by the guardian to reside, he may, subject to the provisions of this section, be taken into custody and returned to that place by any officer on the staff of a local social services authority, by any constable, or by any person authorised in writing by the guardian or a local social services authority.

(4) A patient shall not be taken into custody under this section after the expiration of the period of 23 days beginning with the first day of his absence without leave; and a patient who has not returned or been taken into custody under this section within the said period shall cease to be liable to be detained or subject to guardianship, as the case may be, at the expiration of that period.

(5) A patient shall not be taken into custody under this section if that period for which he is liable to be detained is that specified in section 2(4), 4(4) or 5(2) or (4) above and that period has expired.

(6) In this Act 'absent without leave' means absent from any hospital or other place and liable to be taken into custody and returned under this section, and related expressions shall be construed accordingly.

The effect of this section is most important for a detained patient – if he escapes from detention and remains free for 28 days he is no longer liable to be detained.

Under the 1959 Act, patients suffering from psychopathic disorder or subnormality (now impairment) could be retaken at any time within a six month period. Now in all types of mental disorder the period is 28 days.

For some case studies relating to this Part, see para **11.2.4** *in Part 11 following.*

5   Legal consequences of mental disorder

5.1   Introduction

The 1983 Act is exclusively concerned with 'the reception, care and treatment of mentally disordered patients'. It does not affect the general legal rights and responsibilities of mentally disordered persons to enter into contracts, to make wills, to marry etc except where the patient is subject to the jurisdiction of the Court of Protection. In this section we shall depart from our consideration of the 1983 Act and look at common law rules governing these areas. Before doing so one important point needs to be made clear. Merely because a person falls within the definition of mental disorder in the 1983 Act it does not automatically follow that he is unable to contract, marry etc. Each of these branches of the law have their own tests to establish capacity.

5.2   Contracts

It is an essential requirement of a binding contract that both parties understand the terms of the agreement they are making. If one of the parties cannot understand the consequences of his agreement because of his mental disability he may claim to have the contract set aside. But this claim will only succeed if the other party knew or ought to have known of his mental incapacity. Furthermore the question of a person's mental capacity to understand the consequences of a contract is only relevant at the time the contract is made. If he is fully capable of understanding what he has done at that time then it will not be possible for him to set aside his contracts if he becomes mentally incapable after they have been made. So it is possible for a person who suffers from a mental disorder which allows him 'lucid intervals' to enter into legally binding contracts.

There is another qualification to the general rule about capacity to contract. This relates to what the law describes as contracts for necessaries. These are goods which are essential for the mentally incapable person's survival, eg food, heating, lighting and lodgings. Contracts which relate to necessaries will be binding upon the mentally incapable person even if he is not capable of understanding the consequences of his agreement or if the other party did know that he was incapable through mental incapacity of appreciating the nature of his actions.

Tenancies are particular types of contract and a tenancy of a house in which a person suffering from mental incapacity lives would probably be regarded in law as a contract for necessaries. The usual obligations to be found in tenancies, ie to pay rent and rates, to keep the premises properly maintained, not to use the property for purposes other than those specified in the tenancy, will bind a tenant even if he is suffering from mental incapacity. Similarly the landlord's obligations under the tenancy will not be affected by the tenant's mental incapacity.

Finally there is specific statutory provision concerning the supply of necessaries to a mentally incapable person: section 2 of the Sale of Goods Act 1979 provides that 'where necessaries are sold and delivered to a person who by reason of mental incapacity . . . is incompetent to contract, he must pay a reasonable price therefor.'

5.3 Wills

Similar rules exist concerning the validity of wills made by persons suffering from mental incapacity. For a will to be legally binding upon the testator he must:

(a) understand the consequences of making a will;
(b) be fully aware of the extent of the property he owns and intends to dispose of;
(c) know who his relatives are and who he has responsibilities towards;

(d) understand the manner in which he has attempted to dispose of his property.

A will is not revoked by the testator's subsequent mental incapacity and a will made during a 'lucid interval' is perfectly valid.

If a will, rational on the face of it, is shown to have been properly signed and witnessed it will be presumed to have been made by a person of competent understanding. It is presumed to be valid unless evidence to the contrary is produced by a person seeking to challenge its validity, thus the burden of proving a will to be invalid is on the person challenging it.

5.4 Marriage and divorce

5.4.1 A marriage which took place after 1971 can be set aside *within three years,* if, at the time of the ceremony, the grounds set out in section 12 of the Matrimonial Causes Act 1973 exist:

Matrimonial Causes Act 1973, section 12

A marriage celebrated after 31 July 1971 shall be voidable on the following grounds only, that is to say—
   [(a) . . . ;]
   [(b) . . . ;]
   (c) that either party to the marriage did not validly consent to it, whether in consequence of duress, mistake, unsoundness of mind or otherwise;
   (d) that at the time of the marriage either party, though capable of giving a valid consent, was suffering (whether continuously or intermittently) from mental disorder within the meaning of the Mental Health Act, 1983 of such a kind or to such an extent as to be unfitted for marriage;
   [(e) . . . ;]
   [(f) . . . .]

Proceedings to set aside a marriage are known as nullity proceedings. The proceedings must, if based on paragraphs (c) or (d) of section 12 of the 1973 Act, be started within three years of the marriage ceremony. The effect of a nullity decree is that the marriage is treated in law as never having existed. An exception to the rule is that children of the marriage will not lose their legitimate status if a nullity decree is granted on grounds (c) and (d). Until the marriage is set aside by the court the marriage is perfectly valid. Either party to the marriage may start nullity proceedings under grounds (c) and (d). The following further points on grounds (c) and (d) should be noted:

(1) the object of ground (c) is to ensure that the parties to a marriage fully understand the nature of the obligations they are entering into. The test applied by the courts is set out in the following extract from a case in 1954:

Was the [person] . . . capable of understanding the nature of contract into which he was entering, or was his mental condition such that he was incapable of understanding it? To ascertain the nature of a contract of marriage a man must be mentally capable of appreciating that it involves the responsibilities normally attaching to marriage. Without that degree of mentality, it cannot be said that he understands the nature of the contract.

This test is very similar to the test of capacity to enter into commercial contracts (see paragraph 5.2).

(2) The test for ground (d) is mental disorder *and* unfitness for marriage. Lack of consent is not relevant here – the parties may well be able to understand the obligations of marriage. What is relevant is 'fitness for marriage' and the test here is expressed in the following words from a case in 1969. In this case the husband applied for a nullity decree on the grounds of his wife's mental disorder and unfitness for marriage. It was proved that the wife was suffering from temporary hysterical neurosis which was a mental disorder within the meaning of the Mental Health Act 1959 but the court refused to grant the nullity decree as it was not satisfied as to the wife's unfitness for marriage. In so doing the court laid down the following test: 'Is this person capable of living in a married state, and carrying out the ordinary duties and obligations of marriage?'

5.4.2 *Divorce* The matters considered in the previous paragraph apply only at the time of the marriage ceremony. What is the position if a party to a marriage subsequently suffers from a mental disorder? This may well constitute grounds for divorce. The person seeking a divorce is referred to as the petitioner and the person contesting the divorce is the respondent.

There is only one ground for divorce – that the marriage has broken down irretrievably. Before a court can find that a marriage has irretrievably broken down it must be satisfied that one or more of five facts laid down in the Matrimonial Causes Act 1973 exist. None of these facts contain an express reference to mental disorder but they may be caused by or related to a respondent's disorder:

Matrimonial Causes Act 1973, section 1 (2)

...(a) that the respondent has as committed adultery and the petitioner finds it intolerable to live with the respondent;

(b) that the respondent has behaved in such a way that the petitioner cannot reasonably be expected to live with the respondent;

(c) that the respondent has deserted the petitioner for a continuous period of at least two years immediately preceding the presentation of the petition;

(d) that the parties to the marriage have lived apart for a continuous period of at least two years immediately preceding the presentation of the petition (hereafter in this Act referred to as 'two years' separation') and the respondent consents to a decree being granted;

(e) that the parties to the marriage have lived apart for a continuous period of at least five years immediately preceding the presentation of the petition (hereafter in this Act referred to as 'five years' separation').

There have been several divorce cases involving respondents suffering from mental disorder and the following guidance can be drawn from the decided cases:

(1) behaviour in ground (b) can include negative conduct such as prolonged silences and total inactivity as well as positive conduct and includes involuntary conduct.

(2) a respondent cannot desert a petitioner under ground (c) if she is suffering from paranoid psychosis leading to delusions that her husband was trying to murder her and associating with other women. In one case the wife left her husband because of her delusions and the court found that she was acting under the force of her delusions and could not form an intention to desert.

(3) '... in cases in which a respondent is mentally ill it will rarely, if ever, be possible to make use of [ground (d)] because of doubts as to the capacity to give a valid consent.' This means that where a petitioner relies on living apart from a mentally disordered respondent (who is accommodated in a psychiatric hospital on a long-term basis) as a ground for divorce, it will be necessary for the petitioner to use ground (e) (five years apart) as there is no requirement for the respondent to consent under this ground. There is, however, a further requirement for the petitioner under ground (e) – the divorce must not cause 'grave financial or other hardship' to the respondent.

5.4.3   Marriage Act 1983

The provisions of this Act came into force on 1 May 1984. The changes introduced by the Act relate only to location of marriage. The Act does not give anyone the right to marry who does not already have that right (see above, 5.4.1). For example, many patients detained under the Mental Health Act are capable of understanding the nature and purport of marriage and can consent to it, and marriages of detained patients have taken place under existing law outside hospital.

The Marriage Act now permits the marriage of patients detained in hospital under the Mental Health Act 1983 to take place in the hospital, although it does exclude from these provisions those detained under the shorter-term provisions, ie sections 2,4,5,35,36 and 136. Where a detained patient wishes to be married in the hospital, the notice of marriage required by section 27 of the Marriage Act 1949 must be accompanied by a statement made by the hospital managers

(i) identifying the establishment where the patient is detained, and

(ii) stating that the hospital managers have no objection to that establishment being specified in the notice of marriage as the place where that marriage is to be solemnised.

It must be recognised, however, that health service managers do not have to agree to the marriage taking place on health service premises, and it is thus difficult to justify this as being a new right that has been conferred on detained patients.

5.5   Parenthood

5.5.1   A parent's right to care for his child may be removed or seriously limited if that parent suffers from mental incapacity. The effect of mental incapacity on parental rights can be divided into two parts – local authority powers and custody disputes.

5.5.2   The Child Care Act 1980 places local authorities under a duty to receive into care children within their area who appear to be under 17. One of the grounds for receiving children into care under the 1980 Act is:

> that his parents or guardian are, for the time being or permanently,

prevented by reason of mental or bodily disease or infirmity or other incapacity or any other circumstances from providing for his proper accommodation, maintenance or upbringing;

This power does not allow local authorities to keep children in their care (popularly known as 'voluntary care') if their parents recover and are able and willing to take over the care of their children but it can lead to a local authority assuming parental rights over the children. The effect of such action by the local authority is to deprive parents of their natural parental rights particularly the right to care for their children in their own home. The grounds for assuming parental rights are set out in section 3 of the Child Care Act 1980 and one of these grounds is that the parent suffers from a mental disorder (within the meaning of the Mental Health Act 1983), which renders him unfit to have the care of the child.

There is currently much criticism of the power to assume parental rights because it can be exercised in an almost routine administrative manner by local authorities. Unlike care proceedings the exercise of the power to assume parental rights may never be considered by a court. This is because the local authority exercises the power by passing an appropriate resolution which is effective to transfer the parent's rights to it unless the parent objects. In the event of a parental objection the local authority must apply to the juvenile court for an order that the resolution shall continue in force. The consequences of the parental rights procedure for persons suffering from mental disorder are obvious. The child is likely to remain in care for as long as the parent is suffering from the disorder but there is no automatic discharge of the child from care if the parent recovers. The local authority has power to terminate its resolution but if the child has been in care for some time it will be unlikely to be willing to return the child to its parents. The parent's remedy is to take court proceedings to gain the care of the child.

It is not unusual for a local authority to place a child in its care with prospective adopters if the chances of the child returning to its parents appear remote owing to the parent's mental disorder. If this happens the natural parent may not object until the prospective adopters apply for an adoption order. Such an order cannot be made unless the natural parent consents but consent can be dispensed with on several grounds, three of which are relevant to mentally incapable persons. The first is that the parent is incapable of giving agreement, the second that the parent is withholding his agreement unreasonably and the third that the parent has persistently failed without reasonable cause to discharge his parental duties. The court in adoption proceedings is concerned with the child's welfare rather than parental rights and must give first consideration to the child's best interests in any decision it comes to concerning the adoption. As a consequence the likelihood is that a parent suffering from mental disorder will have his consent dispensed with if the court feels there is little likelihood of him recovering sufficiently to care for the child and that the prospective adopters will be able to provide a satisfactory home for him.

5.5.3 In divorce and separation proceedings the court has power to make orders for the custody of any children of the marriage and again the principle upon which it decides such questions is the child's best interests. Thus a parent who suffers from mental disorder may find that a court makes a divorce order and also awards custody of any children of the marriage to the other parent. The chances of successfully challenging such orders are not great for mentally disordered parents as they will have difficulty in satisfying the court that they can provide the children with adequate care.

5.6   Housing

Local authorities have a general duty to provide an adequate supply of housing within their area but they have a specific duty under the Housing (Homeless Persons) Act 1977 to provide advice, assistance or accommodation for persons who are homeless or threatened with homelessness. The precise duty a local authority is under towards a homeless person will depend upon whether or not that person falls within the priority need category for accommodation. Usually this category does not extend to single persons but persons who are vulnerable as a result of old age, mental illness or handicap or physical disability or other special reason are classed as having a priority need for accommodation. The effect of this is that such persons are entitled to be provided with accommodation on a permanent basis by the local authority.

The reason for a homeless person's homelessness may govern what advice, assistance or accommodation he can demand of a local authority under the 1977 Act. The Act contains the concept of 'intentional homelessness'. If an applicant for housing has freely given up accommodation or has lost it through failure to pay rent the local authority may seek to classify the applicant as intentionally homeless. The effect of this is that even if an applicant can claim priority need, if he is intentionally homeless the local authority's duty is limited to providing temporary accommodation for a reasonable period to enable the applicant to find his own alternative accommodation. As a general rule it would seem difficult to argue that a person suffering from mental disorder can form the necessary intention to fall within the intentionally homeless category but each case will depend upon its own facts, particularly the nature and degree of the applicant's mental disorder.

5.7   The Court of Protection

5.7.1   Introduction

The various rules described above concerning contracts, wills, etc apply only where a person's property and affairs are not under the control and supervision of the Court of Protection. If a Court of Protection order exists in relation to a patient's property his powers to enter into contracts and make wills are seriously curtailed. In this section we will look at the procedures and powers of the Court but first we will consider some deficiencies in the Court and its jurisdiction.

The Court was set up by the 1959 Act and has extensive powers over the property and affairs of persons suffering from mental disorder. It would be reasonable to expect that any review of the operation of the 1959 Act would include consideration of the Court and its powers but the Reviews of 1976 and 1978 contain no reference at all to the Court. Also MIND's important critical analysis of the 1959 Act *A Human Condition* contains but a single paragraph on the Court's extensive powers without any reference to the need for reform. It would be wrong to assume from this lack of attention to the Court that reforms were not required. This is confirmed by the publication in 1983 by MIND of *The Court of Protection. A legal and policy analysis of the guardianship of the estate* by Larry Gostin. In this work the need for reform was clearly stated but too late for inclusion in the 1982 Amendment Act. The main defects identified by MIND were:

(a) Lack of sufficient safeguards in the procedures for scrutinising applications to prevent patients becoming unnecessarily subject

to the Court's jurisdiction;
(b) Over-centralisation of the Court's administration in London leading to remoteness from the patients whose property it protects;
(c) The need for an 'informal' procedure whereby patients could consent to the Court's jurisdiction and still retain some control over their affairs.

MIND's solution to the first defect was a general tightening up of the Court's procedures to provide a far more positive scrutiny of applications which come before it. A particular anomaly is that the Court may act upon a single medical recommendation and no guidance is given in the Act or by the Court as to the form which the medical recommendation should take. MIND quotes from a medical report which had been drawn to its attention which concluded as follows: '*Although I have not myself seen him in a condition of being incapable of managing his affairs by reason of mental illness,* I do feel that in view of the history that I would support a move to appoint a receiver to manage his affairs' [emphasis added].

MIND's recommendation, which we would support, is that the Court should not be able to exercise its jurisdiction unless two medical recommendations have been obtained, and one is from an 'approved doctor'. The procedure for notifying the patient of an application to the Court also requires attention. The patient does not automatically receive full details of the application and the evidence upon which it is based.

His only entitlement is to notice that an application has been made and even this may be dispensed with in cases where the Court is satisfied that service of notice on the patient would be to his detriment.

Finally the patient is given a mere seven days to object to the application. MIND's proposals are that the patient should be given full details of the application and the evidence in support and 21 days should be allowed for the patient to respond to the application, thus giving the patient time to obtain advice and if necessary representation.

Once jurisdiction has been assumed by the Court it fails to provide any system whereby the need for the patient to be subject to its jurisdiction is reviewed. It concentrates entirely upon the function of monitoring the patient's financial affairs and never questions whether the patient still requires its overly paternalistic protection. We feel that the Court should review on an annual basis the need for the patient to continue under its jurisdiction by requiring an annual medical report upon the patient's mental condition and ability to conduct his affairs and property.

The Court and its administration is based entirely in London. Judges and officials never visit the patients under the Court's protection and formal hearings at which the patient may attend are rare. The bulk of the Court's business is conducted by post. Use of the Official Solicitor accentuates this defect as he is also London-based and tends to operate through local agencies such as social services departments rather than by personal attendance upon patients. The effect is to distance the Court from patients and the solution proposed by MIND is to transfer the Court's jurisdiction to the County Court system to provide a local jurisdiction for patients and receivers. Whilst agreeing that there is a need for decentralisation of the Court's jurisdiction we do not think MIND's solution is practical or sound. The County Court system is already heavily overloaded with current work and would need a substantial infusion of judges and supporting administrative staff if it were to undertake the Court of Protection's work. A further objection is that County Courts have no experience of this type of work which is of a specialist nature. If it is dealt with properly it requires the expertise of judges with substantial experience in mental health law. The suggestion that the county courts could be assisted by their existing divorce welfare system is also misconceived, again because of the specialist nature of the work and we are not convinced that the required expertise is available within the divorce welfare system. A better solution would be to require judges nominated to the Court of Protection to sit locally and this could be effected through the present circuit judge system. If such a system were created it would need assistance in considering the patient's social circumstances. This could be provided by Local Social Services Authorities using approved social workers.

The final defect identified by MIND was the need for an informal procedure whereby patients could agree to the Court's jurisdiction but still retain some control over their property and affairs so far as their mental abilities permit. At present the effect of an order placing the patient under the Court's jurisdiction does not permit the patient to participate in any decisions concerning his property even if he has limited ability to understand the issues involved. The informal procedure suggested by MIND would allow such participation by the patient and would also allow the Court to exercise its protective jurisdiction where necessary. The informal status would be similar to the informal status of patients in hospital permitted by section 131 of the Act and which is a central feature of mental health legislation. This would certainly be a useful addition to the Court's powers which we would welcome. The present tendency is to view the Court's role as one which is only appropriate for large and complex estates or for patients with no ability to handle their property and affairs.

Unfortunately, the defects identified above still exist as MIND's constructive proposals came too late for inclusion within the 1982 Amendment Bill. The suggested reforms are awaited with hope rather than anticipation.

We now move on to consider the procedure and powers of the Court contained in Part VII of the Act and the Court of Protection Rules 1982.

5.7.2 Applications

Any adult may apply to place a patient's property and affairs under the Court's jurisdiction. The grounds for an application are that a person 'is incapable, by reason of mental disorder, of managing his property and affairs'. The patient may be accommodated in a hospital, mental nursing home or living in the community. He may or may not be subject to compulsory detention powers or under guardianship. The phrase 'mental disorder' is defined in section 1 of the Act. Persons under the Court's jurisdiction are referred to as patients. The Court prefers applications to be made by relatives of the patient and in the case of a married patient will always require proof that the patient's wife or husband has agreed to an application being made. It is not unusual for an application to be made by a patient's creditors or debtors or by a Local Authority. The Court exercises its jurisdiction through nominated judges but in practice the majority of its cases are handled by its administrative staff. There are rarely formal hearings even when the application is contested. An application must be accompanied by:

1 *An Affidavit of Kindred and Fortune* containing the following information:

(a) Personal details of the patient eg: age, occupation or former occupation, nearest relatives of the patient, former residence of the patient;

(b) property owned by the patient;

(c) income of the patient;

(d) patient's current residence, eg NHS hospital, Local Authority accommodation;

(e) patient's commitments, eg cost of accommodation, maintenance to husband or wife and children or other dependents;

(f) patient's debts;

(g) whether patient's income is sufficient to meet his needs and if not whether the patient is prepared to meet deficit from capital;

(h) whether patient has made a will or executed power of attorney;

(i) a proposed receiver for the patient and a referee as to the proposed receiver's fitness to act;

(j) short history of patient. (This usually includes suggestions as to the arrangements which should be made for the patient's dependents and proposals for the care of the patient if he lives in his own home.)

2 *A medical certificate.* This is given by the patient's medical attendant who need not be a specialist in the diagnosis or treatment of mental disorder. The medical attendant is required to state his qualifications and how long he has acted for the patient. He also must state when he last examined the patient and certify that in his opinion the patient is incapable by reason of mental disorder of managing his property and affairs and the grounds for this opinion. He must also state whether the patient is an informal patient or liable to be detained. Further information required in the medical certificate is:

(a) previous history of mental disorder;

(b) whether the patient is dangerous to himself or others;

(c) patient's bodily health and prospects of life, and

(d) patient's prospects of recovery.

Notice of the application is served on the patient and he is allowed seven days to object. The Court may decide that the notice should not be served on the patient on two grounds: first the patient will not understand the notice or second that the notice would affect his health. In any case copies of the affidavit and medical certificate are not automatically served upon the patient.

5.7.3 Objection by the patient

The patient can object to the application simply by letter to the Court within seven days of receiving the notice of the application. A patient's objection may take several forms – objection in principle to the application or merely to the proposed receiver. He may also use the opportunity to state his own views as to how his property should be handled. How the Court responds to the patient's objection depends upon whether it is satisfied as to the patient's mental competency to form an opinion upon the application. If the Court is not satisfied as to the patient's competence it will probably grant the application. The Court may wish to make further investigations and will usually request a Medical Visitor to visit the patient, examine him, and report upon his mental condition. What happens next depends upon the Medical Visitor's report. If it states that the patient is incapable of managing his affairs then the Court will tell the patient that it intends to make an order and give him the opportunity to produce further evidence in support of his objection. If the Medical Visitor's report confirms that the patient is capable of managing his affairs the application will probably fail.

5.7.4 Receivers

The receiver's role is to collect the patient's income and administer his property. This role is carried out under the close supervision and control of the Court which has extensive powers to deal with the patient's estate and which will be looked at in the next section. The Court prefers to appoint a relative of the patient as receiver where possible. The receiver is usually the means by which the Court carries out its powers. If there is no relative suitable or willing to act then the Court will normally appoint the Official Solicitor or an officer of a local authority (usually the Director of Social Services). The precise powers of the receiver will be set out in the Court order appointing him to act. Unless specifically authorised to do so a receiver should not handle capital, grant leases or tenancies, sell property or make loans or gifts from the patient's property.

Whilst the Court's preference to appoint relatives as receivers is understandable there can be an obvious conflict of interest if the relative also expects to benefit under the patient's will and there is some concern that the Court is not always sufficiently aware of such potential conflicts of interest. The procedures do not provide for any automatic inquiry into this aspect of the relationship between patient and receiver.

5.7.5   Powers of the Court

These are set out in sections 95 and 96 of the 1983 Act:

Section 95 (1) The judge may . . . do . . . all such things as appear necessary . . .
  (a) for the maintenance or other benefit of the patient.
  (b) for the maintenance or other benefit of other members of the patient's family,
  (c) for making provision for other persons or other purposes for whom or which the patient might be expected to provide if he were not mentally disordered,
  (d) otherwise for administering the patient's affairs.

In order to carry out the general functions in section 95 the judge is given specific powers in section 96. These include power to:

(a) control and manage property,
(b) buy, sell lease or mortgage property for the patient,
(c) settle property or make gifts,
(d) make a will for the patient,
(d) allow a suitable person to carry on the patient's trade or business,
(e) dissolve a patient's partnership,
(f) carry out the patient's contracts,
(g) conduct legal proceedings on the patient's behalf.

The Court's powers are wide enough to enable it, through a receiver, to handle the most complicated and also the most simple of estates. There is a special 'short procedure' available for small estates of less than £5,000 which does not require the appointment of a receiver. Instead a Court official is appointed to handle the estate.

*For some case studies relating to this Part, see para **11.2.5** in Part 11 following.*

6 The Mental Health Review Tribunal

6.1 Introduction

Section 65 (1) There shall continue to be a tribunal known as a Mental Health Review Tribunal for every region for which a Regional Health Authority is established in pursuance of the National Health Service Act 1977 and for Wales, for the purpose of dealing with applications and references by and in respect of patients under the provisions of this Act.

*   *   *

If the only way that basic human rights can be preserved is by an articulate presentation of a case, that case must be so articulated, and any funds required for payment must be provided out of public resources. One remembers the famous words of Mr Justice Darling when he said: 'The courts of our land are open to everybody, exactly the same as the Ritz Hotel'. There is no point in saying that the tribunals which will have to decide will be open to everybody, unless there is provision for representation to present a case on its merits. (Lord Elystan-Morgan, Lords, January 1982.)

The Percy Commission, reporting in 1957, recommended that there had to be some safeguard against the unjustified continued detention of patients, particularly as the admission procedure was not the subject of any independent review. It was proposed that a tribunal system be created, consisting of medical and non-medical members, to which a detained patient may have recourse at periodic intervals. The 1959 Act adopted this proposal. Over the years, however, the system was subject to criticisms, notably the following:

(a) The patient's right to make an application to a tribunal arose too infrequently. For example, in the case of detention for treatment, an application could only be made annually during the first two years of detention and subsequently every two years.

(b) Some patients could not apply to a tribunal at all, eg patients subject to restriction orders.

(c) Legal aid was not available for tribunal proceedings.

(d) A tribunal's powers were limited to discharge or reclassification of patients. There was no power to intervene in matters affecting a patient's treatment.

(e) A tribunal was bound to direct discharge if the patient was no longer mentally disordered within the meaning of the 1959 Act, even if this was against the best interests of the patient and society as a whole. This shortcoming of the tribunal system was aptly covered in a speech by Baroness Masham in the House of Lords in January 1982:

I believe that the mental health review tribunals have power to recommend either continued detention or discharge. People who serve on these tribunals have told me that it is an impossible choice. In many cases they do not want to detain the patient but the facilities for him to cope in the community are non-existent. The tribunal should have a third choice so they could indicate the type of resources the patient would need outside the hospital.

For example hostel accommodation, sheltered workshop, social worker support or day centre facilities. Mental Health tribunals will then be able to pinpoint the lack of facilities, and something may be done about improving the areas which are now inadequate.

(f) A tribunal was concerned only with the patient's mental condition at the time of the hearing rather than at the time of the original admission and so did not consider any failure to follow the statutory procedures relating to admission to hospital.

(g) Patients experienced great difficulty in obtaining information to support their case for discharge, eg details of community facilities available on discharge. Also patients were often denied access to information submitted by hospitals to a tribunal.

These and other criticisms were aired during the debates on the 1982 Amendment Bill, and the resulting changes in the law go some way towards improving the tribunal system. Three major reforms have been implemented – legal aid is now available for tribunal hearings, patients now have more frequent access to a tribunal and tribunals have a wider range of powers. The introduction of legal aid, largely the result of strong Parliamentary pressure on the Government during the 1982 Bill debates, has been affected by extending the Legal Aid Acts and not by amending the 1959 Act. However a tribunal is given power to pay the expenses of all persons attending a hearing other than solicitors and barristers:

> **Section 78** (7) A Mental Health Review Tribunal may pay allowances in respect of travelling expenses, subsistence and loss of earnings to any person attending the tribunal as an applicant or witness, to the patient who is the subject of the proceedings if he attends otherwise than as the applicant or a witness and to any person (other than counsel or a solicitor) who attends as the representative of an applicant.

The following points should be noted in respect of patients' increased rights of access to a tribunal:

(a) Where a patient has been detained under section 3 of the Act for six months or more, and his case has not been considered by a tribunal, the hospital managers *must* refer the case to a tribunal (see section 68, para 2.3.7 above).
(b) The time periods for review, renewal of detention and the right to make application to a tribunal have been halved (see section 20, para 2.3.4/5 above).
(c) Patients detained for assessment have a new right to apply to a tribunal (see section 66, para 6.2 following).

The 1981 White Paper envisaged an increase in the number of tribunal hearings from 904 in 1980 to around 4,500 a year after the 1983 Act came into force. To cope with this increased workload the following measures have been taken:

(a) Reviews of patients' cases began in advance of the implementation date of 30 September 1983.
(b) Legal aid became available from December 1982.
(c) The panels from which tribunal members are selected have been enlarged.
(d) More flexible arrangements for tribunal hearings have been introduced in the 1983 Rules. These include granting power to the chairman of a tribunal to deal with preliminary matters and allowing cases to be transferred between tribunals.

6.2 Time periods for making an application

Section 66 lists the types of application and the relevant time periods within which they may be made. They can be summarised as follows:

Section	Relating to	Applicant	Time Limit
2	assessment	patient only	within 14 days of admission
3	treatment	patient only	within 6 months of admission
7	guardianship	patient only	within 6 months of reception
16	reclassification	patient or nearest relative	within 28 days of being informed
19	transfer from guardianship to hospital	patient only	within 6 months of transfer
20	renewal of detention and guardianship	patient only	any time during period of renewed detention/ guardianship
25	restriction on nearest relative's discharge	nearest relative	within 28 days of being informed
29	appointment of acting nearest relative	nearest relative	within 12 months of order for removal and then once every 12 months

It should be noted that only one application can be made in the periods specified above.

In addition to the applications referred to in section 66 the Secretary of State may at any time refer cases of detained patients or patients under guardianship to a tribunal.

6.3   Making the application

The 1983 Rules update the earlier Rules in an attempt to provide more flexibility and fairness in the way cases are handled.

Applications must be made in writing to one of the four tribunals which are located in Nottingham, Liverpool, London and Cardiff. There is now no prescribed form of application but the Rules require applications to contain the following information:

(a) The patient's name and address;
(b) The address of the hospital where he is detained, from which he is conditionally discharged or was last detained;
(c) Where appropriate the name and address of the patient's private guardian or nearest relative;

(d) The section of the Act under which the patient is, or is liable to be detained;
(e) The name and address of the patient's representative if appointed.

Whether the removal of the prescribed form of application is an improvement is arguable. Under the previous Rules it was the practice of hospitals to keep supplies of forms for patients to use. The printed form at least provided a framework within which the patient could construct his application. Now the patient must draft the entire application himself and it must contain the information specified in the 1983 Rules which are unlikely to be readily accessible to patients who will now have to rely on advice from hospitals and in DHSS leaflets for guidance in preparation of the form. If the patient submits an application unaided, there is always the possibility of delays being caused through failure to include the necessary information on the application form. The advantage of dispensing with a prescribed application form is that the patient may make his application without having to reveal his intention to the hospital. There is evidence that patients were reluctant to make applications because they feared their treatment in hospital would be adversely affected if the hospital was aware an application to a tribunal had been made. Although this fear was usually completely unjustified it may nevertheless have persuaded patients not to make applications.

6.4   Procedure following an application

Once an application has been received by the tribunal it must notify the patient if he is not the applicant, and:

(a) the hospital (detained patients); or
(b) the Home Secretary (restricted patients); or
(c) the local social services authority (guardianship patients).

One of the above bodies must then submit a statement to the tribunal within three weeks (six weeks if the patient is conditionally discharged). This statement must include information specified in Schedule 1 of the 1983 Rules. This information is divided into two sections – background information and case history of the patient and reports. The reports must include a medical report and a social circumstances report together with the body's views on the patient's suitability for discharge and any other observations the body wishes to make. The 1983 Rules require a statement relating to conditionally discharged patients to contain similar information and reports. If the body submitting the statement considers that any part of the statement should be withheld from the patient on the ground that 'disclosure would adversely affect the health or welfare of the patient' such material must be set out in a separate document together with reasons why disclosure should not be made. Whilst the tribunal may withhold such information from a patient it must disclose this information to the patient's authorised representative. The tribunal has power to postpone consideration of an application if it considers that to do so will be in the interests of the patient. This power to postpone may not be exercised in respect of certain applications relating to:

(a) reclassification;
(b) renewal of detention or guardianship;
(c) restriction on discharge by a nearest relative;
(d) a change in the section under which the patient is detained.

6.5   The hearing

This will usually take place at the hospital in which the patient is accommodated. A tribunal will normally consist of three persons – a chairman who will be a lawyer, a medical member and a 'lay member' with 'such experience in administration, such knowledge of social services or other such other qualifications or experience as the Lord Chancellor considers suitable.' The 1983 Rules provide that the medical member must examine the patient in order to form an opinion upon the patient's medical condition. The examination may take place in private and the medical member is entitled to access to the patient's medical records. The medical member informs the tribunal of his medical opinion upon the patient's mental condition in private, and the patient or his representative have no right of access to this opinion under the 1983 Rules. The chairman will usually dictate the procedure to be followed at a hearing and the 1983 Rules give substantial freedom to tribunals to conduct their proceedings as they see fit.

Rule 13 Subject to the provisions of these Rules, the tribunal may give such directions as it thinks fit to ensure the speedy and just determination of the application.

Rule 22 (1) The tribunal may conduct the hearing in such manner as it considers most suitable bearing in mind the health and interests of the patient and it shall, so far as appears to it appropriate, seek to avoid formality in its proceedings.

(2) At any time before the application is determined, the tribunal or any one or more of its members may interview the patient, and shall interview him if he so requests and the interview may, and shall if the patient so requests, take place in the absence of any other person.

(3) At the beginning of the hearing the president shall explain the manner of proceeding which the tribunal proposes to adopt.

(4) Subject to Rule 21(4), any party and, with the permission of the tribunal, any other person, may appear at the hearing and take such part in the proceedings as the tribunal thinks proper; and the tribunal shall in particular hear and take evidence from the applicant, the patient (where he is not the applicant) and the responsible authority who may hear each other's evidence, put questions to each other, call witnesses and put questions to any witness or other person appearing before the tribunal.

(5) After all the evidence has been given, the applicant and (where he is not the applicant) the patient shall be given a further opportunity to address the tribunal.

Notwithstanding this freedom to fix its own procedures a tribunal must ensure that it reaches its decision in a fair manner and here the principles of 'natural justice' have some application to the procedure adopted by a tribunal. Although the expression 'natural justice' is vague, and has been described by one judge as 'sadly lacking in precision', it is possible to state briefly the principles which have direct relevance to tribunal hearings:

(a) No man may be a judge in his own cause;
(b) A tribunal must allow a fair hearing to all parties;
(c) Reasons for the tribunal's decision should be given.

Some of the matters covered by the principles of natural justice are also covered by the 1983 Rules. Where this occurs the 1983 Rules prevail. It is within the areas of discretion given by the 1983 Rules to the tribunal (eg Rule 22(1)) that the principles of natural justice may have an application. Particularly important is the principle that the parties must be given a fair hearing. Implicit in this are the following rights of a patient in proceedings before a tribunal:

(a) To know in advance of the hearing the case that will have to be answered;
(b) To present evidence at the hearing in support of his case for discharge, either personally or through his appointed representative;
(c) To challenge evidence presented at the hearing by the hospital,

again either personally or through his representative.

Some of these rights are provided for in the 1983 Rules but in a modified form, eg the right to know the hospital's case is covered by the hospital's duty to submit a statement (see para 6.4). The patient may be denied sight of the full statement; however the principles of natural justice require that the full statement should be disclosed to the patient's representative on condition that the representative does not reveal the 'confidential' parts to the patient. It seems that this is the usual practice and if it is not followed a patient may be able to challenge the tribunal's eventual decision on the ground of breach of natural justice. The principles that 'no man shall be a judge in his own cause' and that notice of the hearing must be given to the parties are covered by Rules 8 and 20 respectively:

Rule 8 (1) . . . the members of the tribunal who are to hear the application shall be appointed by the chairman.

(2) A person shall not be qualified to serve as a member of a tribunal for the purpose of any proceedings where—

(a) he is a member or officer of the responsible authority or registration authority concerned in the proceedings; or

(b) he is a member or officer of a health authority which has the right to discharge the patient under section 23(3) of the Act; or

(c) he has a personal connection with the patient or has recently treated the patient in a professional medical capacity.

This rule ensures that the tribunal is entirely unconnected with either the patient, the local social services authority (in guardianship proceedings) or the hospital or its health authority.

The 1983 Rules provide by Rule 20 that the tribunal must give all parties 14 days' notice of the date, time and place of the hearing (the parties may agree to a shorter period).

Hearings are required by the 1983 Rules to take place in private unless the patient requests a public hearing. This request may be refused by the tribunal on the grounds that a public hearing would be 'contrary to the interests of the patient.' If a public hearing is refused the reasons for the refusal must be recorded and could form a ground of appeal. Whilst it would not normally be expected that a patient would require a public hearing (and in practice they are rarely held) because of the personal nature of the matters which will be considered in the hearing, even in a public hearing no details of the proceedings may be revealed or published without the tribunal's permission. It is difficult to identify what advantages a public hearing would give a patient. The following quotation from the

MIND/LAG Guide *Representing the Mentally Ill and Handicapped* (1980), illustrates the issues involved:

> At a public hearing any person may attend the proceedings, including relatives, friends, observers, Members of Parliament, researchers and members of the press. Nevertheless, at both public and private hearings the tribunal is entitled to exclude from the entire proceedings any person it thinks fit . . .

> A hearing in public may provide the patient with added assurance that the proceedings are fairly conducted. Open proceedings will help to hold the tribunal publicly accountable in respect of its procedures and ultimate decision.

The tribunal is given a wide power to exclude any person including the patient from the hearing or any part of it:

Rule 21 (4) The tribunal may exclude from any hearing or part of a hearing any person or class of persons, other than a representative of the applicant or of the patient to whom documents would be disclosed in accordance with rule 12 (3), and in any case where the tribunal decides to exclude the applicant or the patient or their representatives or a representative of the responsible authority, it shall inform the person excluded of its reasons and record those reasons in writing.

This is another area of discretion of the tribunal to which the principles of natural justice apply as the Rule in question does not require the tribunal to apply any criteria in coming to a decision to exclude. All that must be done is that the tribunal must give reasons for its decision to exclude. The effect of this power to exclude is to override the patient's rights in Rule 22 (4) (see above).

This wide power to exclude, coupled with the freedom (subject to the principles of natural justice) to lay down the procedure which will be followed during a hearing makes for wide variations in practice between tribunals. As stated earlier the tendency is for the chairman to dictate the procedure which an individual tribunal will follow. It is possible for a tribunal to avoid its duty to 'hear and take evidence' from the patient and its duty to allow the patient to question the responsible authority's witnesses by excluding him from the hearing.

Finally the Rules permit the tribunal either to take evidence on oath, to subpoena witnesses to appear at the hearing or to produce documents. In practice evidence is not usually taken on oath and the Rules specifically allow this.

6.6   The decision

The powers of the tribunal are set out in section 72 of the Act:

Section 72 (1) Where an application is made to a Mental Health Review Tribunal by or in respect of a patient who is liable to be detained under this Act, the tribunal may in any case direct that the patient be discharged, and—

(a) the tribunal shall direct the discharge of a patient liable to be detained under section 2 above if they are satisfied—

(i) that he is not then suffering from mental disorder or from mental disorder of a nature or degree which warrants his detention in a hospital for assessment (or assessment fóllowed by medical treatment) for at least a limited period; or

(ii) that his detention as aforesaid is not justified in the interests of his own health or safety or with a view to the protection of other persons;

(b) the tribunal shall direct the discharge of a patient liable to be detained otherwise than under section 2 above if they are satisfied—

(i) that he is not then suffering from mental illness, psychopathic disorder, severe mental impairment or mental impairment or from any of those forms of disorder of a nature or degree which makes it appropriate for him to be liable to be detained in a hospital for medical treatment;

or

(ii) that it is not necessary for the health or safety of the patient or for the protection of other persons that he should receive such treatment; or

(iii) in the case of an application by virtue of paragraph (g) of section 66(1) above, that the patient, if released would not be likely to act in a manner dangerous to other persons or himself.

The tribunal has a discretionary power in any hearing to order the patient's discharge but it must order discharge if it is satisfied as to the matters set out in subsection (1). The criteria which the tribunal must apply are those in the relevant sections relating to the patient's admission to hospital, either for assessment or treatment. The effect of the tribunal hearing is, therefore, to review whether the patient's mental condition, at the time of the hearing, is such as to warrant his continued detention in hospital. The Act also requires the tribunal to have regard to further criteria when deciding whether or not the patient's detention should be continued:

Section 72 (2) In determining whether to direct the discharge of a patient detained otherwise than under section 2 above in a case not falling within paragraph (b) of subsection (1) above, the tribunal shall have regard—

(a) to the likelihood of medical treatment alleviating or preventing a deterioration of the patient's condition; and

(b) in the case of a patient suffering from mental illness or severe mental impairment, to the likelihood of the patient, if discharged, being able to care for himself, to obtain the care he needs or to guard himself against serious exploitation.

The criteria in this subsection only apply when the tribunal is considering the case of a patient detained for treatment. The criteria are the treatability test and, for mentally ill or severely mentally impaired patients only, how far the patient will be able to care for himself in the community.

Section 72 (3) A tribunal may under subsection (1) above direct the discharge of a patient on a future date specified in the direction; and where a tribunal do not direct the discharge of a patient under that subsection the tribunal may—
(a) with a view to facilitating his discharge on a future date, recommend that he be granted leave of absence or transferred to another hospital or into guardianship; and
(b) further consider his case in the event of any such recommendation not being complied with.

The tribunal is given three new powers:

(1) Following consideration of the patient's case under subsection (1) the tribunal may direct discharge at a future date so that preparations can be made for the patient's reception back into the community; or
(2) The tribunal may recommend an alternative placement for the patient, eg guardianship; or
(3) If the tribunal's recommendation is not acted upon then the tribunal may reconsider the patient's case.

It should be noted that the tribunal's power is to recommend and not to direct.

Section 72 (4) Where application is made to a Mental Health Review Tribunal by or in respect of a patient who is subject to guardianship under this Act, the tribunal may in any case direct that the patient be discharged, and shall so direct if they are satisfied—
(a) that he is not suffering from mental illness, psychopathic disorder, severe mental impairment or mental impairment; and
(b) that it is not necessary in the interests of the welfare of the patient, or for the protection of other persons, that the patient should remain under such guardianship.

The criteria which a tribunal must apply in considering an application from a patient under guardianship are exactly the same as the grounds for receiving patients into guardianship in section 7 of the Act (see para 3.2 above).

> **Section 72** (5) Where application is made to a Mental Health Review Tribunal under any provision of this Act by or in respect of a patient and the tribunal do not direct that the patient be discharged, the tribunal may, if satisfied that the patient is suffering from a form of mental disorder other than the form specified in the application, order or direction relating to him, direct that that application, order or direction be amended by subsituting for the form of mental disorder specified in it such other form of mental disorder as appears to the tribunal to be appropriate.

This gives the tribunal power to reclassify the patient.

Communication of the decision

The written decision must be sent to to all the parties, and in the case of a restricted patient, to the Home Secretary. This must happen within seven days of the hearing. The tribunal is given discretion, under the 1983 Rules, as to how it communicates its decision to a patient 'if it considers that the full disclosure of the recorded reasons for its decision to the patient . . . would adversely affect the health or welfare of the patient or others . . .' In other words it can withhold parts of its decision from the patient. This does not authorise withholding parts of the decision from the patient's representative who should be given a copy of the full decision with the reasons upon which it is based.

6.7   The role of the social worker in the tribunal setting

The 1983 Rules contain no reference to social workers (whether approved or otherwise). They are not required to submit reports or give evidence in a tribunal hearing. Does this mean that they have no role in tribunal proceedings? In fact social workers can be involved in tribunals in three different ways:

(a) as hospital social workers;
(b) as approved social workers;
(c) as 'independent social workers'.

6.7.1   Hospital social workers

By this term we mean social workers employed by local social services authorities but based in hospitals. They may or may not be approved social workers.

The Rules require the hospital to submit three reports, one of which is:

an up-to-date social circumstances report prepared for the tribunal including reports on the following:

(a) the patient's home and family circumstances, including the attitude of the patient's nearest relative or the person so acting;

(b) the opportunities for employment or occupation and the housing facilities which would be available to the patient if discharged;

(c) the availability of community support and relevant medical facilities;

(d) the financial circumstances of the patient.

The reports form part of the statement which the hospital must submit within three or six weeks of notice of the application to the tribunal. In practice this report is prepared by the hospital based social worker whose client the patient is.

The importance of this report in the tribunal proceedings cannot be overemphasised. It indicates to the tribunal what possibility there is of the patient successfully caring for himself in the community, and could, in borderline cases, persuade the tribunal to discharge a patient if satisfied that the community support will be sufficient to meet his needs. The problem for hospital social workers in preparing such reports is to preserve their objectivity. The MIND/ LAG Guide referred to earlier (para 6.5) describes the problems in the following terms:

In practice after-care reports are variable in quality. Some reports give no information and some merely state that 'no facilities are available'. This may be attributable to the fact that the report is prepared by a member of the therapeutic team which is opposing discharge. It is sometimes the view of the team that it is not their responsibility to examine rehabilitative programmes and community alternatives until they have decided that discharge is appropriate. Their bias is unlikely to be conducive to a positive and comprehensive report of available facilities or even an active attempt to investigate the alternatives.

Whilst this criticism may be true of individual hospital social workers, as a general comment on their professional independence it is unfair. The hospital social worker's position is quite exceptional within the social services department – he is employed by the local authority but working within a health service establishment. This gives hospital social workers an opportunity to form an independent view upon the best placement in which to treat patients. They have direct access to patients in hospital wards, to the doctors treating those patients and to the community based services provided by their employing authorities. The role of hospital social workers in tribunal proceedings is to ensure that the tribunal is made fully aware of what will happen to the patient if he is discharged. To do this they must investigate all possible alternative placements and form an independent professional opinion upon the ability of the patient to care for himself outside hospital, taking into account what support can, and will, be offered by the local authority. This opinion should then be incorporated within the social circumstances report submitted as part of the statement.

6.7.2 The approved social worker's role

Whilst the hospital social workers will usually provide the social circumstances report which forms part of the hospital's statement they are unlikely to be called as witnesses in the tribunal proceedings unless their presence is requested by the tribunal or the patient to clarify any matters in that report, which the hospital representative is unable to deal with. Because of their involvement in the hospital's case it is unlikely that hospital social workers will be called as witnesses on behalf of the patient but this could happen in the case of a field based approved social worker who has retained contact with the patient and/or his family since the patient's admission to hospital. The approved social worker may also be asked to give evidence on behalf of the patient if he is, or has been, responsible for supervision of the patient during leave of absence. The tribunal has power to subpoena witnesses although this is rarely used. It is more usual for the tribunal to use its power under Rule 15 to 'call for such further information or reports as it may think desirable, and may give directions as to the manner in which and the persons by whom such material is to be furnished.' The approved social worker's role here may be as a witness as to factual information within his direct personal knowledge concerning the patient and/or his family circumstances, or, as an expert witness to give his professional opinion upon the patient's ability to care for himself outside of hospital and upon the local authority and family support the patient can expect to receive. It is in carrying out the 'expert witness' role that some guidance can be given to approved social workers faced with this task.

It is interesting to note that although the approved social worker's role in arranging for a patient's admission to hospital is defined quite clearly in the Act and was the subject of extensive discussion during the Parliamentary debates on the 1982 Amendment Bill, no attention was focussed on whether the approved social worker should have a role in arranging for the patient's discharge from hospital. The 1983 Act, and the majority of commentators upon the legislation, seem to have accepted the implication that the approved worker's role ends at the hospital door and may or may not be resumed, once the decision has been made on medical grounds, to discharge the patient from hospital. But in practice this is not the case – two situations where the approved social worker will, in practice, retain involvement with the patient's case, either through contact with the patient himself or his family, have been identified earlier (at para 4.1). The argument can therefore be put forward that the approved social worker's role as an expert witness in tribunal proceedings is to ensure that the case for discharge of the patient is clearly presented to the tribunal. Just as the approved social worker's statutory role under section 13 (see para 2.8.7 above) involves him in challenging any assumption that hospital is the only place in which an individual patient can receive the treatment he requires, so his role as a witness in tribunal proceedings requires him to challenge any assumption that the patient must remain in hospital because, in the opinion of the hospital, that is the only place where he can continue to receive his treatment. The approved social worker must be able to give full information to the tribunal upon the range of support services which can be made available to the patient if he is discharged. This information must include full details of services available from all local authority departments, particularly housing, and from voluntary organisations within the area the patient will be discharged to. The role also requires the approved social worker to negotiate with other local authority departments and the DHSS to ensure that the patient receives all services and benefits to which he is entitled. It is also a role that could not reasonably be expected of a hospital based social worker.

6.7.3   The role of the independent social worker

The growing use of so-called independent social workers in child care proceedings can probably be traced back to the making available of legal aid funds to pay their fees and expenses. The introduction of legal aid for patients applying for discharge to tribunals can be expected to produce a similar development in tribunal proceedings. What will be the independent social worker's role, and how will it differ from that described above for the approved social worker?

The first point to make is that the description 'independent' is misleading as the social worker will be called, and paid, by the patient, or the legal aid fund on the patient's behalf. To quote the MIND/LAG Guide:

> The independent social worker's principal responsibility is to the patient and his representative. In this capacity the social worker must not be compromised by conflicting interests between agency function and responsibility and his client's interests . . .

> The independent social worker must, through exhaustive enquiries, aim to eliminate every impediment to the patient's discharge, so that the tribunal's conclusions and recommendations are influenced primarily by consideration of the patient's mental state and behaviour and not by the lack of suitable accommodation or occupation.

Whilst agreeing with the first quotation we have reservations about the second. It seems to imply that the independent social worker should attempt to divert the tribunal from considering what facilities are available to support the patient in the community. This does not appear to be a very professional attitude to adopt – it suggests that the tribunal should be persuaded to discharge at all costs and ignore the consequences for the patient if there are, in fact, no or insufficient community resources available to support him outside the hospital. It also ignores the statutory duty of the tribunal in section 72 (2)(b) concerning mentally ill or severely mentally impaired patients, namely, to have regard 'to the likelihood of the patient, if discharged, being able to care for himself, to obtain the care he needs or to guard himself against serious exploitation.'

The purpose of the independent social worker in tribunal proceedings must be to provide the tribunal with an alternative view upon the question, 'Can the patient be discharged into the community, and if so, are there sufficient community based services to enable him to live a relatively independent existence?' This view will be an alternative to that of the hospital which by refusing to discharge the patient is arguing that his treatment can only be given in a hospital.

It is not for the independent social worker to comment upon the medical issues involved in the patient's mental condition – if independent opinion on these matters is required then an independent psychiatric report should be obtained on behalf of the patient and this may also be funded through legal aid.

It will be seen from the above that the independent social worker's role differs little from that of the approved social worker giving evidence on behalf of his client, the patient. Both are submitting their expert opinion upon the most appropriate placement for the patient.

6.8   Conclusion

At the beginning of this Part, seven criticisms of tribunals and their proceedings were listed. Only three have been resolved and the revised procedures of tribunals still leave the patient at a disadvantage in seeking to challenge the hospital's case against his discharge. These procedures are, in several instances, contrary to the principles of natural justice and therefore unfair, a particular example being the tribunal's power to withhold parts of the hospital's case from the patient.

A further concern lies in the absence of any procedure by which the tribunal can obtain a truly independent report upon the social aspects of the patient's case. The parallel with child care proceedings is obvious; here a procedure for independent representation of the child has eventually been implemented.

For a case study relating of this Part, see para **11.2.6** *in Part 11 following.*

7 The offender patient

7.1 Introduction

> According to a press report, Lord Lane, the Lord Chief Justice observed
> in relation to a mentally sick person who came before him:
> 'We are forced to do what we know to be wrong, put her in prison,
> because not enough hospitals are available. We see this type of case every
> week and nobody has done anything about it'. (Baroness Fisher, 'Lords,
> 1 December 1981.)

This, not untypical, statement by a judge reflected a growing
concern that the system of hospital orders for offender patients was
not working either for the benefit of the patient or the community as
a whole. Ordinary psychiatric hospitals in the 1960s and early 1970s
were becoming increasingly reluctant to admit patients who were
either untreatable or unmanageable in the absence of specialist
staff, and the special hospitals were thus filled to capacity. Two
reports were commissioned: 'Report on the Review of the
Procedures for the Discharge and Supervision of Psychiatric
Patients subject to Special Restrictions' (The Aarvold Committee)
and the 'Report of the Committee on Mentally Abnormal
Offenders' (The Butler Committee). The 1983 Act contains some
but not all of the recommendations made by these Committees, but
the major problem of the availability of hospital beds is likely to
continue to cause difficulty, unless sufficient secure unit
accommodation is made available. Strong pressure brought to bear
for the inclusion of an amendment in the Bill to oblige Regional
Health Authorities to supply beds was resisted by the Government
and replaced by the less onerous provisions of section 39:

Section 39 (1) Where a court is minded to make a hospital order or
interim hospital order in respect of any person it may request—

(a) the Regional Health Authority for the region in which that person resides or last resided; or

(b) any other Regional Health Authority that appears to the court to be appropriate,

to furnish the court with such information as that Authority has or can reasonably obtain with respect to the hospital or hospitals (if any) in its region or elsewhere at which arrangements could be made for the admission of that person in pursuance of the order, and that Authority shall comply with any such request.

This duty, which presumably will be delegated to District Health Authorities, is not a duty to supply a bed but to supply a report about the availability of beds. However it will mean that the court is provided with up-to-date information which may lead to a reduction in delays, and a spokesman for the Health Authority could well be required to justify a decision not to admit an offender to hospital.

7.2   Remands to hospital

7.2.1   For Report.

One of the difficulties experienced by the courts under the 1959 Act was that reports on an accused's mental condition could only be obtained whilst the patient was remanded in custody or on bail. The accused could only be placed in a hospital (as opposed to a prison) if this was made a condition of bail. The problem was that the hospital had no power to detain the accused if he should decide to break a condition of his bail. Section 35 of the 1983 Act adopts the recommendation of the Butler Committee that courts should have the option of remanding the accused to hospital so that a report can be prepared on his mental condition. Section 35 did not come into force on 30 September 1983 but is scheduled to come into force on 1 October 1984.

This implementation date is sooner than was expected – some commentators expected that as the provisions 'have significant resource implications' they were unlikely to come into force for two to three years.

7.2.2   Section 35 (1) Subject to the provisions of this section, the Crown Court or a magistrates' court may remand an accused person to a hospital specified by the court for a report on his mental condition.

(2) For the purposes of this section an accused person is—

(a) in relation to the Crown Court any person who is awaiting trial

167

before the Court for an offence punishable with imprisonment or who has been arraigned before the court for such an offence and has not yet been sentenced or otherwise dealt with for the offence on which he has been arraigned;

(b) in relation to a magistrates' court, any person who has been convicted by the court of an offence punishable on summary conviction with imprisonment and any person charged with such an offence if the court is satisfied that he did act or made the omission charged or he has consented to the exercise by the court of the powers conferred by this section.

This is a new power. Note that the magistrates' court's power is exercisable without the need to convict the accused and also if the accused consents.

7.2.3   When can an order under section 35 be made?

Section 35 (3) Subject to subsection (4) below, the powers conferred by this section may be exercised if—

(a) the court is satisfied, on the written or oral evidence of a registered medical practitioner, that there is reason to suspect that the accused is suffering from mental illness, psychopathic disorder, severe mental impairment or mental impairment; and

(b) the court is of the opinion that it would be impracticable for a report on his mental condition to be made if he were remanded on bail;

but those powers shall not be exercised by the Crown Court in respect of a person who has been convicted before the court if the sentence for the offence of which he has been convicted is fixed by law.

(4) The court shall not remand an accused person to a hospital under this section unless satisfied, on the written or oral evidence of the registered medical practitioner who would be responsible for making the report or some other person representing the managers of the hospital, that arrangements have been made for his admission to that hospital and for his admission to it within the period of 7 days beginning with the date of remand: and if the court is so satisfied it may, pending his admission, give directions for his conveyance to and detention in a place of safety.

(5) Where a court has remanded an accused person under this section it may further remand him if it appears to the court, on the written or oral evidence of the registered medical practitioner responsible for making the report, that a further remand is necessary for completing the assessment of the accused's mental condition.

The following points should be noted:

(a) evidence from a single doctor is sufficient

(b) remand on bail must be considered impractical by the court
(c) the wider definition of mental disorder which includes any other disorder or disability of mind is not included in the list of disorders
(d) the power cannot be used where a person has been convicted (as opposed to charged with) murder
(e) the person remanded cannot be given treatment without his consent
(f) the court must be satisfied that the hospital will take the accused within seven days.

7.2.4 How long can the order last?

Remands are made for periods of up to 28 days. They can be extended for further 28 day periods up to a maximum of 12 weeks if the doctor responsible for making the report gives oral evidence to the court that further time is needed to complete the report.

7.2.5 Rights of accused persons whilst remanded for report

The position of accused persons remanded under section 35 is unsatisfactory in several aspects because they do not benefit from many of the safeguards in the Act which apply to the majority of detained patients. The consent to treatment provisions do not apply to them. Nor have they any right to apply to a Mental Health Review Tribunal for discharge yet they can be remanded for up to 12 weeks. Compare this with the position of patients detained in hospital for assessment under section 2 of the Act who do have a right to apply to a tribunal and whose maximum period of detention is 28 days. A remand can be renewed on two occasions without the accused being present in court provided he is legally represented and his representative is given an opportunity to speak on his behalf. It is to be hoped that this power will only be used in cases where the accused is genuinely unfit to take part in the proceedings and will not become an automatic procedure to suit the administrative practice of hospitals and courts. Section 35 gives the hospital power to detain accused persons on remand therefore they are liable to restriction upon and interference with their correspondence, provisions which are described elsewhere (para 4.3). Two further consequences of their detention are that:

(a) persons remanded for report are entitled to be given the information hospitals are required to give patients under section 132 (see para 4.1.2) and

(b) if persons remanded for reports abscond they are liable to arrest and to be brought back before the court which remanded them. In such circumstances the court can terminate the remand and deal with the accused 'in any way in which it could have dealt with him if he had not been remanded'.

Finally the accused is given the right to obtain an independent medical report upon his mental condition and use it to support an application to terminate his remand. This right was grudgingly conceded by the Government during the 1982 Amendment Bill's passage through Parliament. It was not in the original Bill, because, the Government argued, the right existed without the need for express provision. The unfairness lies in the requirement that the report must be obtained at the accused's own expense. A patient applying to a Mental Health Review Tribunal may obtain similar report at the expense of the legal aid fund now that legal aid is available in tribunal proceedings.

7.2.6 For treatment

Section 36 (1) Subject to the provisions of this section, the Crown Court may, instead of remanding an accused person in custody, remand him to a hospital specified by the court if satisfied, on the written or oral evidence of two registered medical practitioners, that he is suffering from mental illness or severe mental impairment of a nature or degree which makes it appropriate for him to be detained in hospital for medical treatment.

Here is another new power for courts dealing with mentally disordered offenders. It also did not come into force on 30 September 1983 but is scheduled for 1 October 1984. It allows an accused to be remanded for treatment, is only available to the Crown Court and provides an alternative to section 48 (transfer directions) (see para 7.5.6 following).

7.2.7 When can an order be made?

The circumstances are set out in section 36(2) and (3):

Section 36 (2) For the purposes of this section an accused person is any person who is in custody awaiting trial before the Crown Court for an offence punishable with imprisonment (other than an offence the sentence for which is fixed by law) or who at any time before sentence is in custody in the course of a trial before that court for such an offence.

(3) The court shall not remand an accused person under this section to a hospital unless it is satisfied, on the written or oral evidence of a

registered medical practitioner who would be in charge of his treatment or of some other person representing the managers of the hospital, that arrangements have been made for his admission to that hospital and for his admission to it within the period of 7 days beginning with the date of the remand; and if the court is so satisfied it may, pending his admission, give directions for his conveyance to and detention in a place of safety.

Note the following points:

(a) the order cannot be made where the charge is murder
(b) the opinions of two doctors are required
(c) the diagnosis must be mental illness or severe mental impairment
(d) a hospital bed must be available within seven days
(e) 'place of safety' means, unless the accused is a child, an hospital willing to receive the accused temporarily, police station, prison or remand centre. If the accused is a child the definition of place of safety in child care legislation applies.

7.2.8   How long can the order last?

Section 36 (6) An accused person shall not be remanded or further remanded under this section for more than 28 days at a time or for more than 12 weeks in all; and the court may at any time terminate the remand if it appears to the court that it is appropriate to do so.

7.2.9   What are the accused's rights?

As with remands for reports the accused may be re-remanded in his absence provided he is represented in court. He has no right to apply to a Mental Health Review Tribunal but the consent to treatment provisions do apply to him and he may apply to the court for his remand to be terminated based upon an independent medical report which he must pay for.

7.3   Hospital and guardianship orders

7.3.1   The powers of the Crown Court and magistrates' courts to make hospital and guardianship orders are not new; they were contained in section 60 of the 1959 Act. Changes have been made to the grounds for making these orders to bring them into line with the new civil provisions of the 1983 Act, eg the grounds refer to the new definition of mental disorder and the treatability test has been introduced. Because they are not new powers they *did* come into force on 30 September 1983. Unfortunately the old problems of lack of hospital places and community provision for offenders have not been attacked in the Act. This is disappointing but not surprising given central government's failure to accept that the objectives of the Act will not be achieved without the commitment of substantial resources for the care and treatment of the mentally disordered.

7.3.2   Section 37 (1) Where a person is convicted before the Crown Court of an offence punishable with imprisonment other than an offence the sentence for which is fixed by law, or is convicted by a magistrates' court of an offence punishable on summary conviction with imprisonment, and the conditions mentioned in subsection (2) below are satisfied, the court may by order authorise his admission to and detention in such hospital as may be specified in the order or, as the case may be, place him under the guardianship of a local social services authority or of such other person approved by the local services authority as may be so specified.

A court can only make orders under this section (described as hospital orders or guardianship orders) if the offender has been found guilty of an imprisonable offence and the sentence is not fixed by law (eg murder). Once a hospital or guardianship order has been made the civil detention provisions apply and the criminal court loses control over the offender's care and treatment.

7.3.3   When can an order be made?

Section 37 (2) The conditions referred to in subsection (1) above are that:
   (a) the court is satisfied, on the written or oral evidence of two registered medical practitioners, that the offender is suffering from mental illness, psychopathic disorder, severe mental impairment or mental impairment and that either—
   (i) the mental disorder from which the offender is suffering is of a nature or degree which makes it appropriate for him to be detained in a hospital for medical treatment and, in the case of psychopathic disorder or mental impairment, that such treatment is likely to alleviate or prevent a deterioration of his condition; or
   (ii) in the case of an offender who has reached the age of 16 years, the mental disorder is of a nature or degree which warrants his reception into guardianship under this Act; and
   (b) the court is of the opinion, having regard to all the circumstances including the nature of the offence and the character and antecedents of the offender, and to the other available methods of dealing with him, that the most suitable method of disposing of the case is by means of an order under this section.

The main points to note are:

(a) two doctors' reports are required;
(b) the categories of mental disorder coincide with those in section 1

of the 1983 Act and the treatability test is applied in cases of psychopathy and mental impairment;

(c) a hospital or guardianship order must be the most suitable way to deal with the offender;

(d) juvenile courts can make hospital orders in proceedings under the Children and Young Persons Act 1969, and guardianship orders if the child is over 16;

(e) the magistrates' court can make hospital and guardianship orders without convicting the offender;

(f) hospital orders can only be made if the court is notified by the hospital that a place will be available for the offender within 28 days. During that 28-day period the offender can be kept in a place of safety as defined above (see para 7.2.7);

(g) the Home Secretary has power to direct that the offender is to be placed in another hospital if an emergency arises during the 28-day period.

7.3.4 Guardianship orders

Section 37 (6) An order placing an offender under the guardianship of a local social services authority or of any other person (in this Act referred to as 'a guardianship order') shall not be made . . . unless the court is satisfied that that authority or person is willing to receive the offender into guardianship.

Unlike the provisions relating to hospital orders there is no specific requirement for the court proposing to place an offender under guardianship to hear evidence that the proposed guardian is willing to receive the offender into guardianship. In practice the court will expect to be addressed by a representative of the local social services authority (or the proposed private guardian) on this point and in the case of local social services authorities this duty will normally fall upon their approved social workers.

7.3.5 Interim hospital orders

The Butler Committee recognised the difficulties experienced by doctors in recommending full hospital orders on the basis of a brief examination in a prison hospital. More time was required before recommending such a major step. The solution is in section 38, a new section which is not in force at the time of writing. In essence, where a person has been convicted by a Crown Court or a magistrates' court of an imprisonable offence the court may make an interim hospital order for a maximum period of sixth months.

Before making the order the court must hear written or oral evidence from two doctors to the effect:

(a) that the offender is suffering from mental illness, psychopathic disorder, severe mental impairment or mental impairment; and

(b) that there is reason to suppose that the mental disorder from which the offender is suffering is such that it may be appropriate for a hospital order to be made in his case

and the object of the procedure is to help the court to decide whether or not it should eventually make a full hospital order. The offender may be treated during the interim hospital order and the consent to treatment provisions apply to such treatment. The possibility of a prison sentence following treatment under the interim order will arise again if the treatment is successful.

7.4 The effect of hospital, interim hospital and guardianship orders

7.4.1 Section 40 (1) A hospital order shall be sufficient authority—

(a) for a constable, an approved social worker or any other person directed to do so by the court to convey the patient to the hospital specified in the order within a period of 28 days; and

(b) for the managers of the hospital to admit him at any time within that period and thereafter detain him in accordance with the provisions of this Act.

(2) A guardianship order shall confer on the authority or person named in the order as guardian the same powers as a guardianship application made and accepted under Part II of this Act.

(3) Where an interim hopsital order is made in respect of an offender—

(a) a constable or any other person directed to do so by the court shall convey the offender to the hospital specified in the order within the period mentioned in section 38(4) above; and

(b) the managers of the hospital staff shall admit him within that period and thereafter detain him in accordance with the provisions of section 38 above.

(4) A patient who is admitted to a hospital in pursuance of a hospital order, or placed under guardianship order, shall, subject to the provisions of this subsection, be treated for the purposes of the provisions of this Act mentioned in Part I of Schedule 1 to this Act as if he had been so admitted or placed on the date of the order in pursuance of an application for admission for treatment or a guardianship application, as the case may be, duly made under Part II of this Act, but subject to any modifications of those provisions specified in that Part of that Schedule.

7.4.2   The effect of this section is to place offenders in the same position as civil patients so far as possible. This means that, amongst other things, the consent to treatment provisions (see para 4.2) apply to them and that their periods of detention are controlled not by the sentencing courts but by the responsible medical officer and Mental Health Review Tribunals, subject to the provisions referred to later in para 7.6.

7.5   Restriction orders

7.5.1   One of the greatest areas of controversy created by the 1959 Act arose from the restrictions on discharge of certain categories of offenders. The attempt to provide a balance between the offender and the non-offender by creating parallel powers to review the cases of both categories of patients clearly failed when the restriction order was imposed on an offender.

7.5.2   Uppermost in the minds of MPs during the debates upon the criminal provisions in the 1982 Amendment Bill was the case of *X v United Kingdom,* a case which came before the European Court in Strasbourg in June 1981. X spent two-and-a-half years in Broadmoor, having been convicted of a serious attack on a fellow employee before being conditionally discharged in 1971. After three years living in the community with no apparent difficulty he was recalled in April 1974 following reports that his mental condition had deteriorated. It later transpired that these 'reports' consisted of information X's wife had passed on to his supervisor when announcing her intention of leaving him.

Having failed to secure his release from hospital by an application for habeas corpus, he instituted proceedings in Strasbourg. The European Court concluded that X's recall to hospital as a person of unsound mind was lawful under the relevant provisions of the European Convention on Human Rights, but the Court upheld his claim that he was entitled to a judicial review of the substantive grounds of his detention under Article 5(4) of the Convention:

> Everyone who is deprived of his liberty by arrest or detention shall be entitled to take proceedings by which the lawfulness of his detention shall be decided speedily by a court and his release ordered if the detention is not lawful.

Habeas corpus proceedings were unsuccessful as he had been unable to show that the Home Secretary had acted either unreasonably or outside of his powers. His right to apply to a tribunal for review did not arise under section 66(8) of the 1959 Act until he had been back in Broadmoor for 6 months, and in fact a hearing did not take place until the time that his legal representatives learned of the 'reason' for his recall. The tribunal recommended conditional discharge, but this was not granted until July 1976, although he was granted leave in February.

In the view of the European Court, the continued 'lawfulness' of the detention of anyone held on the ground of mental disorder must depend upon the continuation of a degree of mental disorder justifying that detention; and since the extent of mental disorder may change over time, there has to be a mechanism for periodic independent review. Habeas corpus was concerned entirely with whether the procedures laid down for detaining persons were properly complied with and not with whether or not the grounds for detention existed. In short, the mechanisms for periodic independent review of the cases of restricted offenders were inadequate, particularly where the period of detention was of unlimited duration.

7.5.3 The new law

Section 41 (1) Where a hospital order is made in respect of an offender by the Crown Court, and it appears to the court having regard to the nature of the offence, the antecedents of the offender and the risk of his committing further offences if set at large, that it is necessary for the protection of the public from serious harm so to do, the court may, subject to the provisions of this section, further order that the offender shall be subject to the special restrictions set out in this section, either without limit of time or during such period as may be specified in the order; and an order under this section shall be known as ' a restriction order'.

(2) A restriction order shall not be made in the case of any person unless at least one of the registered medical practitioners whose evidence is taken into account by the court under section 37(2)(a) above has given evidence orally before the court.

7.5.4 The following points should be noted:

(a) A restriction order can only be made when a hospital order is made.
(b) The power is only available to the Crown Court.
(c) A restriction order can only be made to protect the public from serious harm. In deciding this the Crown Court must take into

account the offender's past criminal record and the risk of further offences. The phrase 'serious harm' was inserted to meet a recommendation of the Butler Committee and to prevent the repetition of a case in 1976 where a restriction order was made upon a woman who had been convicted of damaging two window-panes in a telephone kiosk. There was no evidence that she was liable to be violent.

(d) The order may be for a specified period or without limit of time.
(e) One of the doctors giving evidence must appear in court.

7.5.5 Effect of a restriction order

If the Crown Court makes a restriction order then some of the rights the offender would have under an unrestricted hospital order are qualified in the following ways:

(a) The hospital does not have to carry out the automatic periodic review of his detention under section 20.
(b) A Mental Health Review Tribunal cannot order his discharge without the Home Secretary's permission.
(c) Transfers and leave of absence need the Home Secretary's permission.
(d) As long as the restriction order is in force the offender remains liable to detention whereas under unrestricted hospital orders offenders can only be recalled within six months of leave of absence being given.

In summary the Home Office retains control over discharge of restricted offenders although in response to a recommendation of the Butler Committee the Act does require that the responsible medical officer must review the restricted offender's case at least once a year.

Once the Crown Court has made a restriction order it loses all control over the offender's placement and discharge. This control lies primarily with the Home Secretary who can order the offender's discharge as soon as he feels that it is no longer necessary to detain the offender to protect the public from serious harm. The Home Secretary can order a restricted patient's discharge absolutely or on conditions. Under a conditional discharge a patient is liable to recall at any time and is usually subject to supervision in the community by a probation officer or a social worker. The major reform in relation to restriction orders is that the patient can, for the first time, apply to a Mental Health Review Tribunal for a conditional discharge to be made absolute (see paragraph 7.6 following).

Although restriction orders can only be made by the Crown Court a magistrates' court may commit an offender over 14 to the Crown Court for it to consider how to deal with the offender. The magistrates' court must have convicted the offender for this procedure to operate. The Act also lays down how convicted offenders may be accommodated whilst awaiting sentence by the Crown Court. The magistrates' court may direct the offender's detention in any hospital ready to admit him. This will normally be the local receiving hospital for a particular magistrates' court which takes offenders who are sentenced to an unrestricted hospital order. If a hospital does accept the offender it becomes liable to ensure his attendance at the Crown Court and to provide fresh medical reports for the Crown Court when it sentences the offender. The Crown Court can make a hospital order (restricted or unrestricted) in the absence of the offender if he is unfit to appear but before doing so it must hear oral evidence from two doctors that he is suffering from mental illness or severe mental impairment of a nature or degree making it appropriate for him to be detained in a hospital for treatment.

7.5.6 Transfers from prison to hospital

The 1983 Act gives the Home Secretary power to transfer prisoners suffering from mental disorder from prison to hospital under Transfer Directions. Medical reports are required stating that the prisoner is suffering from one of the four categories of mental disorder and that it warrants the prisoner's detention in hospital. The treatability test must be satisfied if the prisoner is suffering from psychopathic disorder or mental impairment.

Transfer directions last for 14 days and are usually issued where the prisoner's need for treatment is urgent.

· 7.6   Tribunal rights for offenders

7.6.1   Powers to discharge restricted patients

Section 73 (1) Where an application to a Mental Health Review Tribunal is made by a restricted patient who is subject to a restriction order, or where the case of such a patient is referred to such a tribunal, the tribunal shall direct the absolute discharge of the patient if satisfied—
   (a) as to the matters mentioned in paragraph (b)(i) or (ii) of section 72(1) above; and

(b) that it is not appropriate for the patient to remain liable to be recalled to hospital for further treatment.

(2) Where in the case of any such patient as is mentioned in subsection (1) above the tribunal are satisfied as to the matters referred to in paragraph (a) of that subsection but not as to the matter referred to in paragraph (b) of that subsection the tribunal shall direct the conditional discharge of the patient.

(3) Where the patient is absolutely discharged under this section he shall thereupon cease to be liable to be detained by virtue of the relevant hospital order, and the restriction order shall cease to have effect accordingly.

Thus a restricted patient can apply to a Mental Health Review Tribunal for discharge and if the tribunal is satisfied that he is not suffering from one of the four categories of mental disorder warranting his detention in hospital or that detention is not necessary to protect the patient or others the tribunal must order the patient's discharge unless it thinks a conditional discharge is called for.

If the tribunal grants a conditional discharge the patient will be liable to recall by the Home Secretary and he must comply with any conditions imposed by the tribunal at the time of discharge or later by the Home Secretary. The tribunal can defer a conditional discharge until it is satisfied that any arrangements it considers necessary to supervise the patient have been made. Special provision is made where a patient under a Transfer Direction applies to a tribunal for his discharge. If the tribunal decides that the patient no longer needs treatment it cannot order his discharge – the patient then becomes liable to resume his prison sentence or to stand trial. The tribunal has several choices – it can inform the Home Secretary that the patient could be absolutely or conditionally discharged or if this is not appropriate it can recommend that the patient continues to be treated in hospital. If the patient who applies to the tribunal is on remand the Home Secretary must transfer the patient back to prison unless the tribunal recommends that he continues to receive treatment in hospital.

7.6.2 When may an offender patient apply to a Mental Health Review Tribunal?

Section 69 (1) Without prejudice to any provision of section 66(1) above as applied by section 40 (4) above, an application to a Mental Health Review Tribunal may also be made—

(a) in respect of a patient admitted to a hospital in pursuance of a hospital order, by the nearest relative of the patient in the period between the expiration of 6 months and the expiration of 12 months beginning with the date of the order and in any subsequent period of 12 months; and

(b) in respect of a patient placed under guardianship by a guardianship order—

(i) by the patient, within a period of six months beginning with the date of the order;

(ii) by the nearest relative of the patient, within the period of 12 months beginning with the date of the order and in any subsequent period of 12 months.

This rather complicated section gives the nearest relative a right to apply in respect of a patient subject to a hospital or guardianship order but not in the first six months of a hospital order. This is a change from the 1959 Act under which the nearest relative could apply during the first six months of a hospital order. It should be remembered that a patient also cannot apply for discharge during the first six months of a hospital order. The reason for this restriction is given in the Explanatory Memorandum as: 'because their case will have been examined at the outset by a court which must have considered medical evidence from two registered medical practitioners.' Apart from this difference the rights of patients subject to hospital orders now run parallel to the rights of civil patients and represent an attempt to remedy the defect in the old law identified in *X v United Kingdom* bearing in mind that under the 1959 Act the Mental Health Review Tribunal's powers were only advisory in relation to restricted patients. The nearest relative's right to apply in respect of a patient under a guardianship order can be exercised at any time during the first 12 months of the guardianship and then annually.

7.6.3 **Section 70** A patient who is a restricted patient within the meaning of section 79 below and is detained in a hospital may apply to a Mental Health Review Tribunal—

(a) in the period between the expiration of 6 months and the expiration of 12 months beginning with the date of the relevant hospital order or transfer direction; and

(b) in any subsequent period of 12 months.

Again, put simply a restricted patient can apply betweeen six and 12 months from the making of the restriction order and then once a year. The definition of a restricted patient holds no surprises – it means a patient who 'is subject to a restriction order or restriction direction'.

For completeness it is necessary to look briefly at a set of provisions which create parallels to the automatic referral procedures introduced by the 1983 Act for non-offender patients. The provisions may be summarised as follows:

(a) The Home Secretary is given a discretion to refer a restricted patient's case to a tribunal at any time.
(b) The Home Secretary *must* refer a restricted patient's case to a tribunal if it has not been considered by a tribunal for three years.
(c) If a person who has been made subject to an order under the Criminal Procedure (Insanity) Act 1964 does not apply to a tribunal within six months of the order the Home Secretary must refer his case to a tribunal. Under that Act a court must make a hospital order if an offender has been found guilty by reason of insanity.

8 The Mental Health Act Commission

8.1 Introduction

> I have very mixed feelings about the Commission, because I am not sure
> whether it is supposed to be acting as a policeman in the mental hospital,
> seeing that the law is upheld and protecting the patients' interests or
> whether it will be judge and jury and brought into play if the law is
> broken (Baroness Fisher, Lords, December 1981.)

Examples of the role of the new Mental Health Act Commission
have already been provided in relation to the consent to treatment
provisions and other rights of the patient compulsorily detained in a
hospital. It is our intention at this point to provide a clearer identity
and focus for the Commission and some of the background to its
creation:

> There is a strong case for an appointed body to inspect and monitor
> closed institutions such as Rampton and other special hospitals, or
> indeed wherever patients are subject to detention under the Mental
> Health Act. The exact powers and functions of such a body would be for
> further consideration, but we think it might be constituted on the lines of
> the old Board of Control or the Scottish Mental Welfare Commission. Its
> functions might include the review of patient care and treatment, the
> independent investigation of more serious complaints (from whatever
> source) and a general protective function on behalf of detained patients
> which need not necessarily cut across the functions of Mental Health
> Review Tribunals. Such a protective function might include some
> responsibilities in connection with the difficult problem of consent to
> treatment in respect of detained patients. (Report of Rampton Hospital
> Management Review Team 1980).

The 1982 Amendment Bill introduced the MHAC in order to implement this recommendation.

> **Section 121**(1) Without prejudice to section 126(3) of the National Health Service Act 1977 (power to vary or revoke orders or directions) there shall continue to be a special health authority known as the Mental Health Act Commission established under section 11 of that Act.

Using existing powers under the National Health Service Act avoided the need to take separate powers in the Amendment Bill to make provision for membership. It was to be designated by an Order in Council as an authority subject to the Health Service Commissioner's jurisdiction, and much concern was expressed in debate about the composition and jurisdiction of such a body.

The Bill was, and was to remain, silent regarding composition, although Parliament was informed in the 1981 White Paper that membership would be drawn from the ranks of lawyers, doctors, nurses, psychologists, social workers and laymen who would probably be visiting each of the 300 or so local hospitals and mental nursing homes in England and Wales once or twice a year and each of the four special hospitals once a month (presumably as a result of the disturbing findings of the Rampton Inquiry). Parliament was further informed (although again there was nothing in the Bill about this) that there would be a total of 70 members (72 was the final number) split into 5 regional panels, and the Government appeared to envisage that each panel would consist of 2 lawyers, 2 nurses, 2 psychologists, 2 social workers, 2 laymen and 4 psychiatrists – making 14 in all with a heavy preponderance of doctors.

It was considered by some to be inappropriate to create a health authority of the same category as those provided by the National Health Service Act. The Commission should be distinct, particularly as the fields of mental disorder and physical illness were distinct, and its powers were to directly affect the liberty of the subject in a way that no regional health authority was able to do.

A number of other concerns were expressed during Parliamentary debate:

(a) There was already hospital service visiting. How efficient had this been in the past? In addition there were hospital management committees and tribunals. Would the creation of MHAC merely lead to a heavy bureaucratric machine?
(b) How would the Commission be monitored, ie who would

inspect the inspectors? The publication of reports would be one answer but evidence was adduced that the Scottish Commission upon which the English one was modelled had only published three reports in its 20-year history, thus tending to convey the impression of an aloof, insular and impenetrable body.

(c) Rather than the creation of yet another quango, could not a widening of the powers and composition of mental health review tribunals which are multi-disciplinary and to which patients already have direct access, prove the better way forward?

(d) Would the Commission be able to adopt an *independent* stance in relation to facilities available to patients following discharge?

(e) Would the cost of providing this extra layer of bureaucracy prove acceptable?

(f) Would the Commission have powers to protect the interests of informal patients? All patients in hospital, whether detained or not, are deprived of the normal social relationships and control over many decisions affecting their lives. Informal patients would, therefore, have just as great a need for an effective watchdog to investigate complaints and to ensure that they were informed of their rights. On the other hand, it was argued that informal patients already benefited from a large number of bodies, such as the Health Service Commissioners, The Health Advisory Service, the development team for the mentally handicapped, the Court of Protection and Community Health Councils. Were these not enough to provide protection for this group of patients who, in theory, were free to leave hospital at any time?

(g) How could only 70 individuals working part-time (a day-and-a-half a week) meet their statutory commitments? This was, and remains, the major area of doubt.

8.2 The statutory provisions

The result of the extended debate was section 121 of the 1983 Act:

Section 121 (2) . . . the Secretary of State shall direct the Commission to perform on his behalf –

(a) the function of appointing registered medical practitioners for the purposes of Part IV of this Act and section 118 above and of appointing other persons for the purposes of section 57(2)(a) above; and

(b) the functions of the Secretary of State under sections 61 and 120(1) and (4) above.

Section 121 (2) contains a series of functions which must be delegated to the Commission. They are divided into four groups:

(1) appointing doctors who will give certificates as to a patient's consent and also a second opinion on proposed treatment under the consent to treatment provisions. The Commission is also to appoint members of the multi-disciplinary team with whom the doctor must consult before giving his second opinion. The doctors and laymen involved in the consent to treatment provisions may be members of the Commission;

(2) advising the Secretary of State on the content of the Code of Practice to be prepared under section 118;

(3) requiring reports to be submitted on treatment given under the consent to treatment procedures and upon the patient's condition, and issuing certificates prohibiting further treatment upon particular patients under section 61(3) of the Act;

(4) general protection of detained patients under section 120. In particular the Commission is required to visit and interview detained patients in private, and investigate individual complaints made by patients. Power to examine patients is given to doctor members of the Commission and to the Commission as a whole to require documents relating to a patient's detention and treatment to be produced and inspected.

Section 121 (4) The Secretary of State may, at the request of or after consultation with the Commission and after consulting with such other bodies as appear to him to be concerned, direct the Commission to keep under review the care and treatment, or any aspect of the care and treatment, in hospitals and mental nursing homes of patients who are not liable to be detained under this Act.

Much concern was expressed in Parliament that the original Bill did not require the Commission to supervise informal patients. This subsection is a response to this concern. It is a discretionary power, unlike that relating to detained patients, and only exercisable on the initiative of the Secretary of State or the Commission. The Commission's powers to interview and examine detained patients are extended to informal patients by section 121(5).

Section 121 (7) The Commission shall review any decision to withhold a postal packet (or anything contained in it) under subsection (1)(b) or (2) of section 134 . . . if an application in that behalf is made–
   (a) in a case under subsection (1)(b), by the patient; or

(b) in a case under subsection (2), either by the patient or by the person by whom the postal packet was sent;
and any such application shall be made within 6 months of the receipt by the applicant of the notice referred to in subsection (6) of that section

Section 121 (8) On an application under subsection (7) above the Commission may direct that the postal packet which is the subject of the application (or anything contained in it) shall not be withheld and the managers in question shall comply with any such direction.

This power to review the withholding of mail should be read together with the provisions of section 134 (see para 4.3.2 above).

Section 121 (10) The Commission shall in the second year after its establishment and subsequently in every second year publish a report on its activities; and copies of every such report shall be sent by the Commission to the Secretary of State who shall lay a copy before each House of Parliament.

Again, Parliamentary concern over the Commission's accountability bore fruit. Those who favoured an annual report eventually accepted that such a time period would prove difficult for such a small body to produce a detailed report.

Section 120 contains further provisions:

Section 120 (2) The arrangements made under this section in respect of the investigation of complaints may exclude matters from investigation in specified circumstances and shall not require any person exercising functions under the arrangements to undertake or continue any investigation where he does not consider it appropriate to do so.
(3) Where any such complaint as is mentioned in subsection (1)(b)(ii) above is made by a Member of Parliament and investigated under the arrangements made under this section the results of the investigation shall be reported to him.

It will be possible for the Commission to decline to investigate a complaint which has already been investigated either by the hospital managers or possibly the Health Service Ombudsman where no new evidence is supplied by the complainant.

Summary

The regular statutory functions of the Commission may be summarised as follows:

appointing approved doctors; visiting and interviewing patients;

investigating complaints by patients, non-patients and MPs; reviewing reports from doctors (although the Commission has no power to discharge patients – that is a matter for the Mental Health Review Tribunals); reviewing the position of informal patients (although it is uncertain how frequently this activity will be carried out); reviewing the withholding of postal packets.

8.3   The code of practice

One final and singular function given to the Commission concerns the drafting and revision of the Mental Health Act Code of Practice.

> **Section 118** (1) The Secretary of State shall prepare, and from time to time revise, a code of practice–
>> (a) for the guidance of registered medical practitioners, managers and staff of hospitals and mental nursing homes and approved social workers in relation to the admission of patients to hospitals and mental nursing homes under this Act; and
>> (b) for the guidance of registered medical practitioners and members of other professions in relation to the medical treatment of patients suffering from mental disorder.
>
> (2) The code shall, in particular, specify forms of medical treatment in addition to any specified by regulations made for the purposes of section 57 above which in the opinion of the Secretary of State give rise to special concern and which accordingly should not be given by a registered medical practitioner unless the patient has consented to the treatment (or to a plan of treatment including that treatment) and a certificate in writing as to the matters mentioned in subsection (2)(a) and (b) of that section has been given by another registered medical practitioner, being a practitioner appointed for the purposes of this section by the Secretary of State.
>
> (3) Before preparing the code or making any alteration in it the Secretary of State shall consult such bodies as appear to him to be concerned.

Thus the code, which has not been published at the time of writing, will be for the *guidance* of all those professionally qualified to have powers under the new legislation and it will be noticed that it will relate to admissions and the medical treatment (which includes nursing, care, habilitation and rehabilitation) of patients suffering from mental disorder. Presumably this will be to the benefit of all patients, detained and informal.

In relation to the Code, the Explanatory Memorandum states that:

> The Secretary of State has directed the Mental Health Act Commission

to submit proposals as to the content of the Code, and the Commission will also be responsible for submitting proposals for revisions to the Code. In particular they may want to propose revisions to it when developments in professional practice, or particular issues where guidance is needed, have come to their attention . . . The Code does not have the force of law, but everyone involved in the care of mentally disordered patients, including treatment in the community, should have regard to it whenever it is relevant. *Failure to do so could be evidence of bad practice.*

The indication is, therefore, that although the Code of Practice will have no direct statutory significance, it could be used in court proceedings to provide evidence as to what might be considered bad practice, ie negligence.

9 After-care

9.1 Introduction

> . . . there are many people detained in mental hospitals who need not be there if adequate facilities for residential and day care were available . . . [If] the Mental Health Act Commission does its job (and indeed I wish it well) then the demand for greater facilities such as those I have mentioned will increase, and there is of course the problem of discharge after care. Many patients who may be discharged . . . will in fact face discharge after some periods of detention in a mental hospital, and as such will face great problems in acclimatising themselves to the great world outside which has changed considerably since they went in. It is a problem we have to face as a result of this Act. (Lord Wallace of Coslany, Lords December 1981.)

The 1982 Amendment Bill, as first introduced into Parliament was silent on the matter of after-care. When the question was raised, it was argued by the Government that any amendment dealing with after-care would provide an unnecessary duplication of existing legislation. Paragraph 2(1) of Schedule 8 of the National Health Service Act 1977 states that 'A local social services authority may, with the Secretary of State's approval, and to such an extent as he may direct, shall, make arrangements for the purpose of the prevention of illness and the care of persons suffering from illness and for the after care of persons who have been so suffering.' This provision was considered to be of too general a nature and an amendment creating a specific duty in relation to individual patients was successfully moved. It is too early to say how effective the after-care provisions will prove to be, but the vagueness of its terms suggest it is unlikely to generate much positive action by the authorities concerned.

9.2   The statutory provisions

9.2.1   **Section 117** (1) This section applies to persons who are detained under section 3 above, or admitted to a hospital in pursuance of a hospital order made under section 37 above, or transferred to a hospital in pursuance of a transfer direction made under section 47 or 48 above, and then cease to be detained and leave hospital.

The limitations of the duty are immediately apparent from this subsection which lists the categories of patients to whom the duty applies:

(a) patients detained for treatment;
(b) patients detained under hospital orders;
(c) patients transferred to hospital from prison.

Patients detained for assessment and informal patients are not within the scope of the after-care provisions. Nor, it seems, are detained patients who remain in hospital on an informal basis after their period of detention ends and then leave hospital.

If the limited extent of the duty is unsatisfactory then the vagueness of its terms is the cause of even greater concern:

9.2.2   **Section 117** (2) It shall be the duty of the District Health Authority and of the local social services authority to provide, in co-operation with relevant voluntary agencies, after-care services for any person to whom this section applies until such time as the District Health Authority and the local social services authority are satisfied that the person concerned is no longer in need of such services.

There are a number of points upon the duty in subsection (2) which raise potential difficulties for patients who seek to obtain the after-care services which they require:

(a) The joint nature of the duty. The manner in which the duty is laid down depends upon district health authorities, local social services authorities and voluntary agencies agreeing upon the services required in their area. If they cannot agree, either generally upon the type of services to be provided within their area, or upon the requirements of an individual patient, there is no procedure for resolving such disputes in the 1983 Act. If such a dispute causes delay in provision of services or even total failure to provide services at all, what can the patient do? The answer must be for him to complain to the Secretary of State and request him to exercise his default powers in section 124 of the 1983 Act (see para 9.3).

(b) What services must be provided? The term 'after-care services' is not defined in the 1983 Act and therefore the extent of and the manner in which they are provided is left to the discretion of district health authorities and local social services authorities. This will inevitably lead to uneven provision throughout the country and as there is no minimum standard laid down in the 1983 Act nor in DHSS guidance it will be difficult for a patient to argue that the authorities are failing to carry out their statutory duty. The district health authority and the local social services authority may decide only to provide regular visits by an approved social worker or a community psychiatric nurse. It would seem that the patient cannot demand more if the authorities are satisfied that such provision is adequate for the patient in question.

(c) The duty only lasts as long as the district health authority and the local social services authority are satisfied the patient needs the services. The patient cannot appeal if services are withdrawn.

9.2.3 Section 117 (3) In this section 'District Health Authority' means the District Health Authority for the district, and 'the local social services authority' means the local social services authority for the area in which the person concerned is resident or to which he is sent on discharge by the hospital in which he was detained.

Problems will arise under this subsection if the patient is not returned to the area in which he was resident prior to his detention in hospital. The subsection suggests that the hospital has a power to choose the area to which it will send a patient on discharge, without reference to the district health authority and local social services authority which will be obliged to provide after-care services for the patient. This point is not free from doubt. If hospitals discharge patients without ensuring that arrangements for their after-care have been made by the authorities for the areas to which the patients are sent, the whole purpose of this section, limited as it is, will be defeated. Before discharging a patient, a hospital should consult the district health authority and local social services authority for the area in which the patient was resident before admission to hospital and ensure that arrangements for his after-care have been made. If it is the hospital's intention to send a patient to an area in which the patient was not resident before admission, such consultation by the hospital is even more essential to ensure that the patient's welfare is not affected by administrative disputes over responsibility to provide after-care services.

9.3 Enforcing a statutory duty

The problems that patients seeking to obtain after-care services under section 117 may encounter can be divided into two types:

(a) those arising from the inability of the various authorities involved to agree upon responsibility to provide the services in a particular case, and
(b) disagreement between patient and authority upon the level of services a particular patient requires.

There is clearly a need for an independent body to adjudicate upon all these matters and ensure that the objectives of section 117 are achieved. A patient could attempt to enforce his rights under section 117 by means of court action but he is certain to fail unless he has first exercised any default powers in the 1983 Act. These are contained in section 124 of the Act:

Section 124 (1) Where the Secretary of State is of the opinion, on complaint or otherwise, that a local social services authority have failed to carry out functions conferred or imposed on the authority by or under this Act or have in carrying out those functions failed to comply with any regulations relating to those functions, he may after such inquiry as he thinks fit make an order declaring the authority to be in default.

(2) Subsections (3) to (5) of section 85 of the National Health Service Act 1977 (which relates to orders declaring, among others, a local social services authority to be in default under that Act) shall apply in relation to an order under this section as they apply in relation to an order under that section.

A patient who is dissatisfied with the services offered to him under section 117 must first refer the matter to the Secretary of State. Under this section and the National Health Service Act 1977, the Secretary of State can order the local social services authority and the district health authority to provide such services as he deems necessary to comply with their obligations towards the patient. If they fail to comply with the Secretary of State's order, he may provide the services himself and charge the authorities who are in default for doing so. This power is rarely, if ever, used and given the vague nature of the after-care duties, it is unlikely that the Secretary of State would use his default power to enforce this section. Despite this, a patient who wished to enforce the duties in section 117 through court action would first have to refer his complaint to the Secretary of State. Only if the Secretary of State refused or failed to take action could the patient then commence court proceedings.

10   Miscellaneous

10.1   Removal and return of patients within the UK

10.1.1   Under sections 80 to 85 of the 1983 Act patients may be moved between England and Wales, Scotland, Northern Ireland, the Channel Islands and the Isle of Man and still remain under detention or guardianship. Once a patient enters a different country within the UK he is treated as if an application has been made in the country into which he is moved, and becomes subject to the mental health legislation of that country.

10.1.2   The Secretary of State must be satisfied that a move under these provisions would be in the interests of the patient and that, where relevant, suitable arrangements have been made for admitting him into hospital or receiving him into guardianship.

10.1.3   Section 86 of the 1983 Act gives the Home Secretary power to authorise the removal from the UK, of a patient who:

(a) is neither a British citizen nor a Commonwealth citizen, and
(b) has no right to live in the UK, and
(c) is receiving treatment for *mental illness* as an in-patient in a hospital.

To exercise this power the Home Secretary must be satisfied that proper arrangements for the patient's care and treatment have been made in the country to which he is to be removed. A Mental Health Review Tribunal must approve the exercise of the Home Secretary's powers.

10.2 *Miscellaneous*

10.1.4 Sections 87–89 permit patients who are absent without leave from hospitals in Northern Ireland, The Channel Islands or the Isle of Man to be retaken if found in England and Wales. These sections include reciprocal provisions to provide for the return of patients absent without leave from hospitals in England and Wales.

The powers in these sections are given to approved social workers and police officers. They do not apply to patients under guardianship.

10.2   Criminal offences

10.2.1   Mental Health Act 1959, section 128
(1) Without prejudice to section seven of the Sexual Offences Act 1956, it shall be an offence, subject to the exception mentioned in this section,—
 (a) for a man who is an officer on the staff or otherwise employed in, or is one of the managers of, a hospital or mental nursing home to have unlawful sexual intercourse with a woman who is for the time being receiving treatment for mental disorder in that hospital or home, or to have intercourse on the premises of which the hospital or home forms part with a woman who is for the time being receiving such treatment there as an out-patient;
 (b) for a man to have unlawful sexual intercourse with a woman who is a mentally disordered patient and who is subject to his guardianship under this Act or is otherwise in his custody or care under this Act or in pursuance of arrangements under . . . Part III of the National Assistance Act 1948, or the National Health Service Act 1977, or as a resident in a residential home for mentally disordered persons within the meaning of Part III of this Act.
(2) It shall not be an offence under this section for a man to have sexual intercourse with a woman if he does not know and has no reason to suspect her to be a mentally disordered patient.

The DHSS Guide gives advice upon the effect of this section and the procedure to be followed if an offence is suspected:

297 . . . The Section makes it an offence for a man to have 'unlawful sexual intercourse' with a woman or to commit homosexual acts with another man, if he is employed in a hospital or mental nursing home where the woman or man is being treated for mental disorder, or if he is the guardian of the mentally disordered person, or if the person is otherwise in his custody or care under this Act, and under certain other circumstances . . . Where there is reason to believe that an offence has been committed under this Section, the Chief Constable should be

194

informed as soon as possible. The police will then decide what is the right course, in consultation with the doctor in charge of the patient's treatment where the patient is resident in or on leave of absence from the hospital (except where the doctor is named as the assailant).

10.2.2 The 1983 Act contains specific safeguards to prevent forgery of the various documents and forms required for the purposes of admission to hospital etc. These safeguards are set out in section 126:

Section 126 (1) Any person who without lawful authority or excuse has in his custody or under his control any document to which this subsection applies, which is, and which he knows or believes to be, false within the meaning of Part I of the Forgery and Counterfeiting Act 1981, shall be guilty of an offence.

(2) Any person who without lawful authority or excuse makes or has in his custody or under his control, any document so closely resembling a document to which subsection (1) above applies as to be calculated to deceive shall be guilty of an offence.

(3) The documents to which subsection (1) above applies are any documents purporting to be—

(a) an application under Part II of this Act;

(b) a medical recommendation or report under this Act; and

(c) any other document required or authorised to be made for any of the purposes of this Act.

(4) Any person who—

(a) wilfully makes a false entry or statement in any application, recommendation, report, record or other document required or authorised to be made for any of the purposes of this Act; or

(b) with intent to deceive, makes use of any such entry or statement which he knows to be false, shall be guilty of an offence.

Three offences are created by this section:

(a) making a false entry in a document required under the Act;

(b) making use of such an entry;

(b) being in possession of a forged document.

The definition of 'false' in the Forgery and Counterfeiting Act 1981 is extremely wide and includes documents which appear to have been authorised by a person with authority under the 1983 Act but which have not, in fact, been so authorised and documents apparently made by a person who does not, in fact, exist. In the case of each offence the person concerned must know or believe that the entry he is making or the document he possesses is false.

10.2.3 Section 127 of the 1983 Act creates specific offences of ill-treating or wilfully neglecting patients in hospital or under guardianship. The Director of Public Prosecutions must authorise prosecutions under this section.

10.2.4 The 1983 Act creates specific offences of assisting or harbouring patients who are absent without leave:

> **Section 128** (1) Where any person induces or knowingly assists another person who is liable to be detained in a hospital within the meaning of Part II of this Act or is subject to guardianship under this Act to absent himself without leave he shall be guilty of an offence.
>
> (2) Where any person induces or knowingly assists another person who is in legal custody by virtue of section 137 below to escape from such custody he shall be guilty of an offence.
>
> (3) Where any person knowingly harbours a patient who is absent without leave or is otherwise at large and liable to be retaken under this Act or gives him any assistance with intent to prevent, hinder or interfere with his being taken into custody or returned to the hospital or other place where he ought to be he shall be guilty of an offence.

Again several offences are created within a single section of the 1983 Act:

(a) to assist a patient to absent himself without leave;
(b) to assist a patient to escape from custody.
(c) to harbour a patient who is absent without leave.

10.2.5 An offence of obstructing persons in the execution of their duties under the Act is created by section 129:

> **Section 129** (1) Any person who without reasonable cause—
>   (a) refuses to allow the inspection of any premises; or
>   (b) refuses to allow the visiting, interviewing or examination of any person by a person authorised in that behalf by or under this Act; or
>   (c) refuses to produce for the inspection of any person so authorised any document or record the production of which is duly required by him; or
>   (d) otherwise obstructs any such person in the exercise of his functions,
> shall be guilty of an offence.
>
> (2) Without prejudice to the generality of subsection (1) above, any person who insists on being present when required to withdraw by a person authorised by or under this Act to interview or examine a person in private shall be guilty of an offence.

The following points should be noted concerning this section:

(a) subsection (1)(a) would apply if a private guardian refuses to allow an approved social worker to inspect the patient's residence;

(b) subsection (1)(b) would apply if an approved social worker is prevented from interviewing a patient prior to considering whether an application for admission to hospital should be made;

(c) subsection (1)(c) could apply if an approved social worker requires a person claiming to be a nearest relative to produce documentary evidence of this status.

(d) An approved social worker has no specific right to interview a patient in private. The duty in section 13 (see para 2.8) is to interview 'in a suitable manner'. This may imply that if the approved social worker forms the opinion that the interview cannot be properly conducted unless it takes place in private he should seek to exclude all persons present. But if those persons refuse to do so they will probably not commit an offence under section 129(2) although the statutory provision is not free from doubt.

10.3 Pocket money

The 1983 Act gives the DHSS power to pay pocket money to in-patients to meet 'occasional personal expenses' where they have no other resources to meet these expenses. Patients who are receiving any State benefits will not be entitled to pocket money. The payments are discretionary – patients have no statutory entitlement to pocket money. The patient may be detained or informal and must be in a psychiatric hospital.

10.4 Pensions

The 1983 Act permits any periodic payments due to a patient from central government funds to be paid direct to the hospital in which the patient is accommodated or to anyone who has care of the patient. The patient must be 'incapable by reason of mental disorder of managing and administering his property and affairs', and the periodic payments must be pensions or employment-related. The payments may be divided between the patient, his dependants and his creditors. This could prove a useful alternative to the Court of Protection procedure although its use is limited by the fact that the power only applies to State pensions and payments.

10.5   Definitions

Section 145 of the 1983 Act defines a number of words and phrases used throughout the Act. These definitions have been referred to at appropriate points in the text with the exception of the following:

'approved social worker' means an officer of a local social services authority appointed to act as an approved social worker for the purposes of this Act.

'hospital' means

(a) any health service hospital within the meaning of the National Health Act 1977; and
(b) any accommodation provided by a local authority and used as a hospital by or on behalf of the Secretary of State under that Act.

local social services authority means a council which is a local authority for the purpose of the Local Authority Social Services Act 1970.

patient (except in relation to the Court of Protection provisions) means a person suffering or appearing to be suffering from mental disorder.

10.6   The approved social worker and the private patient

It may be that the approved social worker is faced with a dilemma in this situation. It is not unknown for a social worker to be summoned to a private institution to carry out an assessment. If an application is made and accepted this will lead to the compulsory detention of the patient at his own expense. Here the approved social worker must pay particular attention to the provisions of section 12 (3) and 5(d) concerning medical recommendations:

Section 12 (3) Subject to subsection (4) below, where the application is for the admission of the patient to a hospital which is not a mental nursing home, one (but not more than one) of the medical recommendations may be given by a practitioner on the staff of that hospital, except where the patient is proposed to be accommodated under section 65 or 66 of the National Health Service Act 1977 (which relates to accommodation for private patients) . . .

(5) A medical recommendation for the purposes of an application for the admission of a patient under this Part of this Act shall not be given

by—
  (a) the applicant;
  (b) a partner of the applicant or of a practitioner by whom another medical recommendation is given for the purposes of the same application;
  (c) a person employed as an assistant by the applicant or by any such practitioner;
  (d) a person who receives or has an interest in the recipt of any payments made on account of the maintenance of the patient; or
  (e) except as provided by subsection (3) or (4) above, a practitioner on the staff of the hospital to which the patient is to be admitted,
or by the husband, wife, father, father-in-law, mother, mother-in-law, son, son-in-law, daughter, daughter-in-law, brother, brother-in-law, sister or sister-in-law of the patient, or of any person mentioned in paragraphs (a) to (e) above, or of a practitioner by whom another medical recommendation is given for the purposes of the same application.

The effect of this is to limit the circumstances in which a medical recommendation can be given by a doctor on the staff of the private institution. It should be remembered that it is the approved social worker's duty to see that there are no obvious defects in the medical recommendations supporting the application and he should guard against medical recommendations which may contravene the above provisions. A situation may also arise where a patient (possessing adequate funds) is willing to accept treatment, but not in a NHS hospital. In such circumstances it should not be necessary for the patient to be compulsorily detained and the approved social worker should arrange for his informal admission to the private institution of his choice. A compulsory admission in such a situation would be wrong as the patient would be willing to be admitted on a voluntary basis.

10.7   Powers of entry

Section 115 An approved social worker of a local social services authority may at all reasonable times after producing, if asked to do so, some duly authenticated document showing that he is such a social worker, enter and inspect any premises (not being a hospital) in the area of that authority in which a mentally disordered person is living, if he has reasonable cause to believe that the patient is not under proper care.
Note. This power is only to be used for inspection of premises, *not* for removal of patients. It only operates within the area of the social worker's employing authority and cannot apply to hospitals.

11   Case study material

11.1   Introduction

As mentioned in the Preface, we believe that the use of case study material is an essential element in the training of social workers. Not only does the use of such material assist in the understanding of often complex legal issues, but it also allows the social worker to be confronted by practical situations thus enabling the consequences of action proposed to be understood and critically appraised.

What follows is a selection of case study material which is intended to address those aspects of the legislation considered to be of particular significance. It is, perhaps, inevitable that certain parts of the text, such as those relating to admission procedures, receive more attention in the case studies than others which are less directly and immediately relevant to the role of the approved social worker.

It will be noted that each case study concludes with specific questions. Although these are primarily intended to deal with legal issues, they may also form a basis for discussion of social work practice. In any event, it is anticipated that trainers will feel free to modify or add to the questions posed.

Note. The material which follows has been compiled in close collaboration with Mike Hewitt, Training Officer with Birmingham Social Services Department, whose important contribution is gratefully acknowledged.

11.2   The case studies

11.2.1   Classification of mental disorder

JANE

Jane, mentally handicapped and 23 years old, attends an Adult Training Centre three days a week. She is a popular girl at the Centre and joins in most activities. She lives with her parents in a quiet residential suburb of the city where her father is employed in a secure job, and her mother works part-time on the mornings Jane attends the Centre.

Late one morning, an approved social worker is called to the Centre to find that Jane has seriously assaulted two other trainees having 'gone berserk' without warning. One girl has a black eye, whilst the other has a head wound from being hit with a chair. Jane has also smashed up furniture. Her mother is at the Centre and has admitted that there have been several incidents of violent temper at home of late. She says the family cannot cope, and thinks that Jane should be in hospital. She asks the approved social worker to make an application for compulsory admission, since Jane goes into a rage if she tries to take her to the doctor.

Questions

In what way is the 1983 Act relevant to Jane's condition?
If you were the approved social worker, what action would you take and why?

ROGER

You are the approved social worker on duty at 'G' Local Authority Social Services Department when you receive a telephone request from Mrs W to visit her son with a view to 'taking him into hospital'. The son, Roger, is 21 years old and has been living with his widowed mother and 13-year-old sister for the past three months. Previously, he had lived away from home for four years, drifting about the country living in communes, and his mother suspects he has been involved in drug-taking.

He left the family home at 17 years of age, six months after his father died. Mrs W says that she has never been able to understand her son, but his behaviour since his return has been 'so difficult!' He gets up late, lounges about the house without talking to anyone, and will not often go out of the house. Then, at midnight or later, he is banging around his room, playing music and even cooking for himself.

The call for help from Mrs W has been prompted by a worsening of the situation in the last 10 days. Roger has three times woken his sister in the night, frightening her, and he keeps repeating what people say to him. Mrs W says he cannot converse sensibly but talks to himself, saying he is communicating with his friends. Mrs W says she is 'at the end of her tether'.

Questions

What action would you take in this situation, and how would you advise Mrs W?
Is hospitalisation appropriate for Roger?

11.2.2   Into hospital
FRED

Fred is a married man of 45 with no history of psychiatric disorder. He lives with his wife and two children, a son of 19 and a daughter of 13.

An approved social worker is visited one morning by the son who says that Fred has kept the family up all night ranting and raving about the aliens who are coming to get him. He has smashed the TV and his son's radio because they are being used by the aliens to check up on him.

The family are afraid for Fred and for themselves, wondering what he will do next. It is the GP at his surgery who has told the son to ask the social worker to apply for admission to hospital for 'observation', saying he will sign the forms and will phone a psychiatrist he knows to arrange for him to sign them when Fred arrives at the hospital. The GP saw Fred two weeks ago when he called at the surgery complaining of headaches.

Questions

Assume you are the approved social worker who Fred's son sees. How would you respond?
What are your statutory obligations under the 1983 Act? How do

they differ from those under the 1959 Act?
If you refuse to make an application, can Fred's son do anything?
What about Fred's wishes if he agrees to hospital admission?

JIMMY

Jimmy, aged 15, is the son of a single-parent mother and has been in the care of the local authority since he was 11 years old. His mother has shown little interest in him, her last contact having been over a year ago. Her present whereabouts are unknown, and she has previously disappeared for several months at a time.

Jimmy was diagnosed as suffering from a mental disorder three years ago, since when he has from time to time attended an outpatient clinic at the local psychiatric hospital. He has become more withdrawn of late and has been listless and unco-operative during the day whilst being active and disruptive at night.

A social worker has been called as Jimmy has now indicated that the 'voices' are telling him not to eat food because the Deputy at the Home is trying to poison him. Two Registered Medical Practitioners are prepared to say that he is suffering from mental illness.

Question

What are the powers and responsibilities of the local authority?

HENRY

Henry is 26 years old and is mentally handicapped. He lives with his stepfather, Fred J, in an old run-down property in the inner ring area of a large city. Fred J has been unemployed most of his life, but is known locally to make a living out of scrap metal. The home is very sparsely furnished, has no inside toilet and only cold running water. The surrounding area is almost derelict. Mrs J died two years ago, and Fred has kept Henry with him. It is believed by those neighbours left in the street that Fred sends Henry out regularly to steal from shops.

The family GP contacts the social services department requesting an approved social worker to investigate the situation. He has made several attempts to visit Henry after neighbours have reported that he is underfed and ill-cared for. On two occasions, he has found Henry locked in alone. On one other occasion Fred J would not let him in and told him to mind his own business.

The GP considers Henry to be in need of protection and support under the 1983 Act and requests the approved social worker to take appropriate action.

Questions

What action can the approved social worker take if he is unable to gain access to Henry?
Under what section of the Act would action be most appropriate?

JOHN R

John R has been unemployed for 18 months having lost his job as a labourer in a rolling mill for fighting with a workmate. Company policy was adhered to, and both men were dismissed instantly even though the 'fight' was no more than an aggressive argument with some pushing.

John has felt guilty about losing his job and he and his wife, Sylvia, have struggled to maintain their three young children on reduced state benefit. During the past six months he has become increasingly depressed, refusing to eat much and just sitting in a chair. For the past week he has not even bothered to get dressed and has become quite aggressive. The GP has been very supportive and has visited at least every two days.

On Friday morning Sylvia found John trying to cut his wrist with a blunt knife. She telephoned the GP and begged that John be admitted to hospital as she could no longer cope. The GP said he was too busy to come, but would complete the forms for an emergency admission, as he had seen from his visit on Wednesday afternoon that John needed treatment. He would arrange for an approved social worker to have the forms and to visit the home.

The approved social worker arrived at the home about midday and, having interviewed John R and Sylvia R, made an application under section 4 of the 1983 Act. He noticed that the GP had stated that he has last seen the patient on Wednesday at 2.00 pm. Assuming this to be a clerical error, he altered the date to Thursday at 2.00 pm and then added his own signature as appropriate.

The approved social worker was loathe to take the aggressive John R to hospital in his car and waited until 1.30 pm for an ambulance. When he ascertained that there was still likely to be a delay, he telephoned a colleague who came out to assist. John R was finally brought to the correct ward at the hospital at 1.59 pm on that Friday.

Questions

Was this a legal admission?
If not, what were the circumstances which would make it illegal?

ROBERT

Robert is a 26-year-old schizophrenic who suffers frequent paranoid delusional states. He lives with his parents in a quiet residential suburb. Robert is unemployed and has few friends. In an attempt to be friendly and create some interest for Robert, his neighbour invited him to his house to see his new set of video games, with which Robert proved to be skilful.

Several days later, Robert's parents called the GP because Robert was behaving in a bizarre manner, and saying he could not help it as he was being controlled by his neighbour's computer. An approved social worker was called, and, after proper consideration of all the circumstances and appropriate enquiries, an application for compulsory admission under section 2 was made.

Robert was taken to the hospital by the approved social worker and Robert's father. He was quiet and well behaved until reaching the hospital ward. Whilst the approved social worker was speaking to the charge nurse and his father, Robert pushed the nurse looking after him backwards through a door and ran off. He was able to get clear of the hospital grounds and back to his own neighbourhood which was not far away.

Robert did not go back to his home but, instead, called on a friend who agreed to put him up for a few days. By the time Robert's whereabouts were discovered, the application under section 2 was 14 days old. The friend refuses to allow the approved social worker or the police into his house.

Questions

What action would you take as the approved social worker at the point where Robert ran off?
Who was responsible for Robert once the application had been made?

DIANA

Diana is a single woman who lives on the fourteenth floor of a tower block. She becomes easily depressed to a point where she is unable to cope alone. She has a friend on the same landing of the block who will willingly move in with Diana during these fits of depression, and with her help admissions to hospital have been kept to a minimum. There have been only two admissions in the past six years (both voluntary) and on the second admission 18 months ago Diana discharged herself within 36 hours of admission, and would not attend the outpatient's clinic until persuaded by her friend.

During a period of time when her friend was away from home for family reasons the friend contacts the local social services department to say that she is worried about Diana who sounds very depressed on the telephone. She says that Diana seems to be threatening suicide, although she does not think she means it.

The situation is investigated by an approved social worker who, after consideration of all the circumstances and discussion with Diana as well as a further telephone conversation with the friend, decides to procure a voluntary admission to hospital. Diana is in agreement and arrangements are made with the hospital for a bed to be made available.

On arrival at the hospital, the approved social worker and Diana are met by the consultant psychiatrist who says that he will not accept Diana as a voluntary patient and did not himself agree that she should come to the hospital on that basis. He points out that Diana discharged herself once before soon after voluntary admission.

Question

What action is now open to the approved social worker?

MARJORIE

Marjorie is a 48-year-old woman who is separated from her

husband. He left her nine months ago and there is little contact between them. The couple have one son who left home over 10 years ago to set up a business in the Channel Islands. He has returned on visits twice, and keeps in touch with his mother by letters and cards.

Marjorie let a room six months ago to a lady named Vera who works in an office near to Marjorie's home. Vera has her own room and pays for rent and board. She occasionally helps with the cooking and other household chores. During the past three months Marjorie has become very depressed, listless and uncommunicative. Vera has tried to help her become more cheerful and lively, but has been unsuccessful. Vera has now discovered that Marjorie has been hoarding aspirin tablets and has bought a large bottle of whisky – Marjorie seldom drinks alcohol. She admits to Vera that she 'wants to end it all'.

Vera seeks help from a voluntary advice centre and is told that she can ask the social services department to consider her as the nearest relative and apply for her admission to hospital.

Questions

Is Vera Marjorie's nearest relative? Can she ever be her nearest relative?
If not, who is Marjorie's nearest relative?

JOHN

John is 28 years of age and has suffered from a form of mental illness for the past 10 years. He is generally stabilised by regular medication, and attends an outpatient clinic at the local psychiatric hospital. There have been a few occasions when admission to hospital has been necessary; only once was this compulsory. John lives most of the time with his mother on a large council estate in Blanktown. She is a widow and her younger son also lives at home. From time to time John takes himself off to stay with friends in Bromchester. This has become a regular pattern without incident and, therefore, has been accepted by his mother and brother.

One morning, the approved social worker on duty in Blanktown received a phone call from Bromchester. John has been making a nuisance of himself at the home of his friends and has barricaded himself in an upstairs room. He refuses to open the door, and is said to be breaking up the contents of the room and throwing them out of the window.

The social worker in Bromchester is demanding that Blanktown send an approved social worker to deal with the situation, saying it is Blanktown's responsibility.

Question

What are the responsibilities of the approved social workers employed by the respective local authorities?

MR AND MRS R

You are called out as the duty approved social worker to the home of Mr and Mrs R who live comfortably in a pleasant residential suburb of a city. On arrival at the home you find Mrs R talking wildly in sentences which do not link sensibly. She is restless and keeps getting out of her chair, pacing up and down using expansive gestures, before sitting down again for a few short moments.

Mr R is a quiet, mild-mannered man who is clearly out of his depth. He does not know how to cope with the situation and is waiting to be told what to do. He says Mrs R has never been like this before today, but this episode has lasted two or three hours so far.

Also present at the home is the family GP who has known the couple for eight years. They are in their late '40s and are childless. The GP says he has been waiting for you to turn up and has already signed papers for a section 4 compulsory admission. He justifies this by pointing out that he is well-acquainted with Mrs R, that her behaviour is abnormal and that he is the medical expert not you.

Question

An an approved social worker, what would be your response to the GP?

MR SINGH

Mr Singh is a 60-year-old Indian man who lives with his son,

208

daughter-in-law and two teenage children, having lost his wife many years ago. He came over from India 10 years ago at the insistence of his son, who has established himself in a small business in a major English city. The son and his wife have adapted their lifestyle to gain the best from western living, whilst retaining some of their cultural values. The children are in constant conflict with their cultural background, preferring the ways of their English friends.

The family GP has referred Mr Singh to the social services department for help because he has become severely depressed over recent weeks. He will not communicate with the family and has refused to eat for four days. The GP has particularly asked for an approved social worker to see Mr Singh because she thinks that a hospital admission is necessary.

Questions

What are the implications for the approved social worker interviewing Mr Singh?
What cultural factors must the approved social worker take into account?
What may help to explain Mr Singh's behaviour?

JANICE

Janice is 28 years old, divorced from her husband and living with her 9-year-old daughter Karen. Janice works as a secretarial assistant in a primary school. For the past six years she has had regular bouts of hypermania. Hospital admission is seldom necessary and there has been only one compulsory admission and three voluntary admissions in the six-year period. The attacks are usually brought under control by an understanding GP, who has invested a considerable amount of time in Janice's case.

The GP has recently suffered a heart attack, and is expected to be away from the practice for some considerable time. The approved social worker is called to Janice's home one weekday morning because Janice has had another attack and has been in a highly manic state for some two hours.

When the approved social worker arrives, Janice is much more calm, but the locum GP, who is still there, insists that she should go to hospital. Janice is unwilling and says that she is now all right. The approved social worker interviews Janice and Karen and is satisfied that hospital admission is not necessary. However, in further discussion, the GP is still insistent that Janice could have a further manic episode and could be a danger to her child. He has spoken to the headmistress of the school where Janice works, who has described her as 'very unpredictable'. The GP has also discovered that Janice walked out of her out-patient appointment with the psychiatrist two weeks ago. The psychiatrist is now prepared to sign an application for admission.

When the approved social worker pursues the matter of reconsidering admission with the GP, the doctor states that, if the approved social worker refuses to sign the papers, he will ensure that the newspapers get to realise how irresponsible social workers are in placing a 9-year-old child at such great risk.

Question

What would you do as the approved social worker?

MRS T

An approved social worker is called to the home of Mr and Mrs T, following a message that the GP and a consultant psychiatrist have paid a domicillary visit earlier that day. They have left papers for an application for admission to hospital under section 2.

When the approved social worker arrives at the house, Mr T answers the door. He invites the social worker in and apologises for his wife's behaviour, saying that 'the silly bitch is at it all the time these days and should be locked up'. Mrs T is in the kitchen sobbing loudly at intervals, and occasionally throwing crockery. She has locked herself in. There are two eight-year-old-girls in the living room, looking well-dressed and cared for, but appearing frightened and confused. Mr T tells them that the social worker has come to take their mother away until she is better.

He explains that Mrs T has had regular bouts of crying and 'bad temper' for about a month and such bouts have become increasingly frequent. He says he can't find out why. She won't tell him and he has even tried knocking some sense into her. She has not yet failed to look after the children, but he says that she can no longer be trusted to pay the bills, something he should not have to be bothered with. He asks the social worker to hurry up and take her away so that he can take the children to a neighbour and get back to work.

After interviewing Mrs T, the approved social worker becomes convinced that she is a desperately unhappy woman caught up in a worsening domestic situation, although all the family have good health and their contact with the GP has been minimal in the last five years. Mrs T says that she feels so frustrated that her husband will not talk to her, merely dismissing her as a 'bad-tempered bitch'. She admits that up to two months ago she was coping, but became very weepy and distressed. The periods of temper followed when her husband kept ignoring her and talking to the children as if she was not there.

The approved social worker is convinced that Mrs T is not mentally disordered, and that compulsory admission to hospital would be wrong.

Questions

How would you deal with the situation as the approved social worker?
What resources would you wish to use?
How would you approach the GP and psychiatrist?
In this situation what would you see as interviewing 'in a suitable manner'?

ARTHUR

An approved social worker is called to the police cells in a small market town to interview Arthur, a man of about 45, who has been arrested during the late evening in the High Street for throwing stones at street lamps. It was reported that he had been shouting over and over that he had been chosen to extinguish the light of the world.

When arrested, Arthur had been dressed only in underpants with some material draped round him. He has refused to speak since his arrest, and has been entirely passive. The approved social worker is taken to the cell where Arthur is sitting with a blanket clutched around him staring into space. When interviewed he makes no response and does not move. A mug of cold tea stands beside him untouched.

The station sergeant insists that the approved social worker completes the forms for an emergency admission to hospital which have been left by the police doctor. The social worker refuses to do so, and attempts to contact a psychiatrist who, it seems, will not be available for several hours.

The sergeant points out that Arthur should be in hospital not in a police cell, and again insists on an application being made. Arthur has no known relatives and is not previously known to the police or to the local social services department.

Questions

How can Arthur be interviewed in a suitable manner?
What action would you take as the approved social worker?

11.2.3   Guardianship

JEFF

Jeff is 22 years old and has suffered from simple schizophrenia for three years. His mother is a widow with four other children and, since her husband died four years ago, has found it difficult to manage. She had to go out to work and relied heavily on Jeff in the year before he was taken ill.

Jeff's mother can no longer take responsibility for him. He is rebellious with numerous behaviour problems, including refusing to wash, living his daytime life at night and leaving any jobs found for him within a few days. He has been made the subject of a guardianship order, and now lives with Mrs M, who runs a small lodging house for six ex-patients from the local psychiatric hospital. They each have their own room, with breakfast and an evening meal provided. A condition of the lodging is that residents either work, attend a day centre or a training scheme.

Mrs M complains to the social services office that she cannot do anything with Jeff. He refuses to go out to work or to the day centre in the mornings, and hides until everyone else has gone. She says that no social worker has been to see her or Jeff for well over three weeks and, in addition, Jeff has been smuggling a girl up into his room. The girl is someone with whom he has had a previous involvement over drugs and Mrs M says the girl will not heed warnings to stay away from Jeff.

Questions

What powers rest with the approved social worker in respect of the guardianship order?
Does Mrs M have any powers under the order?
Can the guardianship order be used to discourage the girl who keeps visiting him?
Should the social services department visit more frequently than every three or four weeks?

11.2.4 The patient in hospital

PAT

Pat is 33 and a farm labourer, admitted to a psychiatric hospital some 35 miles away from home. He was admitted on a compulsory basis under section 4 after he had 'gone beserk' with a piece of farm machinery, narrowly missing causing serious injury to a workmate. The admission was applied for and carried out in an appropriate manner.

Pat is married with two children under seven years of age. There are friends in the village where they live, but no members of either Pat's family or his wife's. Four days after the admission, his wife contacts the approved social worker responsible for the admission, saying that she cannot find out what is happening to Pat. He was admitted on the Friday afternoon, and she was not able to visit until someone looked after the children and she was given a lift to the hospital on the Sunday afternoon. No one at the hospital seemed available to explain to her what was happening, and Pat had only been told that he could not leave the hospital – nothing else.

Questions

What are the rights of Pat and his wife, given the circumstances of the admission?
What could explain why he is still being held after four days?
Who has responsibility for ensuring that Pat is informed of his rights?

EDWARD

Edward is a 32-year-old lorry driver who was admitted to a local psychiatric hospital after he had deliberately driven his lorry into the wall of a house, shouting that it was full of spies.

He was admitted on an emergency application which was later converted to an application for assessment, and has been in hospital for three weeks. The consultant psychiatrist in charge of his treatment has decided that ECT is necessary to aid Edward's recovery, as there has been little progress so far.

Edward has long periods when he can only talk in rambling, incoherent sentences. When he is lucid, however, he will contend vehemently that he is 'not having any electric shocks'. He is becoming increasingly aggressive towards staff and has hit a male nurse.

His wife is very worried about the situation, and is adamant that she does not want her husband to be given this treatment.

Questions

Do the consent to treatment provisions apply to Edward? If so, what are the circumstances which would exclude him?
Must the consultant psychiatrist take any action before giving ECT to Edward?
Can Edward's wife take any action to prevent him being treated by this method?

TOM

Tom is a 38-year-old divorcee who has been living an unsettled life since his marriage ended nine years ago. He drifts from one area of the conurbation in which he has lived to another to find more than casual work, and has now completely lost touch with his ex-wife and children.

Tom was admitted to a large and very busy psychiatric hospital as a voluntary patient suffering from depression. He has not been in hospital before, and after four weeks remains depressed. A hospital social worker has been involved and intends to provide after-care facilities for Tom, working with the consultant and nursing staff on a social care plan for Tom. During a conversation, Tom expressed a fear of having 'electrical treatment', and the approved social worker explained that, as a voluntary patient, he cannot be made to have

ECT. Visiting the ward a few days later, the approved social worker
is told by a distressed Tom that he had been put to sleep and given
the electric shock treatment, although he had been told that he was
being given something to help him relax.

Questions

What action can and/or should the approved social worker take?
Under what circumstances would the Act have allowed for Tom to
have ECT against his wishes?

JACKIE

Jackie is detained in hospital under section 3 of the 1983 Act. She is
a 24-year-old who suffers from a manic depressive illness. Her
family are caravan dwellers living on waste land not far from the
hospital in the inner city ring. The family are well-known to the
social services department, and lose no time in resorting to threats
of litigation if they feel they are not being treated properly. Writing
to the Queen is one of Jackie's father's more regular occupations.

Jackie does not live with her family, having been co-tenant of a flat
rented from the local authority. She and her boyfriend have had
tenancy of the flat for two-and-a-half years. They also have a three-
year-old baby. Whilst Jackie is in hospital, where she has so far been
for two months, the baby is being cared for by its maternal
grandparents. The boyfriend has moved away and there are
substantial rent arrears.

Jackie has written to the MP for the area in which she lives
complaining forcefully, but not threateningly, that she was denied
the right to vote in the recent local elections. The letter has been
intercepted by the hospital authorities – this fact being discovered
when Jackie complained to a social worker that the MP had ignored
her letter just because she was 'in a mental hospital'.

Questions

Was Jackie entitled to vote in the local election, assuming that, by
reason of her tenancy, she is on the electoral roll?
If so, should she have taken any action to ensure that she could
vote?
Were the hospital within their rights in witholding Jackie's letter to
the MP given the family reputation?

VINCE

Vince is a 29-year-old schizophrenic who has been admitted on numerous occasions to his local psychiatric hospital during the past seven years. His admissions have usually been on a voluntary basis, and, apart from one occasion early in the history of his illness when compulsory admission became necessary, Vince has been seen as a model patient.

He lives with his parents, both in their early 50s, and has one brother four years younger than himself who is due to get married in three weeks' time. Vince wants to be able to attend the wedding, and the consultant in charge of his treatment, Dr Y, is taking positive steps to enable this to happen.

At 10.00 pm one evening, the junior doctor on duty is called to the ward. Vince, who is on this occasion again a voluntary patient, is trying to find his clothes because he says he is late for his brother's wedding. The doctor contacts the consultant psychiatrist who says that he is at an important dinner and cannot come to the hospital until later that evening. He does not want Vince discharged or to be allowed to leave, and instructs that the nurses' holding power should be used until he can get to the hospital later.

Vince is restrained and kept on the ward until the consultant eventually arrives at 8.30 the following morning. Vince complains bitterly that he has been held against his will.

Questions

What are the nurses' holding powers under the Act?
What are Vince's rights in these circumstances?

11.2.5   Legal consequences of mental disorder

JENNIFER

Jennifer is 45 years of age, living in a hostel for the mentally handicapped run by a voluntary organisation. She has been following a rehabilitation programme with a view to moving out into sheltered lodgings, and this move is now imminent.

Jennifer's parents were killed in a car crash two years ago. Her only other relative was an aunt who felt that she could not have Jennifer to live with her as she nurses a semi-invalid husband, and lives many miles away from Jennifer's home town.

Jennifer's parents left a will bequeathing a substantial sum of money to her, and it is proposed that she uses some of it towards rent in advance and extra furnishings for her new lodgings.

Jennifer's aunt has kept in touch with her, and has heard about the planned expenditure to improve the quality of Jennifer's life. However, the aunt objects and notifies the social services department in Jennifer's home town that she wishes them to prevent the money being spent.

Questions

Who has the rights and/or responsibilities to help Jennifer administer her finances?
What is the role of the local authority?

OLIVER

Oliver is 37 years old and married with two teenage daughters. He is a civil servant whose promising career was stunted by the onset of a manic depressive illness some ten years earlier. He remains employed, but has frequent periods of sick leave to enter hospital for treatment.

On one occasion, Oliver left home to go to work taking the family car with him, telling his wife that he would need it that day. On the way to work, he took the car, a two year old saloon in very good condition, into a local dealer, saying that God had instructed him to purge himself of mechanical aids to living. The dealer could not accept Oliver's offer to give the car away, but was delighted when Oliver accepted his offer of £750 cash – well below the market value. Oliver then went to a firm of estate agents and negotiated to rent a luxury riverside studio on a minimum tenancy of one year. He paid £600 cash for two months rent in advance and signed a lease. He had told the estate agent at the viewing that the 'voices' told him 'this would be his temple'.

Later Oliver was stopped by the police trying to give away the remaining £150 to passers-by. Before long he was admitted to hospital on an application for admission for assessment.

Questions

What action could Oliver's wife take to retrieve the family property?
Is Oliver liable for his actions?

BILL

Bill rents an upstairs flat in an old mid-terrace house. The house is owned by Jack, an elderly pensioner who lives downstairs. Bill has lived in the house all his life. Since his mother died last year, Bill has lived under the delusion that he owns the house (his mother having given it to him under her will) and has refused to pay Jack any rent. Indeed, Bill has threatened to commence legal proceedings to recover the rent he claims Jack owes him. Jack relied on the rent income from Bill and his mother to supplement his state pension, and is eventually forced to evict Bill for non-payment of rent.

When the court bailiffs arrive, Bill refuses to leave. The police are called. They contact the local Area Housing Office and explain the circumstances, asking Housing to arrange temporary accommodation for Bill. The Housing Office's response is that they have no obligation to provide Bill with accommodation as the Council's policy is not to give single persons council accommodation and also because, by failing to pay his rent, Bill is homeless through his own fault.

The police then contact Bill's GP who visits and examines him. Following the examination, the GP contacts the area social services department, stating that in his opinion Bill requires admission to the local psychiatric hospital for assessment as he appears to be suffering under a delusion that he owns the house.

Questions

You are a member of the intake team to whom the case is assigned.
Would you make an application to admit Bill to hospital?
Can Bill be held liable for the rent arrears?
Has Bill any right to accommodation from the local authority?

11.2.6   The Mental Health Review Tribunal

NORMAN

Norman is a 35-year-old married man who lives with his wife in a smart residential area on the outskirts of a large conurbation. There are no children of the marriage, and both partners have professional careers in local government, working for different authorities. Norman's wife, Marilyn, receives a telephone call at work to say that her husband has been admitted to a psychiatric hospital.

The circumstances of the admission are as follows:

Norman has been increasingly under pressure in his middle-management post following financial constraint and redundancies in his authority. There has been a build-up in the backlog of his work culminating in his sudden loss of equilibrium. He has assaulted an elected member and damaged property and files in his office.

An approved section 12 doctor and an approved social worker were promptly called to the scene, and an application for admission under section 4 was made. This was converted to a section 2 application soon after admission. Norman was given medication immediately following this application on the grounds that treatment was urgently needed.

When Marilyn visited her husband she found him to be totally subdued by the effects of the sedation, and was distressed at seeing his condition. She rapidly became aware that Norman was unable to understand let alone pursue his rights as a detained patient and, therefore, she made an application on his behalf for a review by a Mental Health Review Tribunal. She feels that the medical recommendation on the section 4 application was made by a doctor who did not know her husband, and that, in order to ensure that the matter was dealt with rapidly, not enough consideration was given to the alternatives to compulsory admission.

The hospital-based social worker is asked to prepare a social circumstances report on Norman for the tribunal hearing, and the social worker from Norman's home area could be asked to attend to answer any questions arising from the application for admission.

Questions

This case study could be used as a basis to role play the tribunal hearing. Alternatively, the following questions could be discussed. Given the circumstances of the application for admission, what aspects of good practice may have been overlooked?

What are Marilyn's rights as the nearest relative?

12   The training and assessment of the approved social worker – conflict of opinion

12.1 The 1982 Amendment Bill proposed that the functions of mental welfare officers under the Mental Health Act 1959 should be transferred to approved social workers appointed by local social services authorities. The White Paper – 'Reform of Mental Health Legislation' – which accompanied the Bill explained the proposed change and indicated that guidance on the approval of social workers would be prepared in consultation with professional associations, training bodies, employing authorities and other interested organisations. It will be remembered also that the Code of Practice (referred to in 8.3), covering all the professions involved in compulsory admissions to hospital, is intended to provide general guidance.

In December 1981, at the time the Amendment Bill was introduced into the House of Lords, a small working group organised by the Social Work Service of the DHSS produced a consultative document containing draft guidelines for the approval of social workers. The working group had been asked to suggest approval procedures, including any requirements for the training of those to be approved, and arrangements for continuing approval by the authority giving the original approval or by another authority to which social workers had transferred. The group attempted to describe the general principles to be followed in such a way that a system for the approval and training of social workers could be

220

adapted to fit different local circumstances and the various organisational patterns of provision of social services.

12.2 The 1959 Act did not specify that local health authorities (whose duties were subsequently transferred to local social services authorities) should appoint as mental welfare officers people who were social workers. The role was to fill the gap in making application under the various powers when relatives were unable or unwilling to do so themselves, and to replace the judicial element in former procedures with some lay participation. According to the DHSS Consultative Document:

> Nothing was said about the professional skills or qualifications needed to carry out these duties. With the development of mental health social work in local health authorities, and the appointment as mental welfare officers of some staff qualified in social work and mental health, varying opinion as to their responsibilities under the Act and the way they should be carried out began to develop.

The re-organisation of local authority social services which took place in 1971 brought major changes, and, the Document stated:

> . . . . . it is widely argued that some of the expertise was lost as social services departments were striving to meet new pressures and demands made upon them. At the same time the concept of mental welfare officers simply acting as a substitute for relatives and following statutory procedures at the behest of general medical practitioners and/or psychiatrists was increasingly questioned. Not infrequently there was confusion, misunderstanding and uncertainty which gave rise to inter-disciplinary disagreement especially between family doctors and social workers. More generally there was concern to distinguish between the need for medical assessment of the potential patient's condition, that for independent assessment of the social conditions necessitating compulsion, and the need to protect civil liberties.

The proposals for change, which are now contained in section 13 of the 1983 Act, are intended to clarify the responsibilities of social workers approved for statutory duties, and the working group argued that it followed that to carry out these duties (for example, interviewing 'in a suitable manner') social workers should have appropriate and systematic training.

12.3 It was argued that decline in the use of compulsory powers was a factor to be taken into account in deciding how many social workers an authority would need to train and approve under the amended legislation, but this should be balanced by a proper assessment of the work to be undertaken and an appreciation of the role envisaged for them. There would be no point in authorising more than was necessary as opportunities for gaining experience of statutory work were limited and expertise would suffer if the work was shared among too many. The aim should be to offer training and subsequent approval, if the training programme was to be completed to the satisfaction of the authority, to those keen to develop this special expertise alongside a general professional interest in mental health.

There is no doubt, as this book has striven to make clear, that approved social workers will have a wider role than merely to react to requests for applications for admission to hospital, or to make arrangements as necessary and to ensure compliance with the law, important and necessary though these elements are. They are envisaged as specialists, capable by virtue of training and experience in dealing with mental disorder, of making an informed contribution to multi-disciplinary teams which are handling crises. According to the Consultative Document:

> They should have sufficient knowledge and skill to gain the confidence of colleagues in the health services, clients and relatives, and they should fully understand the contribution of members of other disciplines and of the relevant facilities provided by the services for which they work.

The problem was, and is, how such sentiments could be translated into training and assessment programmes which were reasonably uniform across the country, capable of being resourced, and acceptable to the social work profession.

The working group recommended that each local social services authority should set up a panel which would have two functions. The first would be to recommend to that authority a suitable training programme based on a universal common core. The second would be to commend to the local social services authority for approval social workers who are considered to have completed the training programme satisfactorily. Each authority would be guided by its panel in the setting up of a training programme and would make use of any local facilities which may already exist in educational establishments. CCETSW should be approached for advice and it could be convenient for two or more authorities to organise a joint training programme in order to make the best use of available resources.

The programme that follows is the one suggested by the DHSS Working Group and is included in its entirety as a backdrop to subsequent events:

12.4   The programme

Phase A

This phase is intended to give social workers the opportunity to have close contact with mentally disordered people and to experience at first hand life in various residential and day-care settings. The social worker would be present mainly in an observational capacity but could participate in appropriate tasks provided these further the primary objective of gaining an awareness of the effects of mental disorder and its treatment. Phase A should consist of:

(1) One month's placement in a residential or day care setting catering for mentally ill people exclusively. The placement might be in a hospital, a day hospital or day centre.
(2) One month's placement in an adult training centre, hospital or hostel for mentally handicapped people. An especially suitable placement would be an establishment which caters for behaviourally disordered mentally handicapped persons.

Phase B

Social workers should undertake a three-month full-time equivalent period of supervised practice and a formally organised teaching programme. The two components of this phase will be:

(1) A supervised practical work placement of at least three months in a multi-disciplinary setting such as a psychiatric hospital or a mental health centre where there is an established social work department. Social workers should carry their own cases under supervision, attend case conferences and participate in any teaching programmes which the placement can offer.

(2) A formally organised teaching programme consisting of seminars and lectures on all aspects of mental illness. The seminars should be focussed on discussing case material preferably from social workers' own work loads to enable them to learn about the social aspects of mental illness. The formal teaching can be organised in a variety of ways, perhaps using appropriate local education facilities and should be tutored by an experienced social worker calling on psychiatrists,

psychologists and people from other disciplines to contribute to the programme.

Phase C

This phase concerns itself with all aspects of relevant legislation and is a fundamental requirement of the training programme. It should consist of teaching on the Mental Health Act and on the law as it affects a person in our society with special emphasis on issues concerning the rights of citizens. The teaching should be geared to placing the Mental Health Act in perspective with other legislation and the law as a whole, especially that governing hospitals and other social institutions.

Phase D

The content of earlier phases has been planned in order that, in addition to those preparing for approval, it may also meet the needs of managers and social workers who require knowledge of mental disorder without proceeding to full approval under the Act. The components of this phase include the more specialised experiences required by social workers who are preparing for approval.

(1) Participation in the emergency duty rota and undertaking referrals under the supervision of an approved social worker or during the two years following the passing of the Act a suitably experienced mental welfare officer. During this time the social worker should have the experience of undertaking statutory work under the Act as well as developing his skills in crisis intervention work. This has to be seen in the context of the provision of comprehensive care and future management of cases. It is important that the trainee should be able to follow the future progress of clients including relevant psychiatric opinion about them.

(2) Social workers should be provided with information about local resources and how to use them. They should visit all relevant health and personal social services facilities (including both statutory and voluntary provision), become acquainted with the staff and be aware of the services agencies are able to offer, including information about clients' rights to benefit. Approved social workers will need direct access to appropriate services in order to properly discharge their duties under the Act, and senior managers should ensure that approved social workers

are aware of the extent of their powers and the means of acquiring access to local resources.

Phase E

(1) Recommendation by the panel and subsequent approval by the local social services authority.
(2) All social workers who are approved should have some long-term mental health cases on their work load and should continue to receive supervision or consultation.

Phase F

A process of reappraisal will be necessary in order to make certain that approved social workers are continuing to receive practical experience of the right type and amount, that they are up to date with service developments and developments in the management of mental disorder and also that they are aware of changes in local policies and provision. Local authorities should therefore institute a system by which the formal approval of an individual social worker is revalidated every five years. Revalidation will depend upon a specific recommendation by the panel to the local social services authority to the effect that the social worker should continue to be approved under the Act.

12.5 The draft proposals became public in January 1982, and according to a report in *The Times*:

> The proposals arise from the Mental Health (Amendment) Bill, progressing through the Lords, which says that only approved social workers will be allowed to undertake such jobs as committing people compulsorily to mental hospitals. Until now social workers with no special training in mental health were able to do that. Moreover there has been confusion about the role of social workers in relation to the client and the doctors involved in the case. Under the guidelines a national register of approved social workers will be established and a crash training programme organised before the new Act is implemented.

Throughout the early months of 1982 much consultation and discussion took place involving, among others, BASW, the AMA and the ACC. CCETSW was also involved to assess what its role might be. However, by mid-1982 it became clear that the DHSS guidelines had failed to find the support necessary for their implementation. The main reasons for this would appear to be that the training programme was in itself too grandiose and much too heavy on resources. In addition, the DHSS itself did not appear willing to finance such an operation (see 12.12 following). So much for 'a crash training programme organised before the new Act is implemented.'

12.6   On October 28 the 1982 Amendment Act reached the statute book, the only part of it to be implemented at that time being the crucial transitional period of two years during which the move from mental welfare officer to trained approved social worker was to take place. The DHSS guidelines having foundered, time was now becoming of the essence.

Also in October, CCETSW had begun a series of consultations with individuals and organisations in order to attempt to determine the way forward. It became clear that although the importance of the new legislation as far as the patient was concerned was widely appreciated, the implications for the social work profession were not, and it was at this time that CCETSW took control. By January 1983, CCETSW was able to issue a Press Release to this effect:

> Since the Mental Health (Amendment) Act 1982 became law, CCETSW has begun the consultation and planning necessary to ensure that enough mental health social workers are available to be considered by local authorities in England and Wales for approval by October 1984. Directions to be issued by the Secretary of State this year will make it clear that the Council is responsible for promoting training opportunities and assessing social workers to be approved by their employers under the new legislation.

> Local authorities will provide the training in collaboration, where possible, with educational institutions and professional interests. In the interim, schemes will be based, where possible, on existing training provision relating to current mental health legislation but in any case the objective will be to improve and maintain quality and standards . . .

> CCETSW will prescribe the content of assessment of workers who will need to demonstrate essential knowledge and competence in the following areas:-
> - the provisions and implications of mental health legislation
> - the nature of mental disorder and its social and family context
> - available local facilities and resources.

> All three units will need to include assessment of workers' capacity to make professional judgements required to perform the functions of 'approved' social workers under the law. Appropriate opportunities for observation and supervised practice in specific settings will be an integral part of the assessment . . .

Social workers will be assessed according to requirements which will be prescribed by CCETSW within the next few months. Experienced social workers who have been warranted as mental welfare officers under existing legislation may be exempted from parts of the complete training, but *all* will be assessed in the essential knowledge and competence required to carry out functions of approved social workers.

12.7 Which form or forms of assessment procedure would CCETSW choose? The DHSS guidelines had been rejected and time was moving on. At the beginning of March 1983 CCETSW held a three-day workshop attended by representatives of the social work, psychiatric and legal professions together with representatives of MIND. Many who attended saw this as an important opportunity to improve at least one aspect of social work training at a post-experience if not at post-qualification level. One factor was clear – there was hardly any national uniformity in the training of mental welfare officers. On the other hand, it would be quite unfair to suggest that this was true of all areas of the country. Bedfordshire Social Services Department had for some years run a wide-ranging training scheme culminating in a written examination. Equally, the well known 'Skillmill' course jointly organised by a number of authorities in the Northern Region had attracted much favourable attention. Skillmill, established in 1980, consists of two residential weeks and a practice period during which the student is supported by his own line manager and an agency-appointed adviser. The student's workload is reduced in order to accommodate five selected cases chosen by the line manager (in consultation with the student and adviser). These cases are chosen to give the student a variety of experience of work with mentally disordered people, with a balance between acute and chronic conditions. New referral situations must be included in the five cases chosen. Other elements involved include a tape/video interview by the student with a client, and a local network resources project identifying the need for and existence of local resources. As far as assessment is concerned, there is an external assessor, and the assessment procedure is in five stages leading to an assessment panel which considers: reports on the practice period, evaluation of the local network resource project, comments of group leaders and the external assessor's report, but without a formal written examination.

However, time and the projected number of candidates for the whole of England and Wales made it clear that, at least until

October 1984, such schemes were too ambitious to be assessed on a national basis. What emerged from the three-day workshop was CCETSW Paper 19:1, extracts of which stated as follows:

> CCETSW has concluded that it can most effectively contribute to the preparation of social workers to be approved under the Act by the establishment of national criteria for their assessment. To this end, CCETSW will:
> - arrange a centrally organised system of assessment
> - prescribe the content of assessment
> - establish standards for assessment.
>
> Although as much help and guidance as possible will be given to social service authorities as resources permit, CCETSW will not itself provide training nor approve training programmes . . .
>
> CCETSW is in the process of establishing a central examination board to oversee the examination of social workers selected by their employing authorities. The board will consist of individuals appointed by and accountable to the (CCETSW) Council and drawn from management and practice and from teaching and training. The central examination board will be responsible for planning the examinations and for establishing and maintaining overall standards.
>
> . . . the assessment at this stage, although in the form of questions related to practice, will allow less opportunity for individualised assessment than CCETSW would have preferred. The Council, however, intends to keep assessment arrangements under review.

A decision had been made. There was to be a national examination spread over a series of sittings (five, as it subsequently transpired between November 1983 and November 1984), preparation for which was to rest solely with each local authority. Further information on the matter (Paper 19:2) was sent to all Directors of Social Services in England and Wales in May 1983 to the effect that CCETSW regulations would require that, apart from those warranted before 28 October 1982, all candidates put forward for assessment would have to be social workers holding the CQSW, or its equivalent, with two years' post-qualification experience. Further,

> CCETSW has decided that, to ensure the maintenance of adequate and consistent standards of assessment, it must restrict the number of candidates to be assessed in the period up to June 1984 to 2,500.

Social Services authorities were also invited at this point to submit estimated numbers of candidates that they intended to put forward. These arrangements were given statutory effect by the issue of Directions under section 114(3) in Circular LAC(83) 7 issued in

June 1983 (see para 1.2.8 above).

12.8   Neither CCETSW nor its board of examiners ever said then or subsequently that this was the ideal form of assessment, but the tight time period imposed by the Act probably ruled out anything other than a 'stand or fall' examination.

The format of the paper that subsequently emerged consisted of two two-hour examination papers designed to test knowledge, competence and capacity to exercise judgement in all areas of social work practice relative to mental disorder. Paper One was divided into two parts – a list of 10 multiple-choice questions on those sections of the Act which were considered essential to the powers and duties of approved social workers, followed by a choice of three out of four cameo case studies designed to test the application of legal and clinical knowledge to social work practice. Paper Two consisted of a longer case study, the case material for which would be received by the candidates some weeks before the examination date in order to stimulate discussion. On the day, questions would be provided which were designed to test: social work practice and methods; use of local and national provision, including community networks, statutory and voluntary resources; roles and responsibilities of other people, including other professionals, who may be involved with the ongoing work; reference to other legislation when appropriate; ability to show evidence for decisions of judgement.

Not unexpectedly, the scheme received a cool response. The composition of the examination board was criticised, the contents of the paper were criticised (particularly when specimen questions began to appear), and the requirement for any form of assessment, let alone by examination, gave rise to considerable debate. On the other hand, training courses did begin to emerge, albeit somewhat limited in nature and scope, and from August 1983 onwards, courses were mounted, usually of between 8 to 10 days in length, which did attempt to address the criteria designed to be tested by the examination, and more than 500 candidates attended the first examination sitting in November.

12.9   By this time one serious difficulty had begun to emerge. It has been stated earlier that although the implications of the new legislation for the patient were widely appreciated and understood, implications for professional practice were not fully appreciated in the initial stages. NALGO, to which the majority of social workers belonged, made no submission to the Commons Standing Committee during the passage of the 1982 Amendment Bill, and so it is impossible to say whether at that stage they appreciated the implications for proposed assessment plans. In any event, before the end of 1983 NALGO expressed strong opposition to the idea of the examination. They urged, amongst other things, that it was divisive and could well damage the employment prospects of those who either were not selected by their employing authorities to sit the examination or who sat the examination and failed. They argued that all those who were currently operating as mental welfare officers on 28 October 1984 should be 'blanketed in' and that assessment procedures should only apply to the newly qualified social worker. From the beginning of 1984 NALGO had instructed its members to boycott the examination. The February examination reflected this in the low number of candidates who appeared on examination day. NALGO also expressed concern about lack of resources.

We feel that if a line of consultation between the DHSS and NALGO had been established earlier, much of the subsequent bitterness could have been avoided, particularly as the form and contents of the examination itself have by this time gained a wider acceptance than many originally anticipated, and in any event, CCETSW may well review its assessment procedures with a view to arriving at a more effective form of assessment of professional knowledge and skills which may not concentrate on an examination as the only form of assessment.

12.10   Another DHSS Working Party, which included representatives from CCETSW, ACC, AMA and NALGO was formed around Easter of 1984, and the subsequent report (published in May) attempted to appease critics of the system. The examination would stay in place during an interim period of 18 months beginning in October 1984 but at the same time, as an alternative, each local authority (either by itself or jointly with other authorities) would assemble its own training package and submit it to CCETSW for validation. These courses would then be mounted, but their management and assessment would be externally moderated by CCETSW. At the conclusion of the interim period the alternative examination procedure would cease and would be replaced by the courses which had been validated by CCETSW.

Hopes were high that this would gain acceptance, but the latest information available to us is that NALGO is continuing to object to the existence of the examination or indeed to the existence of any form of assessment for the reasons rehearsed above.

12.11 The debate upon what constitutes the most appropriate form of training and assessment for approved social workers continues, and at the present time of writing it is difficult to predict what the eventual outcome will be. However, it is clear to us that a minimum national standard of training must be laid down and monitored either by the Secretary of State or by CCETSW on his behalf. The attempt to set such a standard by means of a written examination alone has not provided a complete answer. What is required is for the existing deadline of 28 October 1984 to be extended for two years. During this time local authorities should be directed under section 114(3) to submit, either individually or jointly, locally based training programmes for validation by CCETSW. In addition, CCETSW should issue guidelines upon the content of such programmes in order to avoid abortive work by local authorities and to ensure no further delays occur in setting up a national training scheme. Schemes should be reviewed at regular intervals by CCETSW. Regrettably, it will be necessary to 'blanket in' existing mental welfare officers during this interim period but if directions to this effect are not made, local authorities will be unable to carry out their statutory duties under section 114(1) in some parts of the country.

12.12 Far more important than extending time-limits is the need for Government to recognise that section 114 has significant resource implications for local authorities. Present staffing levels in social services departments are already affected by constraints on expenditure to such an extent that local authorities will be unable to release sufficient numbers of social workers for extended periods of training which will be required to satisfy the standards the 1983 Act seeks to achieve. The view of Government in 1982, expressed in the following words of the Minister of Health, must change if progress is to be made. Unfortunately there is little present evidence that the Government does realise the resource implications of the 1983 Act as a whole let alone those of section 144:

> . . . many local authorities already provide training to the level we have in mind. The Bill is making sure that practice everywhere is brought into line with the best practice of local authorities. For that reason alone those local authorities already specialising in the training of their social workers will find that there is little, if any, increased expenditure

required. What is more, because we are going over to this corps of approved social workers there will tend to be fewer of them than at the moment there are mental welfare officers, the latter being drawn from the wider ranks of social workers all over the country.

Our present estimate is that, although it is extremely important that we are developing this corps of approved social workers, the extra public expenditure involved in training and approving them will be minimal. Nevertheless, we are consulting local authorities on the guidelines that we have set out for training and approval. We shall review any financial problems when we discuss standards of training. (Kenneth Clarke, Minister of Health, Commons, Second Reading March 1982.)

Whilst these consultations did take place, they did so in the context of an examination-based assessment scheme which laid down few requirements as to the manner in which staff who were to take the examination, were to be trained. If, as we have advocated, comprehensive training packages are introduced by local authorities, these will be costly and this must be recognised by Government.

Index

Bold type for 2-figure numbers indicate more major discussions of subjects

Index

Mental Health Law and Practice
for Social Workers